the earliest ships

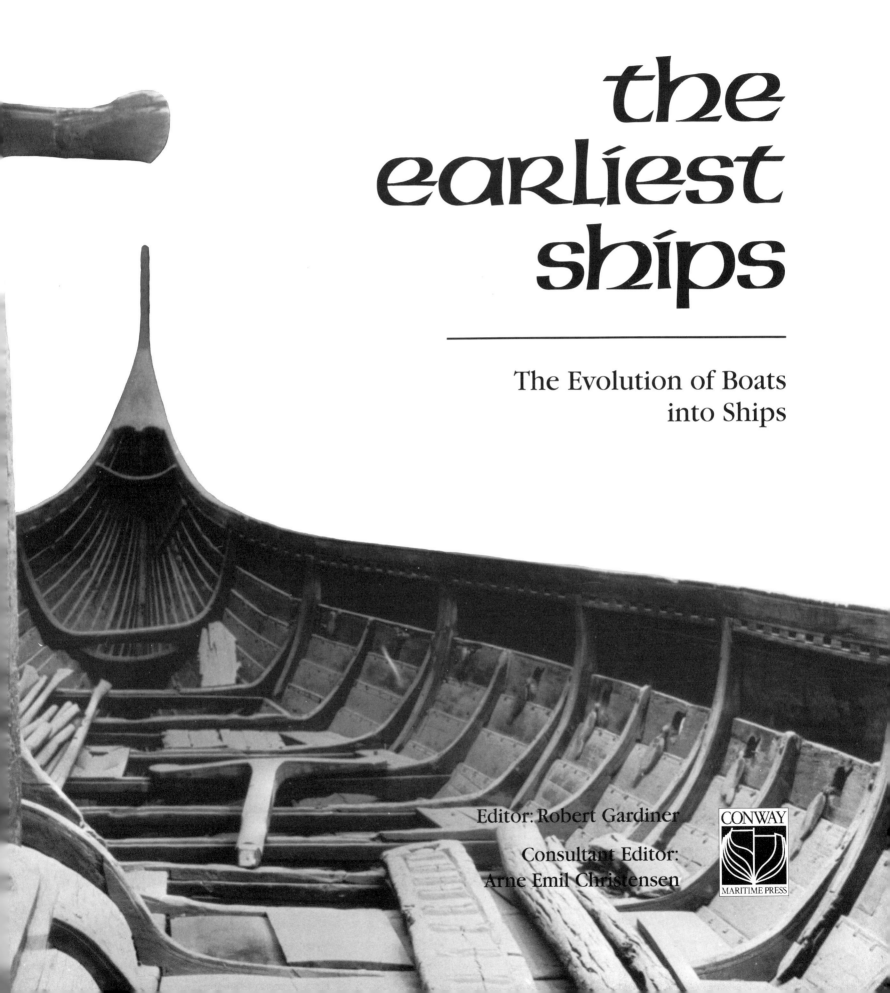

the earliest ships

The Evolution of Boats into Ships

Editor: Robert Gardiner

Consultant Editor:
Arne Emil Christensen

CONWAY
MARITIME PRESS

Series Consultant	DR BASIL GREENHILL CB, CMG, FSA, FRHistS
Series Editor	ROBERT GARDINER
Consultant Editor	ARNE EMIL CHRISTENSEN
Contributors	LIONEL CASSON ARNE EMIL CHRISTENSEN OLE CRUMLIN-PEDERSEN PROFESSOR DR DETLEV ELLMERS JEREMY GREEN PROFESSOR SEAN MCGRAIL DR BASIL GREENHILL DR EWE SCHNALL

Frontispiece: The Gokstad ship, perhaps still regarded as the Viking ship par excellence. Thanks to a unique combination of literary sources and archaeological finds in rich abundance, vessels of the Viking era are the earliest for which a reasonably detailed development history is now possible. (Oldsaksamling, Oslo)

© 1996 Brassey's (UK) Ltd

First published in Great Britain 1996 by
Conway Maritime Press, an imprint of Brassey's (UK) Ltd
33 John Street, London WC1N 2AT

British Library Cataloguing-in Publication Data
Earliest Ships: Evolution of Boats into Ships
(Conway's History of the Ship Series)
  I. Christensen, Arne Emil II. Gardiner, Robert
  III. Series
  623.809

ISBN 0 85177 553 5

Typesetting, design and page make-up by Tony Hart
Printed and bound by The Bath Press, Bath

Contents

Preface

THIS TITLE completes an ambitious programme of twelve volumes intended to provide the first detailed and comprehensive account of a technology that has shaped human history. It has been conceived as a basic reference work, the essential first stop for anyone seeking information on any aspect of the subject, so it is more concerned to be complete than to be original. However, the series takes full account of all the latest research and in certain areas has published entirely new material. In the matter of interpretation care has been taken to avoid the old myths and to present only the most widely accepted modern viewpoints.

To tell a coherent story, in a more readable form than is usual with encyclopaedias, each volume takes the form of independent chapters, all by recognised authorities in the field. Most chapters are devoted to the ships themselves, but others deal with topics like 'Shiphandling and Navigation' that are more generally applicable, giving added depth to the reader's understanding of developments. Some degree of generalisation is inevitable when tackling a subject of this breadth, but wherever possible the specific details of ships and their characteristics have been included. With a few historically unavoidable exceptions, the series is confined to seagoing vessels; to have included boats would have increased the scope of an already massive task.

The history of the ship is not a romanticised story of epic battles and heroic voyages but equally it is not simply a matter of technological advances. Ships were built to carry out particular tasks and their design was as much influenced by the experience of that employment – the lessons of war, or the conditions of trade, for example – as purely technical innovation. Throughout this series an attempt has been made to keep this clearly in view, to describe the *what* and *when* of developments without losing sight of the *why*.

The series is aimed at those with some knowledge of, and interest in, ships and the sea. It would have been impossible to make a contribution of any value to the subject if it had been pitched at the level of the complete novice, so while there is an extensive glossary, for example, it assumes an understanding of the most basic nautical terms. Similarly, the bibliography avoids very general works and concentrates on those which will broaden or deepen the reader's understanding beyond the level of the *History of the Ship*. The intention is not to inform genuine experts in their particular area of expertise, but to provide them with the best available single-volume summaries of less familiar fields.

Each volume is chronological in approach, with the periods covered getting shorter as the march of technology quickens, but organised around a dominant theme – represented by the title of the book – that sums up the period in question. In this way each book is fully self-sufficient, although the completed twelve titles link up to form a coherent history, chronicling the progress of ship design from its earliest recorded forms to the present day.

For this volume we are almost entirely in the hands of archaeologists, since the period largely predates documentary history. Although archaeology is the principal source of evidence, we have avoided the details of the actual excavations, concentrating instead on the results and implications of the work for the history of the ship. Naturally this places great emphasis on particular finds, which may or may not be representative, but such has been the progress of archaeology in the last half-century that coherent threads of ship development are now emerging for many areas of the world. The ancient maritime cultures of Europe are the most studied, and consequently form the core of this volume, but there is growing interest in the rapidly developing areas of the Pacific rim, and these non-European traditions are accorded their own chapter by a man who has done as much as any single individual to make these discoveries more widely known.

To make a coherent story from a relatively small number of finds is akin to tackling a child's join-the-dots drawing with most of the dots missing. It is inevitable, therefore, that some of the chapters may seem overly speculative: our defence must be that it is the scholar's task to make sense of the evidence, and as long as a theory fits the known parameters, is internally consistent, and does not stretch credulity, then it may stand until further and awkward evidence requires a new theory. Furthermore, because there are so few to call upon, the same archaeological discoveries may be quoted in support of different strands of development in more than one chapter, leading to the appearance of repetition and overlap. This has been accepted in pursuit of readability since the only alternative is far more cross-referencing, which can prove irritating to the keenly interested reader who will be continually directed to other parts of the book.

Besides archaeology, the other prime tool is ethnographic analogy. In some parts of the world what would once have been called 'primitive' methods – and certainly some of great antiquity – have survived to be examined by contemporary scholars. The reasons why certain design features *are* still employed can throw light on why they *were* adopted in the distant past, and the techniques of ethnographic comparison are now well established in the study of early water craft.

Most of the vessels dealt with in this volume are by almost any definition boats rather than ships, but in tracing the origins of seagoing craft this is an inevitable and understandable departure from the restraints of the series.

Robert Gardiner
Series Editor

Introduction

THIS volume, the first in time sequence of the twelve volumes of 'Conway's History of the Ship', gives in summary an account of the current state of our knowledge of the early forms of water transport in different parts of the world, but predominantly in northern Europe, and how from them were developed, or not developed as the case may be, structures which constituted significant elements in the economies of the societies which built and operated them. To such economically and socially significant floating mobile nautical structures may be given the name of 'ship'.

By this definition of economic and social significance the big Scandinavian-built vessels of the so-called Viking period of all their various types which carried people and goods, with whatever object in view, were ships, as were, later, the cogs of north Germany and the holcs of Britain, and, in due course, the early two- and three-masted vessels of western Europe in the late 1300s and early 1400s. All these vessels represented significant capital investment, large use of scarce resources of materials and labour, on structures which were very important in the activities of the societies which produced them. Such structures we may call ships and, for purposes of convenience perhaps, describe all less significant mobile floating structures as boats, whatever their construction and their lineage.

So far so good. But if we go further back in time, or into societies in a relatively early stage of technical development, we cannot really use this definition. In earlier and in poor societies a logboat may well represent an important capital investment. It can be argued that in such

a situation the logboat will be the only vehicle of water transport there is and there will consequently be no 'boats' and 'ships'. We simply have no idea of how earlier societies rated their vessels. Were the British Bronze Age big sewn vessels of which fragments of varying sizes have

been found in Humberside, in Gwent and in Kent regarded as boats or ships? Indeed, did the language used by their builders allow of any distinction? How were Hjortspring or Graveney regarded by those who used them? It can, I think, be argued that the real answer to

A model of the larger of two vessels found at Kvalsund in western Norway and thought to date from around AD 700. The hull form is suitable for sailing, but there is no surviving evidence that the craft was propelled by any method other than oars. Although conventionally described as 'boats', by the criteria of size and economic significance these craft might be better seen as 'ships'. (Norsk Sjøfartsmuseum, by courtesy of Basil Greenhill)

The Graveney boat as originally excavated from the Kentish marshes of southern England. The vessel is believed to be a workaday coaster dating from the early tenth century. In the last thirty years, highly important archaeological finds like this one have revolutionised understanding of early water craft, to the point where it is said that the sum of knowledge on such subjects has virtually doubled in that time. (Basil Greenhill)

this not very important question of what is a boat and what is a ship is simple. A ship is what her contemporaries called a ship. A boat is what they called a boat.

Despite all the work which has been done in different parts of the world in the last thirty years on the archaeology of boats and ships, the account of the development of boats and ships in prehistory available to us now is still fragmentary. The subject has been studied and recorded as chance has brought informed observers into circumstances in which they could record in some degree the details of the structures of boats and ships from their actual remains. Sometimes, rarely, such remains have been properly excavated, even more rarely still adequately recorded and published. There is iconographic evidence, pictures in one form or another of boats and ships at various periods. There are a few written descriptions. There is ethnographic evidence.

Important evidence has been provided by the intense but localised archaeological work centred on the Danish National Maritime Museum's research centre at Roskilde which has been going on since the late 1950s. Here a considerable body of knowledge has been built up about the development of some Scandinavian and north European boats and ships between roughly 800 AD and about 1200 AD. Aided, as it has been by numerous archaeological finds of fragments of boat and ship structures preserved in the peculiarly favourable conditions which exist in the shallow, sandy, sheltered waters of Denmark, it has been the most extensive and intensive work of its kind and, developed now with the building of hypothetical reconstructions of some of the finds and their extensive testing under oars and

sails, it has set the pace and established standards for its kind of archaeology throughout the world. It has also, perhaps, tended to overemphasise the significance of the particular building traditions with which it has dealt and some very important finds have not yet been fully published. It is important to remember that there remain very many areas of the world where there exist all the geographical features and historic, social, and economic conditions necessary for the fostering of boatbuilding traditions which have been studied relatively little, if at all.

The work at Roskilde has been largely, but by no means entirely, archaeological. The remains of a boat or ship are a first class prime source. But the problems that these remains present are almost always considerable because the remains are never complete. Usually the upper parts of the vessel have been destroyed. Often the remains are in a shattered state and there will be a great deal of hypothesis in any possible attempt at re-assembling, made the more difficult because the wood fragments are often distorted, water logged, and perhaps in a fragile state of decay. Over the last thirty years techniques have been developed for hypothetical reconstruction on paper, or, more likely now, on computer, of the form and structure of an entire boat or ship from remains which may resemble those of a crashed aircraft.

If the primary source for the study of the evolution of boats and ships is archaeological, there are others. Probably the most significant, most thoroughly prepared, best recorded and best published maritime archaeological experiment ever conducted has been the building, rowing and sailing of a Greek trireme of the period from the early fifth century to the

second half of the fourth century BC. The subject itself is one for the next volume in this series,[1] but it is highly relevant here because there is almost no archaeological evidence for the construction of the trireme. The sources have been iconographic and literary. But prolonged and intense study of this evidence headed by John Morrison, and the subjecting of the results to the rigorous analysis of the naval architect John Coates, has resulted in an Anglo-Greek enterprise which has led to a very substantial accession to our knowledge of a type of ship which played a fundamental part in the development, not perhaps so much of other ships, but, through the role it played in the Greek fighting forces, in the history of Europe and of European thought.

A further source of information on the development of boats and ships is ethnographic. Indeed ethnographic descriptions of boats used in modern (that is recent non-industrial generally illiterate small-scale) societies are, as Professor Sean McGrail has said:

> . . . of great use in the technological interpretation of excavated material as they enable the archaeologist to escape the bounds of his own culture and become aware of other technologies. There are problems in using analogies cross-culturally but the more alike in environmental, technical and economic terms two cultures (one ancient, one modern) can be shown to be, the greater the likelihood that ethnographic studies will be of relevance to the understanding of ancient cultures.

Nevertheless,

> Ethnographic analogies must be treated with great caution . . . It must be borne in mind that, however persuasive arguments based on indirect evidence may be, they cannot constitute proof . . . with the rider that, in the present state of knowledge no answers may be possible and any answer will be probabilistic rather than definitive.[2]

This point of probability must be borne in

1. *The Age of the Galley*, chapters 3, 9, and 11.

2. S McGrail, *Ancient Boats in NW Europe: The Archaeology of Water Transport to AD 1500* (London 1987), p3.

mind in all studies of the development of the boat and ship and it is apparent in the chapters which follow. Dr Detlev Ellmers examines the earliest forms of water transport, the devices used in pre Bronze Age Europe, while the next two chapters deal with the water transport of the Bronze Age interpreted broadly, the first in the Mediterranean and the second studying the separate boats cultures of northwest Europe. Detlev Ellmers then examines the evidence for

Besides archaeology, the other prime source of evidence for the design and construction of early ships is ethnographic craft – relatively 'primitive' structures like these Bangladeshi sampans and logboats which have survived into the present century provide technological analogies that help to explain features of ancient craft that would otherwise remain mysterious. (Basil Greenhill)

a Celtic wooden shipbuilding tradition in northern Europe in the period 500 BC to 1000 AD. This is a new field of study, the more important in view of the great problems usually associated with the disparate nature of the source material. Drawing together literary, iconographical and archaeological evidence, Dr Ellmers has produced what is probably the first coherent account of Celtic maritime developments, connecting both inland and seagoing craft in a unique and identifiable tradition that stands apart from the better known Mediterranean and Scandinavian techniques.

Arne Emil Christensen, who has been editorial consultant to this volume, then examines the vessels of the Scandinavian expansion and their predecessors. These are boats and ships about which we now know a great deal as a

result of the ethnographic and archaeological experimental work done in the last thirty or so years in Norway and Denmark and particularly at Roskilde. The development of the boats of Arabia and China, although the latter have been published in some detail by Needham,[3] have not received the same degree of attention in European writing. Jeremy Green examines the evidence for the history of their evolution up to the beginning of the sixteenth century in the next chapter.

The remaining chapters of the book deal with a couple of subsidiary topics. A great deal of work has been done at Roskilde on problems of reconstruction of boats and ships of the period

3. J Needham, *Science and Civilisation in China*, Volume 4, Part 3 (Cambridge 1971), pp379ff.

of the Scandinavian expansion and on the practical trials of reconstructions leading to a scientific estimation of performance possibilities. This important subject is dealt with by the man who has been the main inspiration for this work, Ole Crumlin Pedersen, in a short chapter.

The very important question of early pilotage and navigation is dealt with in another chapter. The study of this subject demands not merely a purely academic approach; the most important contributions have perhaps been made by practical seamen of an earlier generation who were themselves familiar with the intricacies of stellar and solar navigation and the use of all the ancillary methods of calculating dead reckoning, drift, and of weather prediction, which were in use until the middle of the twentieth century. It has been said that adequately to study primitive navigation it is necessary yourself to have been dependent professionally at sea on methods of navigation in use before the development of radio and all that has followed.

The doyen of the study in Britain of the history of navigation is David W Waters who has recently commented:

> It is very difficult to convince many landsmen scholars that ship-handling, navigation, and hydrography – 'the art of the seaman' – in one word, seamanship, and its history is a discipline as exacting as mastery of the classics or of mathematics. Seamanship has to be mastered to sail a ship in a safe and timely manner; to comprehend also how this was done in the past necessitates no less mastering by study knowledge of the seamanship of the past.[4]

Another practical seaman, Captain Søren Thirslund, a man brought up in the four-masted schooners of the Danish Greenland trade before the Second World War, has, working with the archaeologist C L Vebaek, recently established[5] on archaeological evidence that the Scandinavian settlers of Greenland probably used a wooden or stone bearing dial as a device to assist solar navigation and that this was a significant factor in the development of Norse trans-Atlantic navigation.

The relatively small size of Viking vessels and the unparalleled knowledge of their construction has encouraged scholars to build replicas that can be used to establish the sailing and handling qualities of these craft. The Viking Ship Museum at Roskilde in Denmark has been in the forefront of this experimental archaeology movement, an example being the two reconstructions shown here preparing for a series of trials at Roskilde in 1992.

Finally there is the question of the actual employment of early ships, generally touched upon throughout *The Earliest Ships*. It is perhaps relevant at this stage to make the point that although this volume is the first in time sequence of the most comprehensive history of the ship which has yet been published in the English language, the study of the building and operation of boats and ships is only part, though a very important one, of the maritime sub-discipline of archaeology. Again to quote Professor McGrail:

> But such technological study of rafts and boats, isolated from the study of their use, their geomorphological, climatic and economic environments, and without some consideration of the land-based facilities they require, can easily become over-specialised, uninfluenced by and uninfluencing the rest of the archaeological and historical disciplines.[6]

The broader setting of the development of the boat and ship involves the study of the use of all types of water transport in all sorts of environments. For instance, although we are a very long way from having a complete picture, through the archaeological study of remains of vessel structures found underwater in recent years – most notably perhaps at Red Bay in Labrador where the almost intact structure of a Basque whaler of the mid sixteenth century has been thoroughly examined by Robert Grenier and his team – we have begun to learn more of the vastly complex process by which the skeleton-built sailing ship evolved probably in the period between the late 1400s and the mid 1600s. This was a development of immense importance to European civilisation since it gave mankind for the first time a vehicle capable of regular oceanic voyaging on a commercial basis and it led to the development in the eighteenth century, with the further development of navigational techniques, of the beginnings of world trade with all that has followed.

But, important as it is for us to know in some detail how and where these technical developments took place, and wise as it would be in any modern study not to neglect the significance of the development of the ship at this period, nevertheless the development of the ship was only part of what was going on and must be considered against the broader economic and social European scene of the period, both in general and in detail, and against other technological developments, in navigation, harbour facilities and land transport, and against industrial development generally and the development of financial structures.

But the historian, almost whatever his or her specialism, must be aware and take account of the maritime dimension in its broader sense, and at the heart of this is the ship herself. It is to be hoped that the publication of these volumes will help to lead to a general historical awareness of the ship and her significance, her limitations, her background and her fundamental role in the development of the modern world.

Dr Basil Greenhill

4. *The Mariner's Mirror* 79/1 (1993), p97.

5. C L Vebaek and S Thirslund, *The Viking Compass* (Humlebaek, Denmark 1992).

6. S McGrail, *Ancient Boats in NW Europe*, p1.

1

The Beginnings of Boatbuilding in Central Europe

TO ESTABLISH the earliest stages of ship construction in central Europe it is necessary to look at the question from a different angle: when and under what circumstances did men first travel on water? It is the business of archaeologists to find the evidence which can answer this question, and they have exploited ingenious detective skills in wringing information from that evidence. The search for traces of the origins of Linear Pottery before about 5000 BC is a relatively simple matter because pottery fragments hardly decay at all, but the situation is much more difficult when dealing with boats. Boats were built exclusively of organic materials which decay in the ground and have only survived under exceptional conditions in a more or less fragmentary state. Boat discoveries are therefore rare. Even the oldest boat find – excavated close to Husum, and dating from the ninth millennium BC – does not necessarily come at all close to the origins of boatbuilding.

Yet the Husum boat fragment does go back to the final phase of the last Ice Age, when men were still hunters and gatherers and lived by hunting reindeer and catching fish in the cold steppes of the time, just as the Caribou Eskimos of Canada still exist today. The Eskimos use boats not only for fishing but also for hunting caribou – an American species of reindeer – because these are easy to kill by spear when they swim across rivers.

This current application of boats under Ice Age conditions suggested to the writer the important idea that the origins of boatbuilding could be established, at least approximately, by studying the first appearance of those fishing and hunting devices which could be used from a boat.

There is plenty of evidence to show that early men consumed fish, not least from the presence of fish bones in camp waste sites. However, initially they had to catch the fish with their bare hands with a quick grab from the river bank or in shallow waters. This situation did not change until around 16,000 years BC. Around this time the residues of the rein-

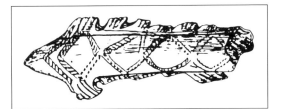

Tip of a fishing spear in the form of a fish in a net. Carved in mammoth ivory, found near Döbritz in Thüringen, Germany.

deer hunters of the Magdalene period (named after a French archaeological site) suddenly include large numbers of harpoon tips and pointed fishing hooks, carved from reindeer antler, which is relatively strong and reasonably durable. There is even evidence of fishing nets from the Magdalene; naturally the fine cords have not survived, but the tip of a fishing spear found in Thüringen shows the net so clearly that it is possible to see exactly how the fish was caught in it. Suddenly, around 16,000 BC, the reindeer hunters are using all the important fishing implements still in use today (fishing spear, hook, net) as well as the spears required for reindeer hunting. For a while they will have used these devices from the bank. Then it became clear that they could increase their catch enormously by using their tools from shallow water – and the desire to float out from the land onto the open waters like a reindeer and to use their hunting apparatus there became irrepressible.

The first boats

The thought processes which led to the first use of boats can be deduced. The reindeer hunters of around 8000 BC were following the reindeer returning to Norway as the ice melted, and these hunters engraved the results of their thinking on the rock in the form of a reindeer-shaped boat, and in so doing left the oldest known boat pictures. In the pictures the bow ornament in the form of a small reindeer's head can be clearly seen. The stern finishes in the same small stub tail which is characteristic

of the reindeer: the boat was an 'artificial' swimming reindeer in which the hunter could sit, in order to hunt real reindeer and catch fish. That was the crucial idea which drew land-based man onto the water and finally made a seaman of him.

Modern man, who was able to follow on television the first steps into space, or even a previous generation who experienced man's first attempts at flight, is in a better position than men of earlier epochs to understand the significance of this step. In fact, only three times in human history has man succeeded in leaving his natural habitat – dry land – and penetrating into other dimensions. On each occasion a special 'apparatus' was required: first the boat, then the aircraft and finally the rocket and space capsule. The boldness and pioneering spirit of the original boatbuilders can only be guessed at, but those characteristics must have been no less pronounced than in the men involved in the comparable enterprises of the twentieth century.

Equally the technical achievement of the Ice Age hunters with their primitive stone and bone tools should not be underestimated. Many books on early shipbuilding still insist that early man simply had to hollow out a tree trunk and paddle away, but this was by no means the case, for during the late Ice Age trees tall and thick enough to make dugouts simply did not exist. Hunters of the time also lacked the tools required for hollowing and shaping dugouts. But they were practised at using stone tools to make hunting weapons and other implements out of reindeer antlers. They were also capable of carving and smoothing bows and arrows, harpoon shafts and tent poles from the paltry birches and spruces of their environment. And they could tan animals' skins and, using sewing needles made of bone or antler, sew together garments and tent panels, so that they could produce completely weatherproof tents of skins stretched over an internal framework of wooden rods. Thus the reindeer hunters of the early Magdalene not only had at hand the most important fishing apparatus, but

Fisherman or hunter and his catch in an open skin boat, other hunting boats and a dolphin. Rock carving from Evenhus on the Trondheimsfjord, central Norway.

also the whole range of technologies which they needed to make skin boats, with the possible exception of the problem of absolutely watertight seams, which had yet to be solved.

One essential requirement for producing a waterproof seam was the sewing needle and plenty of experience in using it. However, one of the Magdalene Culture's new inventions – in addition to the fishing implements mentioned above – was the sewing needle. This is the final link in the chain of evidence: since skin boats could not be constructed without sewing needles, the lack of such implements before the Magdalene period means that skin boats could not have existed previously. At the same time the invention of fishing apparatus (also dating from the start of the Magdalene period) brought with it the first real need for boats. For these reasons it can be stated with reasonable confidence that the first waterborne vessels – at least in western and central Europe – were built at the time of the reindeer hunters of the Magdalene period (16,000-10,000 BC). Of course, boats did not immediately leap into existence in the early phase of this culture. It is reasonable to assume that there was a fairly long period during which the hunters gained experience with their fishing apparatus and the women practised the use of the needle, until finally at an advanced stage the time was ripe for the waterborne vessel.

It may seem surprising to suggest the rela-

tively complex skin boat as the first stage in the development of boatbuilding, at least in northern latitudes. But the great innovation in this was far more fundamental than the astonishing variety of technologies required to construct the boat; it was the fact that mankind created in the skin boat the first vessel in which he dared venture out onto the water – an element which was entirely foreign to him. With this move man became able to exploit for himself the food reserves of the great waters, formerly only available to him at the waters' edge, and at the

same time launched himself into a new dependency on technology, of which he had never dreamed. For man's survival on the water depended solely on the functional capability of his boat.

Evidence for the construction of these early skin-covered boats is provided by Norwegian rock carvings which, although dating from many millennia after the original invention of

A skin boat of about 9000 – 8000 BC. Reconstruction based on a fragment of a boat frame found at Husum, Germany.

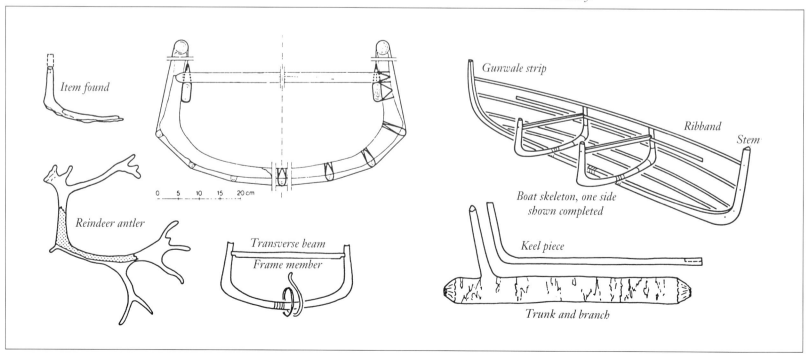

Item found

Reindeer antler

Transverse beam
Frame member

0   5   10   15   20 cm

Gunwale strip

Ribband

Stem

Boat skeleton, one side shown completed

Keel piece

Trunk and branch

these boats, were nevertheless scratched by reindeer hunters who had followed the reindeer as the ice melted. These rock pictures show that the skin boats were open, *ie* were not enclosed kayaks, so that the tension of the skins had to be withstood by a very strong framework. The smallest of these boats were designed for a single fisherman or hunter and had only two frames. This is the simplest possible method of constructing such boats, for the two frames can be made exactly the same size, and their width and spacing adjusted to suit the size of the hunter. With only one frame the boat's natural shape would not be so good, and the fisherman would not be able to sit in the centre of the vessel. On the other hand more than two frames would have to differ in size, and as a result they would have to be arranged quite accurately to produce a well faired shape. Larger vessels of this type were certainly built later for reindeer hunting, but were not present when development started.

Unfortunately the rock pictures only show a side elevation of the boats. It was not possible to develop ideas about their cross-section until an implement from the Ahrensburg Culture (ninth millennium BC) made of reindeer antler, excavated close to Husum in Schleswig-Holstein, was recognised to be a fragment of a boat frame. Reconstructing the frame produced an internal beam at the top of 45-50cm, just wide enough for a man wearing an animal skin garment to sit in. Experts at the German Maritime Museum were keen to develop these ideas, and decided to reconstruct a boat based on the rock pictures and archaeological evidence. The flexible wood strip skeleton used in present-day Eskimo kayaks was copied and lashed tightly to the frames with leather thongs to give the boat its final shape. Arrow shafts from the Ahrensburg Culture had been excavated, and like these carefully shaped and smoothed items all the wooden parts for the Museum's boat were made of pine using the stone tools available at that time. However, on its first trial run the boat's framework immediately failed: the pine was simply too brittle for the purpose. In the second experiment birch wood was used, and, in spite of the very small cross-section of the individual timbers, this proved to be the optimum material for this type of skin boat. The arrangement of the components is shown in the accompanying diagram. The watertight seams in the skin covering were also made after the pattern of Eskimo boats,

Two men in a boat hunting a swimming reindeer. Rock carving from Kvalsund on the Repparfjord, north Norway.

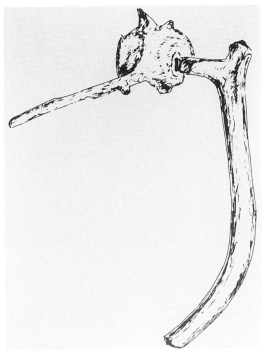

Reindeer skull with a hole in the forehead caused by an antler hatchet; both were found at Stellmoor near Ahrensburg, Germany.

using needles carved from antler of paleolithic shape, although the needle points had to be sharpened frequently. The completed skin boat is so light in weight than one person can comfortably lift it out of the water and carry it. As a result of these experiments the German Maritime Museum at Bremerhaven now houses a reconstruction of the world's oldest boat. It represents the stage in the development of boatbuilding reached about 10,000–11,000 years ago and as such comes very close to the origins of boatbuilding.

Use of the first boats

Once the boat had been invented, it was inevitable that its potential for fishing would be realised. The usefulness of boats for reindeer hunting is clear from a reindeer skull with a battered hole in its forehead, found at Ahrensburg, northeast of Hamburg (approximately 9000–8000 BC). The female animal had been killed by a blow from one of the many short-handled antler hatchets found there. A hunter could only approach this close to a reindeer if the animal was swimming across a stretch of water, in which case it had plenty to do to prevent its heavy antlers pushing its nose under water. Two men could then glide up to the animal in a slim, lightweight skin boat. The man in the stern paddled with quick strokes, while the bow man held the antler hatchet in his right hand and struck its prong into the forehead of the first reindeer they reached. There could be no escape for the animal as the boat was faster. In the water the animal could not defend itself with its antlers, as it had to hold its forehead high up the whole time in order to breathe. One blow on the forehead was fatal. With a small number of boats a single group of hunters could lay in a supply of meat for many weeks during the reindeer's migration

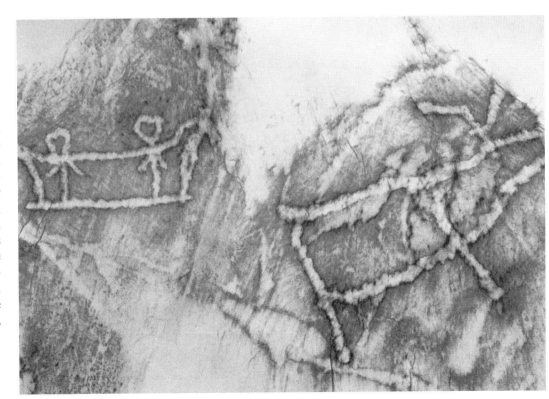

period. The meat could be cut into strips and air-dried, in which condition it remained edible for a long time.

The antler hatchets used for this method of hunting have been found in quite large numbers close to ancient waterways, and provide reliable evidence that reindeer were hunted in this manner, *ie* from boats. The oldest of these antler hatchets so far discovered dates from the late Magdalene period. It was found at the Gönnersdorf hunter camp on the middle Rhine (approximately 10,500 BC). The boat used for this method of hunting was built for a two-man crew, and must therefore have been larger than the fishing version which carried one fisherman only.

A rock picture from Bergbuten near Bossekop in Norway shows a further use of Arctic skin boats. Admittedly this rock carving also dates from a time when the Ice Age was long since past in central Europe, but the animals depicted at Bergbuten leave no doubt that the hunters there were still living under Ice Age conditions. As argued later, it is certainly reasonable to draw conclusions regarding late Ice Age hunter groups in central Europe from these later rock pictures. The rock picture shows a bowman standing in a boat, aiming his arrow at a target on the water's surface at some distance. This is clear from the arrow's intended trajectory, which is flat rather than steeply upward. The picture shows a water bird hunt which is much more successful from a boat than from the bank, where the belt of scrub and reeds may be quite wide.

However, a second person is standing in the same boat, holding two large snowshoes aloft as a sign that he/she is considering continuing the journey over the snow-covered land. It is scarcely possible to imagine clearer evidence that this is a boat intended for travel. It is very much larger than the fishing and hunting boats and has a much larger crew, for the vertical lines indicate men with paddles. Naturally the men who set out in their small boats to catch fish had quickly noticed the great convenience of a boat journey compared with a hard foot march over trackless terrain, and they had developed a large travel boat for transporting quite large groups of people. This means that even in prehistoric times Arctic hunters had developed precisely the two types of boat which represent the Eskimos' standard equipment even in the twentieth century, namely the fishing boat (in Eskimo terms: *kayak*) and the travel boat (in Eskimo terms: *umiak*).

Furthermore the fishermen would quickly have noticed how easy it was to transport their catch once the first boats were in use. Hitherto everything required at camp had to be carried there, often over long distances. If they travelled by water, the boats relieved the fishermen and hunters of the chore of load-carrying. The rock picture shows clearly how the catch and implements were stowed in the front section of the boat while the vessel slipped easily over the water. For these people this must have been an astonishing discovery: suddenly they were able to carry out transport tasks without the hard work of actually carrying the load – with the help of the first vehicle in human history: the boat.

What has been here deduced, primarily from the relatively late pictorial evidence from

northern Scandinavia, is a demonstrable reality in archaeological terms as early as the latter phase of the Magdalene period (approximately 10,500 BC) in central Europe. Careful excavations and the analysis of finds in the Gönnersdorf reindeer hunters' camp (on the east bank of the central Rhine north of Andernach) provide very surprising glimpses of intensive exploitation of the river: from the gravel banks the camp dwellers collected boulders which they used as tools, cooking stones, striking stones and raw materials. They caught fish (the remains of salmon, trout and eel pouts have been found) and hunted waterfowl (goose and swan bones have been found, heron and crane are shown in pictures). They had already developed the antler hatchet with which they could kill their most important source of meat and skins – the reindeer – in the water. Occasionally they also hunted elk in the boggy land close to the river bank.

The fact that simple means were devised for crossing the river, *ie* early ferrying, is indicated at Gönnersdorf by slabs of basalt lava stone which were transported from the Nette valley, which joins the west bank of the Rhine near Andernach. However, there is also evidence that raw materials were transported over long distances along the Rhine. Although 26,000 artefacts made of the local river stone have been found, a further 40,000 have been discovered made of two different types of flint, namely Baltic flint, which occurs naturally near Duisburg at its most southern point (today more than 160km downstream) and Maas flint, which is found in the southern Rhine delta (today about 280km downstream). Both of these sites could be reached by boat. The fact that journeys were made as far as the Rhine delta is also reflected by several pictures of seals on Gönnersdorf slate slabs. In contrast, the haematite deposits at Ahrweiler were comparatively close by (approximately 35km downstream). This material was used extensively to produce red dye, and this again could be obtained and transported by boat. Thus all these deposits of raw minerals, which were exploited regularly and heavily, were always within reach by more or less long boat journeys, which means that the heavy stones and earths could be transported regularly and conveniently by boat, instead of having to be carried over hundreds of kilometres.

However, the archaeological finds also provide indications of individual boat journeys

Archer and a man with snowshoes in a boat used for travelling (as opposed to hunting). Rock carving from Bergbuten, Norway.

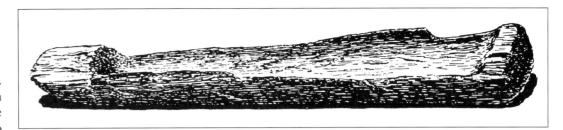

The oldest dugout known to man, in use around 6300 BC as a fishing boat. Length 3m, beam 0.45m, found at Pesse, Netherlands.

by people not obviously transporting goods. For example, a bag probably belonging to a healer contained three fossils which must have been kept for magical purposes relating to hunting. All three fossils had been found close to a river, namely a rhinoceros bone from local deposits, a shark's tooth from the Mainz basin (approximately 110km upstream on the Rhine) and a bored-through Saurian vertebra from Luxemburg (approximately 220km upstream on the Mosel). It is also assumed that the flint oolith used for Gönnersdorf stone implements came from the Mainz basin.

From this evidence it is clear that boats regularly travelled up and down the Rhine and its tributaries (Mosel and Ahr) for distances of up to about 280km, carrying goods and people, fishermen, hunters of water birds and reindeer, and ferry traffic. At each end of these boat journeys there must have been communication with other hunter groups, by means of which objects were exchanged. This is the only way by which the small number of ornamental snails from the Mediterranean and snails in the shape of teeth from the Atlantic could have been brought to the Gönnersdorf hunters. To date no research has shown where these communication points might have been.

The first dugouts

Ten thousand years ago a fundamental climatic change occurred. The great glaciers melted, and the Ice Age came to an end. Central Europe was transformed into forested land, and its natural vegetation remains forest to the present day. This change was an undesirable one for the hunters of the retreating Ice Age, who were primarily specialists in reindeer hunting. Their food reserves – the great reindeer herds – were increasingly migrating to the north. Men had two alternatives: they could migrate to the north in their wake, or make the transition to the entirely different living conditions of dense forest and marshy valley plains. They remained hunters, but had to develop tools and methods for making use of thicker timbers if they wanted to survive. The new technologies they developed were not without consequences for the art of boatbuilding.

It is true that the hunters in the mountain forests appear to have persevered with the skin boat. Of course, it was so light that the traveller could simply lift it out of the water at the rapids and carry it to a point where the river was nav-

igable again. However, in the flatter regions where waterfalls and rapids were not encountered, and where long-distance boat journeys were possible without major problems, a different type of boat slowly but surely came to prominence: the dugout. The only raw material required for the dugout – namely trees of adequate girth – were now available in inexhaustible numbers as far as the hunters were concerned. Moreover, no special implements were required to construct dugouts apart from the tools which men had already developed for other woodworking tasks, such as building huts. These were the axe and adze for felling, hollowing and shaping the tree trunks, and a knife for carving paddles.

However, the transition from the skin boat to the dugout was not simply a matter of continuing the development of existing boatbuilding technology. In fact the dugout represented a significant technological leap and a fundamental innovation involving considerable re-thinking. It was no longer necessary to assemble a boat skeleton from sections of antlers and flexible timbers and then cover the framework with skin. Instead a thick tree trunk was hollowed out by removing material until only a self-supporting shell remained. This new method of construction was not adopted out of bitter necessity; rather it was a matter of opening up a new and supplementary method of boatbuilding, which turned out to be one of the crucial transition points in the history of boatbuilding and water transport. The result of this re-thinking process was a series of heavy but robust boats which were to prove extraordinarily fertile ground for further development. For the succeeding millennia in central Europe the shell method of construction based on the original dugout was the basis of all boatbuilding and shipbuilding. As is now accepted, virtually all the important ship types of this region were developed from early dugouts.

The first dugouts retained the rounded external form of the tree trunk, as a result of which they rolled badly in the water and required much skill to paddle. The oldest example discovered to date was found near Pesse in the Netherlands, and dates from about 6300 BC, *ie* it was built quite close to the time

when the afforestation of central Europe started (around 8000 BC). This relatively crudely worked vessel, cut from a pine tree, was only 3m long with a beam of 0.45m. Its load carrying capacity was small, and it was undoubtedly built as a fishing boat for a single man. Little effort had been made to shape the boat's ends in a particular way; the front end has a vaguely spoon-shaped bow, while the aft end is cut off square, more or less irregularly.

Right from the very start of this new method of boat construction it was the shaping of the ends of dugout boats which presented the boatbuilder with the most difficult problem: he had to cut across the wood fibres, and in so doing created both of the dugout's weak points. If he left too thick a block of wood at the ends, then the timber tended to crack when it dried out. If he left too little material, there was a danger of the structure disintegrating. In the course of time it was discovered that it was necessary to cut through the wood fibres at an angle in order to obtain durable boat ends. The bow of the Pesse dugout shows evidence of this discovery insofar as the outside surface is bevelled to a spoon shape, which allowed the boat to be landed by running up onto a shelving bank. However, the inside of the boat is not bevelled in the same way.

The hunters of the south Scandinavian and central European forests refined the construction of dugouts to such an extent that, when those cultures were in their final phase (fifth millennium BC), dugouts about 10m long were built, hollowed out to a very thin shell. By this time farming cultures were already established in the German central mountains. The boatbuilders were able to shape the spoon bow very precisely, and had also abandoned the rounded outer shape of the tree trunk by providing the boat with a sharp-angled chine, which made the vessels much more stable in the water than the round versions. However, the most amazing feature of this early boat type is the hunters' solution to the problem of the end-grain timber at the rear end. The stern of the dugout had been completed simply as an open channel whose opening was sealed with a transverse board (transom) which was installed separately. This represents the oldest boat found

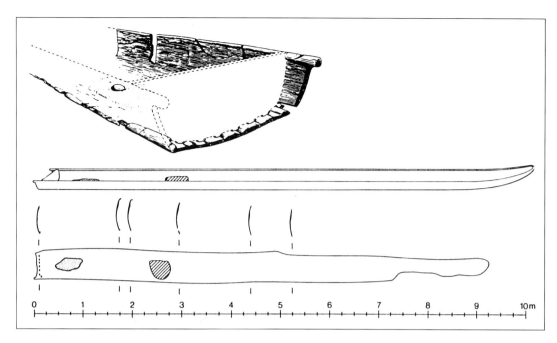

In the fourth millennium BC boatbuilders in northern latitudes assembled for the first time a large wooden boat from several components: a finely worked dugout made of lime wood with separate, inset transom (not extant, but evident from traces of its attachment). Length approximately 10m, beam 0.65m, found at Tybrind Vig, Denmark.

forests were used in exactly the same way as the older skin boats; the smaller examples in particular were used for fishing. By this time the pointed fishing hook characteristic of the receding Ice Age had been significantly improved by the invention of the carved bone fishing hook. The fishing spear was also developed into the more specialised eel spike. This evidence indicates that fishing made an important contribution to the hunters' diet. Transverse arrowheads were developed for hunting water birds, as were thrown wooden implements of the boomerang type. Elk living in the marshy forests were killed from boats when swimming across rivers or fjords, using the same type of striking implement with which the reindeer had been hunted in the Ice Age. However, long dugouts were also built, designed as a convenient method of transporting quite large numbers of persons over distances. For such journeys it was inevitable that food, hunting weapons and perhaps even hunting products (*eg* pelts) would be carried for trading purposes, and as a result there would have come a time when the practical limits of the dugout would be reached – for such boats could not be built wider than the trunks of the thickest trees.

in northern latitudes known to be assembled from multiple wooden components (albeit only two). The significant point of this development is that the boatbuilders were already capable of constructing watertight joints between two wooden parts, even though it has to be admitted that boatbuilding in Egypt was already much more advanced by this time.

The cross-section of this dugout is very similar to the Husum skin boat, and this is one reason why it is now believed that skin boats remained in use for a long period as a complement to dugouts, and thereby influenced their development and shape. A further component of the skin boat worthy of mention was the animal's head at the bow – the boats being constructed largely from animal materials. At least in Scandinavia the animal head was so important to the boatbuilders that they also fixed carved wooden animal heads at the bow of their dugouts, as is evident from Scandinavian rock carvings. From these animal heads it is a direct line of development to the figureheads of the great sailing ships of the nineteenth and twentieth centuries.

The dugouts built by hunters living in the

Boat usage after the Ice Age

Excavations of middle Stone Age settlements and archaeological finds in bogs in the British Isles, Denmark and Schleswig-Holstein have unearthed quite a number of wooden paddles for the first time. The blades of older paddles have a long oval form, while later ones are heart-shaped – a design which eventually disappears altogether. All the excavated paddle

In rock pictures dugouts were depicted as a long, broad line with a large animal's head at the bow and stern. The vertical lines in the boat indicate a crew (sometimes head and arms can be picked out). Below the long dugout can be seen a small, tub-shaped skin boat, also with animal's head bow. From the elks depicted it is clear that both boat types were used by hunters living in the forest. Left of centre: two angled throwing implements; top right is a fishing hook with bait (worm). Rock carving from the island of Brådön in Angermanaelv, northern Sweden.

shafts are broken off in the upper region, but the best preserved are still so long that the crew must have been standing in the boat when paddling.

Archaeologists are particularly well informed about boat usage in the Danish Ertebølle Culture. In this final phase of the hunter-gatherers, when farmers had already settled in central Europe, the coastal population simply threw away the remains of their food, forming large heaps of mussels close to their settlements. Amongst the mussels were found the residues of stone implement manufacture as well as the bones of numerous other animals. From this evidence it is possible to deduce that boats were used as follows: the shellfish banks of the shallow coastal regions were intensively harvested for oysters, cockles and mussels. A sea-floor net was used to catch flat fish such as flounder and plaice from the bottom of the shallower seas, while eels were caught using an eel basket or spear. Cod were also caught, but this would have necessitated paddling out to the open sea. The bait may well have been the marine stickleback, which is only 15cm-18cm long. Other fish caught by the fishermen include cat shark and garfish, herring and mackerel.

Members of the seal family such as the cone seal, common seal and ringlet seal were killed on the beach. White whale, killer whale and dolphin were harpooned at sea from boats, and waterfowl such as swan, geese, numerous types of duck and other birds were shot from boats using bows and arrows. Naturally freshwater fish and water birds were coveted where inland waters were available; water nuts were also gathered, and beaver and otter hunted for their pelts.

There is no evidence relating to long boat journeys for obtaining raw materials, nor about journeys involving groups of people. However, bearing in mind all that is known about fishing, it is an inevitable assumption that very large numbers of sea journeys were carried out, at least within sight of the coast. The open tundra of the preceding Ice Age may have permitted long-range communication by land routes, but the dense virgin forests certainly did not. The only alternative, now exploited much more intensively than previously, was the relatively dense network of rivers of Europe north of the Alps. Thus boat journeys were the method by which the forests were opened up for traffic. In succeeding periods nothing changed in these natural conditions.

The first farmers and skin boats of the coracle type

Seven thousand years ago the circumstances regarding the use of waterborne vessels again changed fundamentally, but this time not as a result of climatic change but due to groups of people migrating from the central Danube region, bringing with them a completely new type of economy: these were the first farmers, penetrating the region of the hunter-gatherers. It is not known whether the latter relinquished their hunting and gathering grounds to the incomers without putting up stout resistance: it is only possible to state that central Europe became a region of settled farmers as a result of this immigration. Until the industrial revolution of around 1800 AD this was the most dramatic economic transition in human history. As such the period is also known as the Late Stone Age revolution or the agrarian revolution, for since then the provision of food for the whole population has no longer depended on the whims of fortune in hunting, and the gathering of wild plants which happened to be growing nearby, but on the thoroughly labour-intensive task of 'manufacturing' food.

The new immigrants brought with them more than just agriculture and breeding cattle. They also brought many other cultural accomplishments, all of which, like the new form of economy, had been developed in the Near East and brought to the central Danube region via various intermediate stages. The farmers thrusting towards the northwest could also spin and weave, and with their cloth garments their appearance was very different from that of the hunters and gatherers who wore clothing of skin and leather. They produced their stone implements by grinding, which meant that they could make them out of quite different raw materials from those used by the hunters, who made their stone tools only by flaking techniques. They also manufactured the first moulded artefacts consisting of vessels and figures made of fired clay. From this period onwards archaeologists are able to differentiate individual cultures by the fragments of pottery vessels found in the ground, usually well preserved, and in each case of characteristic shape. For example, the first farmers of central Europe are members of what is known as the Linear Pottery Culture from the scored, banded decorations on their vessels. To the Linear Pottery Culture clay was virtually the universal raw material. They used it to make vessels for eating, drinking and storage, moulded the weights for their spindles from it, and daubed it on the woven walls between the posts of their great houses. And finally they depicted virtually their entire environment in the form of pictorial clay figures, including their domestic animals (primarily cows and pigs), themselves, occasionally their houses and once even the type of boat they used. This, the oldest model boat found in central Europe, was excavated in a Linear Pottery Culture village in the present-day town of Einbeck, in the region of Northeim in Lower Saxony, and shows an oval skin boat of the coracle type, of which many were still in use in Ireland at the beginning of this century.

Although these vessels are known from Ireland, they were also reported from other regions such as Mesopotamia. Around the year 430 BC the Greek traveller and historian

The oldest model boat found in central Europe looks like an oval pottery vessel with Linear Pottery Culture ornamentation, and represents a skin boat of the coracle type. Found at Einbeck in the Northeim region of Lower Saxony, fifth millennium BC. (Drawing by R Breden)

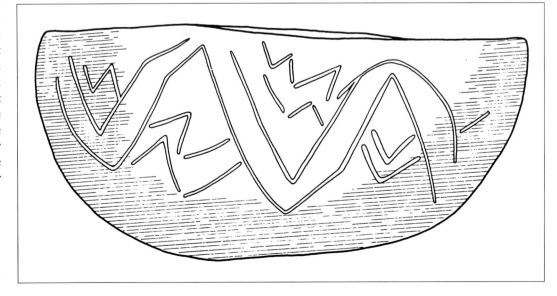

Herodotus described them as

vessels in which people travel down the river to Babylon, round and made of leather. In Armenia, which lies above Assyria, the people cut osiers and make them into a framework for the vessel, which they then cover outside with skins in order to make it watertight. The ship has neither a prow nor a stern, is round like a shield, and is filled entirely with straw. Then they load it and let it float downstream with the current . . . The vessel is steered by two men standing upright in it, using two poles; one of them pulls, the other pushes. The vessels are of varying size, the largest carrying up to five thousand talents. Each boat carries a live ass, probably two on the largest. When they have delivered their load to the man in Babylon, they offer the framework of the vessel and the straw for sale at the same time. The skins, however, are loaded onto the ass, which carries them back to Armenia. For it is not possible to navigate upstream, as the current is much too rapid. For the same reason the vessels are made of leather and not of wood.

Until recently Irish coracles were constructed using cow hides exactly as Herodotus

described. For a long time many suppositions have been made about possible connections between these two identical traditions of boat-building which were separated by thousands of kilometres. In fact the Einbeck clay model shows plainly that some thousand years ago there had been such a connection: the skin boat of the coracle type was brought by the Linear Pottery Culture from the Near East to central Europe 7000 years ago, together with many of their other developments. From that starting point agriculture then spread gradually until it reached Ireland. The coracle was adopted in Ireland at the same time, and happened to survive in that country into the twentieth century, whereas it has long since been forgotten in central Europe, which had been its intermediate point of distribution.

However, the Einbeck model provides more information than just the *where* and *when* of a boat type reaching Ireland from the Euphrates and Tigris. It also gives crucial information on how the Linear Pottery farmers migrated to central Europe from the central Danube area. A family of Linear Pottery farmers would pole its way up the Danube with a small fleet of oval skin boats in the search for suitable land. In this way they could transport all the members of the

family and its essential domestic animals over great distances, safely and without huge effort. At the same time they could transport the fragile pottery storage vessels containing the valuable seed for the various sorts of cereals, pulses and plants yielding oil and fibre (flax). The quantity of grain to be transported should not be underestimated, for there had to be enough to sustain the family until the next harvest in addition to the seed corn. Since the cart had not yet been invented, all this grain would have had to be carried over small beaten paths, and this would have made it impossible to travel long distances in the trackless forests. The skin boats of the coracle type were therefore indispensable and a pre-requisite for the migration of the Linear Pottery Culture to central Europe, and the resultant agrarianisation of that region.

The boats were so small and light that their owners could navigate far upstream even on the minor tributaries of the Danube. However, the major advantage of these lightweight boats was that they could be carried over the watersheds on marches lasting no longer than a few days in order to reach neighbouring river regions, where they could then run more easily downstream to new stretches of fertile land. In this way some Linear Pottery groups penetrated beyond the Danube and March to the upper tributaries of the Oder and Elbe. They travelled down the Elbe as far as the edges of the Magdeburg region, some even crossing the Bode to reach the Braunschweig area. Others journeyed from the Elbe via the rivers of Thüringen to the Werra and the upper Leine, where the Einbeck coracle model provides this glimpse into the water-based communications of the time. Yet others pushed further up the Danube, crossed the watershed to the Neckar valley and from there to the region of the river Rhine. Some of them in turn travelled along the Lahn, over the watershed to the Eder valley and into the Kassel area.

Even after the Linear Pottery Culture groups had taken over the land in this way, this small, lightweight, capable boat type remained in constant use in order to fulfil the settlers' need for supplies of goods from the Danube region. All women and men of any stature wore belt clasps, other items of costume, and ornaments made of the shells of Spondylus mussels; these only occur in the Black Sea and the Mediterranean, and so had to be brought to central Europe in large numbers via the Danube. Axe and adze blades were needed on

A skin-covered boat of the coracle type from the river Boyne in Ireland, around 1900 (after Hornell).

The trans-continental transport network of inland waterways built up by the Linear Pottery Culture of around 5000 BC can be seen from the distribution map of axe and adze blade deposits found close to rivers. All these stone implements were shipped from their Balkan quarries via the Danube and its northern tributaries, then carried over the watersheds and finally shipped again along the rivers flowing into the North Sea (after G Schwarz-Mackensen).

every farm for house building and all other sorts of timber working, and these also had to be transported by boat because the tough stone from which they were ground was only found in the Balkans. There is definite evidence of this trade in the small loads of between two and eight sometimes semi-finished blades made of this type of stone which have been dug up in the vicinity of river banks, probably representing sacrificial offerings by traders in the hope of good business and many happy returns. The distribution map of these sacrificial offerings immediately makes clear the wide-ranging waterway network which was in use at that time. However, not every deposit of these blades was found at places where the boats landed: in some cases the stone implements had been carried by short land routes to the farms located further inland.

This hybrid communications system (utilising natural waterways far upstream, in conjunction with short land routes over watersheds and direct tracks from the river bank to the inland farms) allowed the Linear Pottery Culture to open up an easily navigable network of trans-continental routes just when the first farmers were becoming settled. Even though certain parts of the network were not in constant

intensive use, this system remained the basis of the continually increasing transport operation in central Europe throughout the prehistoric and early historic periods, *ie* for more than 6000 years. It was only the hunger for energy in the Middle Ages (twelfth century and later), when new water mills were built in ever increasing numbers, that inland boat travel was squeezed out of the upper reaches of rivers.

Boats and trade

The first evidence of the way in which trading was organised between the hunters of north Germany and the farmers residing further south dates from the early phase of farming culture (up to about 4000 BC), when the immigrants had occupied the entire mountain area of central and western Europe, but had not yet reached the low plains of north Germany. Archaeological finds from this period show that three small sandy islands in the Elbe, close to Hamburg-Boberg, were used as riverbank markets. This was the region of the Ertebølle/Ellerbek hunter culture, and the islands were used continuously for this purpose for several centuries. All trading parties had to travel to the islands by boat – hunters of the immediate

vicinity, as well as the farmers of the central Elbe-Saale region (around Magdeburg and Halle), who had journeyed at least 300km by river. For the first time it is possible to recognise trading behaviour which was to remain unchanged for several millennia: in every case the members of the more highly developed civilisation visited those of the more primitive cultures in their own region, choosing as meeting points small islands with little or no vegetation. Such an environment offered the foreigners a high level of safety, because ambushes could not be laid, and it was impossible for large numbers of enemy warriors to approach without warning. For example, when the farming way of life had penetrated as far as central Sweden, the Bronze Age farmers from Uppland travelled at least 250km by river and coastal waters to meet the hunters from the north at their island of Brådön in the Ångermannälv region. There they cultivated such good relations that they were allowed to engrave their religious symbols (the sun cult of the farmers) in the rocks which the hunters considered 'holy', and which were covered with drawings concerning hunting and magic. Much later – around 330 BC – Pytheas reported from Massilia (present-day Marseille) that continental merchants landed their ships on an island off the coast of Cornwall with the purpose of trading the tin mined by local people.

At the island markets of Hamburg-Boberg the early farmers of the central Elbe and Saale region wanted to acquire the products of hunting activity, *ie* primarily animal skins, and offered in exchange woven goods, corn and corn products as well as their ground stone axes. At the market site itself the hunters used their pointed-bottom cooking pots to prepare meals from the freshly traded corn, as is clear from the carbonised porridge residues attached to the excavated pottery fragments. A broken ground stone axe was also found at the market site. A smashed Linear Pottery hoe was found at an excavated hunter camp on the mainland near Boberg, and a second was excavated at the Duvenstedt hunter camp which had direct connections by water to the Boberg island market via the Elbe and Alster (40km); both indicate

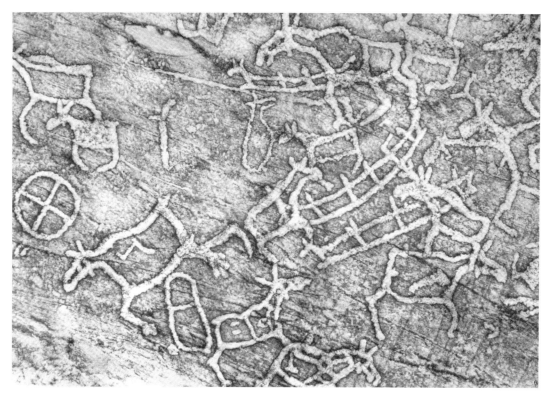

Bronze Age farmers from central Sweden travelled to the island of Brådön in northern Sweden, and carved these religious pictures in the rock.

how the trade goods penetrated into the hinterland after exchange on the island market. The hunters also copied decorative ideas and shapes of pottery items from the farmers' vessels, and introduced them into their own ceramic artefacts. Finally they left behind all kinds of flint tools designed for working timber and skins, which implies that manual work was carried out at the market site as well as trading. Transverse arrowheads were made there, leading us to conclude that the hunters shot waterfowl to provide a change in diet for the farmers and for themselves. The caches of flint hatchets found grouped in small areas most likely represent sacrificial offerings by the hunters (*eg* one hatchet each at the start of a market season).

When they first arrived the farmers of the Rössen Culture also buried an offering in the ground right at the water's edge, in the form of a magnificently decorated clay vessel, presumably with organic contents. This was the only pottery vessel to survive in its entirety on the islands. Like the farmers who had travelled so far, the native hunters would have pulled their boats up onto the sandy beach, and slept in simple tents during the period of their stay, preparing their meals over an open fire. As a result the stratum where the finds were made was interspersed with very large numbers of pieces of charcoal; a small number of fire sites were also found in situ and fragments of numerous cooking pots were strewn all over the area. Local pots were in the majority, of course, but in amongst them were many frag-

ments of vessels belonging to the foreign farmers. This evidence tells us that the island markets were in their turn sought out by representatives of the middle and late Rössen Culture, the late *stitchbandkeramic* peoples (Stroke Ornamented Pottery Culture), the Gatersleben Culture and the early Baalberge Culture over a period of many centuries. At one time a farmer died on the island, and according to the rites of the *stitchbandkeramic* people or the Gatersleben Culture his body was burned and buried at the market site without any further grave accompaniments. During this long, uninterrupted period when the Boberg islands in the Elbe functioned as a market, the way of life of the Ellerbek hunters gradually evolved into the agriculture-based Funnel Beaker Culture. We can therefore assume that, even when the late hunter groups were making the transition to a farming economy, communication sites like the Boberg island markets played an important role as sources of information and trading centres in manufactured goods, seed, breeding cattle and so on.

This early prehistoric river bank market has been discussed in considerable detail because these markets are not yet the subject of general research, even though in the waterborne communications network between cultures without towns they were the nodes or crossing points – roughly the equivalent of ports in later eras. Of these prehistoric river bank markets Hamburg-Boberg has been excavated most extensively, but it is by no means the only example. For

example, in exactly the corresponding topographical position to Bremen on the Weser (near Uesen, 23km by river above Bremen), dredging operations brought up a pottery beaker dating from the fairly early Linear Pottery period, which can surely only be interpreted like the sacrificial beaker from the Rössen Culture of Hamburg-Boberg. In any case we can now see the importance of identifying the major river bank markets archaeologically and defining them as the junctions of waterborne traffic for the various prehistoric periods, and of showing their geographical distribution.

Agriculture did not become so prevalent everywhere in early Stone Age Europe as it did in the regions discussed up to now. In Scandinavia the Pitted Ware Culture (*c*3500-2700 BC) retained far more elements of a hunting society, with the result that boats were used more intensively for obtaining daily food than in agrarian cultures. This is evident not least in the location of their settlements on the ancient beach lines of the sea and the great inland waters, but it was primarily reflected in the artefacts buried in men's graves, which were in stark contrast to the customs of other prehistoric European cultures. Harpoons, fishing spears, fish hooks and arrowheads cover the whole range of application of fishing/hunting boats. Bones found in the settlements confirm that seals were the primary target for the hunters, but fish were caught and waterfowl shot (with bow and arrow), making substantial contributions to the people's food. Implements made of imported flint indicate that travel boats were used for longer journeys. A crucial fact is that flint implements in the graves regularly constituted the basic tool set of axe and adze required to construct dugouts, occasionally supplemented by gouges, knife blades and grinding stones.

Even the men of greater status, honoured in their graves with ornamental artefacts, were still buried with both hunting implements and woodworking tools. Women's graves, on the other hand, contained neither tools nor hunting implements; instead they were buried primarily with ornaments and items of clothing. Weapons of war are only found in men's graves under the influence of the Battle Axe Culture (2800-2300 BC), but they soon supplanted tools and hunting implements in the canon of grave artefacts. From then on, until the time when the custom of burying grave

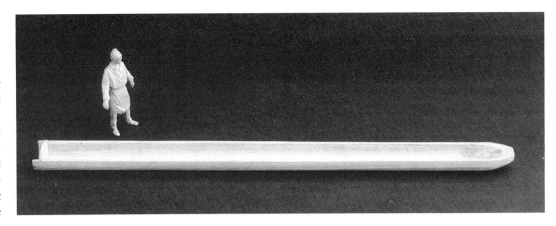

Late Stone Age dugout with spoon bow and inset transom, from the Federsee, Württemberg (length 10.86m).

artefacts fell into disuse in the late Viking period, these objects were dominated by weapons.

These two contrasting facts make it possible to state with some certainty a number of features of the Pitted Ware Culture: it was the men who travelled to hunt animals, occasionally undertook trading journeys by boat and built the boats required for these purposes in the form of wooden dugouts. In no other prehistoric culture of Europe north of the Alps can the gender-specific division of labour in the realm of water travel be proved so unambiguously.

It is quite obvious that the social standing of men was based on the skills and abilities mentioned above, with the result that hunting implements and tools were interred in the grave with them like status symbols. It is noteworthy that the last time that manual ability and hunting success were the foundation of men's social prestige was in this late Stone Age culture. The social upheaval brought about by the Battle Axe Culture was tremendous, and its ramifications must not be underestimated. It completely transformed the structure of society and set entirely new standards, with the result that from that point on a warrior's reputation with weaponry formed the basis of his social esteem.

Developed dugouts

Although the very effective European waterways network had been opened up by the skin boat, this boat type was unable to maintain its dominance over the long term even in central Europe, although in the British Isles it did remain in use in some areas right into the present century. In the early Middle Ages Irish seamen even undertook bold sailing journeys as far as Iceland using seagoing skin boats of this type.

In central Europe, in contrast, the dugout had already been developed by the hunters of the middle Stone Age, and eventually gained the dominant position even amongst the farmers of the Neolithic, after a period of competition with the skin boat. Even though these farmers were able to produce on their farms and in the neighbouring forests the overwhelming majority of their needs in terms of food, clothing, pottery vessels, and heating and building materials, they were still not completely autonomous. In fact they were dependent on the supply of certain indispensable raw materials – amongst which salt for the preservation of meat after the autumn slaughtering was particularly important. However, certain types of stone for making tools and weapons also had to be imported over considerable distances. Jewellery made of amber and jet enjoyed increasing popularity; and when in the fourth millennium BC the first metals were produced in the eastern Mediterranean, gold and copper jewellery items also found their way to the farmers' wives of central Europe. At the same time the farmers acquired copper hatchets and daggers.

Overall there was an increasing rate of exchange of goods over moderate and long distances during the late Stone Age. Furthermore it is obvious that the trans-continental rivers constituted the basic routes for the essential transport activities, and as demand increased, larger and larger boats were called for. To meet this demand the late Stone Age farmers started by basing their vessels on the large travel dugout developed by the middle Stone Age hunters (see the illustration of the boat found at Tybrind Vig, Denmark), and built dugouts of as great a length as possible, featuring a spoon bow and a separate, inset transom.

When they tried to use the thickest tree

Late Stone Age pottery model of a load-carrying dugout with inset transoms at bow and stern, from Telis, Bulgaria.

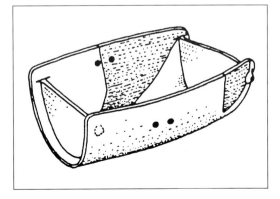

trunks they encountered difficulties in shaping the spoon bow, soon reaching or exceeding the limits of strength of the end-grain timber. That is why the next development was a dugout shaped like a channel, open at both ends, with a separate transom inset not only at the stern but also at the bow.

A clay model from Bulgaria of a load-carrying dugout of this type even indicates the heads of the dowels – probably still made of wood – by means of which the stern and bow transoms were attached. In spite of its rather inefficient shape, this type of load-bearing dugout was widely used for inland traffic within Europe from the lower Danube as far as the Schelde, and remained in use from the fourth millennium BC until the fourteenth century AD. This boat type was in use in Europe for a longer period than any other, and it is likely that the reasons behind its success were its simplicity and robustness.

Although the dugout with separate stern and bow transoms remained in use for an extraordinary length of time, it must not be forgotten that its transport performance was modest because of its inherently high weight, with the result that in the last millennia of its existence it was built and used only for subsidiary transport tasks. By the late fourth millennium boatbuilders were beginning to contrive methods by which they could develop dugout boats larger than the tree trunks from which they were worked. The starting point once again was the typical dugout with its spoon bow and separate, inset stern transom. With the help of two dugouts of this type from the Danish Åmose river we can even follow the steps taken to arrive at a satisfactory solution to this problem. The after side wall of the first dugout had cracked and split in use. In an effort to repair this split fine holes 0.5cm in diameter had been cut through the side wall below the fault (and definitely above it too, although that section of side wall did not survive), in order to close the split again with cords. This would

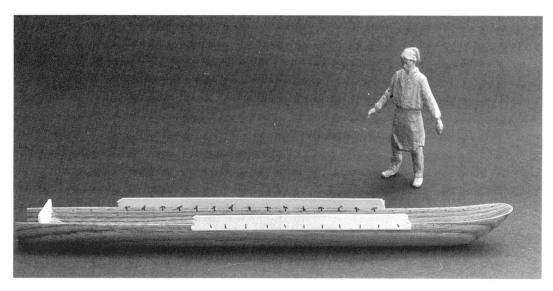

The oldest surviving planked boat from central and northern Europe is a late Stone Age dugout with additional plank strake from Åmose, Denmark (length 5.48m).

have protected the boat from further cracking, and the repair would have been sealed using some method that remains unknown.

The experience gained by such repairs, *ie* lashing together boat parts, evidently led to the crucial realisation that this method could not only make good an accidental split, but could be used as a watertight joint between an additional plank and the top edge of the dugout. In

Sketch of the construction of a broad, flat-bottomed boat from three dugout sections. It shows the principle by which the boat represented by the model from Osikovo, Bulgaria could have been made up of three different parts.

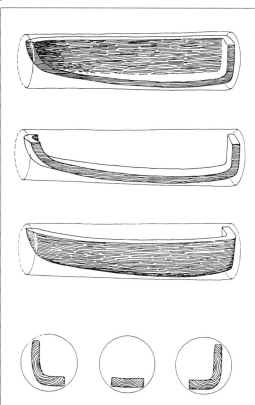

confirmation of this idea the second Åmose dugout exhibits rectangular holes about 2cm in diameter over the entire length of the hull side, at irregular intervals of 10cm to 28cm, just below the top edge. The purpose of these holes can only have been to attach an additional plank. Unfortunately the plank has not survived, so it is impossible to determine how the bow and stern were constructed. In any case no transverse stiffeners (such as frames) were fitted apart from the stern transom, and therefore it is safe to assume in any case that the additional

Late Stone Age pottery model of a wide, flat-bottomed boat from Osikovo, Bulgaria.

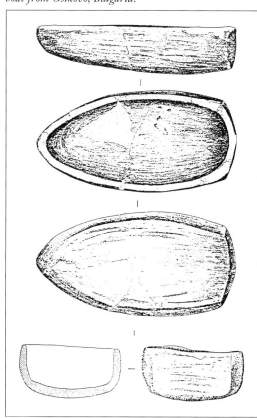

plank overlapped the side wall of the dugout slightly, using what the modern world knows as clinker construction. This is the first boat in which the cord lashing technique can be detected – a technique which differed significantly from the sewing method used on the skin boats. In fact this technique remained the standard method of connecting planks in central European wooden boatbuilding until shortly before the Christian era.

By attaching one or two additional strakes the boatbuilder produced a dugout of greater height, but even with the side walls projecting at an angle the vessel could not be built to much greater width. Once sufficient experience with the cord technique had been accumulated, boatbuilders eventually came up with a downright ingenious method of widening dugouts: the vessel was split exactly along the longitudinal centreline, the two halves separated, and a 'dugout without side walls' fitted in between. The three sections were then joined using the proven cord technique, and the result was a boat which was wider than the tree trunk used for the original dugout.

This technique was used for a while, until boatbuilders learned how to move on a further step: instead of splitting the original dugout, two corresponding halves of the dugout were cut from different trunks, each an exact mirror-image of the other. A further development was to fit more than one centre piece between the shells. Soon it was possible to construct relatively wide flat-bottomed vessels which combined the shallow draught required for small rivers with great longitudinal stiffness, since the two lateral half-shells were of 'angle-iron' section, which prevented the flat bottom from flexing.

This technology was applied to numerous different boat types until well into the fourteenth century AD, but it is difficult to estimate its real origins. For example, a Bulgarian clay model boat dating from the fourth millennium BC is so wide that the full-size vessel could only have been built using three dugout components and the technique described above. Unfortunately it is not certain that the model reproduces accurately the proportions of the original. The next reference point is an early Bronze Age boat (approximately the first half of the second millennium BC) excavated at North Ferriby in the north of England, which displays a highly significant further development of the con-

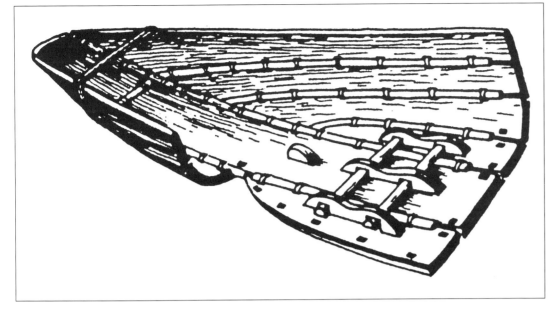

Early Bronze Age ship excavated at North Ferriby, England. Reconstruction of the bow showing a further development in boat construction using three dugout sections.

structional method discussed above. The central part of the vessel still comprises a dugout without side walls, as already described; the cord connection between the timbers by means of twisted yew twigs is also clearly recognisable, but the two lateral dugout half-shells are each assembled from four planks. The vessel could be considered as a standard planked boat were it not for the fact that the front end of each side strake has been cut from the full trunk in such a way that the joined parts together formed a complete spoon bow, as is familiar from Stone Age dugouts. Long before this early Bronze Age boat was built there must surely have been simpler predecessors of similar design, consisting of just the two dugout half-shells and a centre component fitted in-between. The model boat from Bulgaria is the first evidence for the proposition that the date of introduction of this fundamental boatbuilding invention was earlier than has been assumed up to now. Incidentally the model boat has the same form of bow as the North Ferriby boat.

Small clay wheels of model carts, of approximately the same age as the model boat, have also been found in Bulgaria, *ie* it must be assumed that the cart had already been introduced in the course of the fourth millennium BC. Of course, the cart pulled by oxen was used for short-range transport only, *eg* from the farm to the nearest harbour, rather than for long-distance travel, but at some stage it must have become necessary to carry the cart across

a river. Fording places could be sought for small rivers, but fords were not always available on larger rivers, with the result that ferries had to be devised in order to transport carts to the opposite bank. Initially these would certainly have been rafts. But in time boatbuilders realised that the raft trunks could be hollowed out like dugouts and then covered with a platform made of thick timber planks. Naturally a ferry made of hollow tree trunks had greater upthrust than a raft of solid trunks, and could therefore be built smaller. As a result it was also

much easier to use, and therefore quickly became the dominant type.

This technique of connecting several dugouts constitutes the third method by which boats larger than the available tree trunks could be constructed using dugout technology. To date the only trace we have of dugout ferries is individual dugout hulls which served as buoyancy vessels. At both ends they feature quite large rectangular holes in the side walls through which thick rectangular beams were fitted to hold together all the dugouts required to make a ferry. The exact number of dugouts for one ferry is not known. Below the top edge of the hull sides a row of smaller through-holes can be seen. Cords passed through these holes were used to lash in place the plank platform on which the cart would stand.

Early Stone Age farming cultures gave mankind a breakthrough in land-based travel with the invention of the cart. However, at the same time they also helped to develop water-borne transport significantly by devising vessels based on dugouts which were larger than the tree trunks available.

Detlev Ellmers

Ferry for carts composed from several dugouts with a platform on top, found in the river Weser near Minden. Crossbeam and platform are reconstructed to fit the pattern of holes in the sides of the dugout (not dated).

2

The Bronze Age in Northwest Europe

ALTHOUGH there is indirect archaeological evidence from northwest Europe that rivers were used and seas were crossed well before the beginning of the Bronze Age, there are only insubstantial remains of the water transport used: simple logboats (sometimes known as dugout canoes) dated to the Mesolithic and Neolithic periods in the Netherlands, Switzerland and Denmark (see previous chapter). Other forms of water transport undoubtedly remain to be discovered from these pre–Bronze Age times.

There are more remains from the Bronze Age (say, 2400 to 600 BC), and these are more complex than the earlier craft and, as one would expect, display more advanced technology. The technological achievements of Bronze Age people in other, non-boating, aspects of life in northwest Europe indicate that theoretically they could have built all the basic types of water transport ever known:[1] rafts of logs, bundles and floats; and log, bundle, hide, bark and plank boats. Furthermore, they had ready access to all the raw materials that they would have needed, except for the long rolls of quality bark required for bark boats and the bitumen for bundle boats.[2]

No rafts or hide/skin boats have been excavated from Bronze Age contexts. It seems likely, however, that rafts *were* used in the Bronze Age, although only on inland waters in these latitudes, but their remains have not yet been recognised in the archaeological record. This is probably because the materials from which they are made are, to a degree, ephemeral; furthermore, rafts may easily separate into their constituent parts when abandoned for, unlike boats, they do not have to be securely fastened together to make them watertight.

Hide boats

There are also reasons for thinking that hide boats were probably used in Bronze Age northwest Europe.[3] The excavated evidence is, however, insubstantial: antler fragments from

Husum, Schleswig-Holstein[4] of doubtful provenance; enigmatic evidence from an Early Bronze Age grave at Barns Farm, Dalgety, Fife;[5] possibly a small shale bowl from Caergwrle, Wales;[6] and minute boat models of gold from Nors, Denmark which some believe may represent Bronze Age hide boats, whilst others consider them to be sixth-century AD representations of extended logboats.[7] Rock carvings in Scandinavia of doubtful date and difficult in interpretation[8] may include representations of hide boats;[9] however, the reconstruction or 'replica' of the boat depicted on one of the carvings from Kalnes, Norway, built for Marstrander, is unconvincing.

The representation of boats in Scandinavian rock carvings are often very enigmatic, making interpretation difficult and often controversial. These examples from Norrköping, Sweden have been dated to the Bronze Age and are considered by many authorities to depict skin boats. (By courtesy of Basil Greenhill)

On the other hand, from the sixth century BC to the present day there is documentary and representational evidence – intermittent yet persistent – for the use of hide boats at sea, as well as on the rivers and lakes of Ireland and Britain.[10] Such a long-standing tradition does suggest firm roots which could well stretch back to the Bronze Age and even earlier in Britain and Ireland and adjacent parts of the Continent. Hide boats were also used in recent centuries in the circumpolar zone, so it would

1. S McGrail, 'Boats and boatmanship in the southern North Sea and the Channel', in S McGrail (ed), *Maritime Celts, Saxons and Frisians*, CBA Research Report 71, (London 1990), pp32-34.

2. S McGrail, *Ancient Boats in NW Europe* (London 1987), pp89-90, 163-5.

3. S McGrail, *Maritime Celts, Saxons and Frisians*, pp36-37; 'Early sea voyages', *International Journal of Nautical Archaeology* 20 (1991), pp80-93; 'Prehistoric seafaring in the Channel', in C Scarre and F Healy, *Trade and Exchange in Prehistoric Europe*, Oxbow Monograph 33 (Oxford 1993), pp199-210; 'Celtic seafaring and transport', in M Aldhouse-Green (ed), *The Celtic World* (London 1995), pp254-81.

4. Detlev Ellmers, 'Earliest evidence for skin boats in late-Palaeolithic Europe', in S McGrail (ed), *Aspects of Maritime Archaeology and Ethnography* (Greenwich 1984).

5. T Watkins, 'Prehistoric coracle in Fife', *International Journal of Nautical Archaeology* 9 (1980), pp277-286.

6. G T Denford and A W Farrell, 'Caergwrle bowl', *International Journal of Nautical Archaeology* 9, (1980), pp183-192; H S Green, A H V Smith, B R Young and R K Harrison, 'Caergwrle bowl: its composition, geological source and archaeological significance', *Report of the Institute of Geological Science* 80, (1980), pp26-30.

7. S Muller, 'Votivfund fro Sten og Bronzealderen', *Aaboger for Nordisk Oldkyndighed og Histoire* (Copenhagen 1886); P Johnson, *The Seacraft of Prehistory* (London 1980), p126; O Crumlin-Pedersen, 'Boats and ships of the Angles and Jutes', in McGrail, *Maritime Celts, Saxons and Frisians*, pp99-104, fig 14.5.

8. S Marstrander, *Ostfolds Jordbruksristninger Oslo: Skjeberg* (Oslo 1963); P Johnson, 'Bronze Age sea trial', *Antiquity* 46 (1972), pp269-74; J Coles and A Harding, *Bronze Age in Europe* (London 1979), p317.

9. J M Coles, 'Boats on the rocks', in J Coles, V Fenwick and G Hutchinson (eds) *Spirit of Enquiry* (Exeter 1993), pp23-31.

10. S McGrail, *Ancient Boats in NW Europe*, p186; *Maritime Celts, Saxons and Frisians*, p36.

The experimental skin boat built in 1971 under the auspices of Professor Marstrander of Oslo University and Paul Johnstone based on a rock carving from Kalnes, Norway. Recent opinion finds it unconvincing, but it did prove that it was possible to to build a seaworthy craft capable of carying a substantial load in smooth water with the materials available in the Bronze Age and earlier periods. (Paul Johnstone, by courtesy of Basil Greenhill)

not be surprising if evidence were to be found in future for their use by the earliest inhabitants of Norway, Sweden and Finland.

The hide boat fits well into an environment which has not been over exploited or over developed by man, where there are few, if any sizable trees, and where life can be sustained by sea fishing and hunting, with a good supply of hides from land or sea animals: this is virtually a crofter economy and more or less matches the generally accepted reconstruction of life in Mesolithic northwest Europe. Moreover, hide boats can be built with the tools and techniques known to have been used in the Mesolithic. Hide boats are quickly and relatively cheaply built and are readily repaired. They can be used on almost any type of coast from informal landing places and they are more buoyant, seaworthy and seakindly than equivalent plank boats.

Although twentieth-century hide boats are virtually keel-less and have a framework of laths fastened together, seventeenth-century Irish curachs had woven wicker framework and an external keel; there are good reasons for believing that Iron Age and earlier hide boats also had these features.[11] Such a framework is resilient and energy-absorbent yet holds the

shape of the boat and gives strength to the hull for least weight. An external keel allows a hide boat to be sailed closer to the wind than the modern curach which, without a keel, makes

much leeway, as Tim Severin found when he sailed the keel-less hide boat *Brendan* across the Atlantic.[12] Although *Brendan*'s frame had lost some of its sheer and her skin of forty-nine oxhides had developed corrugations at the end of her six-month oceanic voyage, she was in good shape. She may not have been an authentic reconstruction of a prehistoric seagoing hide boat, nevertheless her voyage did demonstrate that a large hide boat generally built by pre-industrial methods had reasonable seakeeping qualities and was reliable. Her voyage does, therefore, give some support, from a

11. S McGrail, *Maritime Celts, Saxons and Frisians*, pp36-9.

12. T Severin, *Brendan Voyage* (London1978).

A late seventeenth-century drawing by Captain Phillips of Irish curachs. The top view shows the 'Portable Vessell of Wicker, ordinarily used by the Wild Irish' and the lower demonstrates 'The Method of Workeing up y^e s^d vessel . . .'. Original in the Pepys Library. (By permission of the Masters and Fellows, Magdalene College, Cambridge)

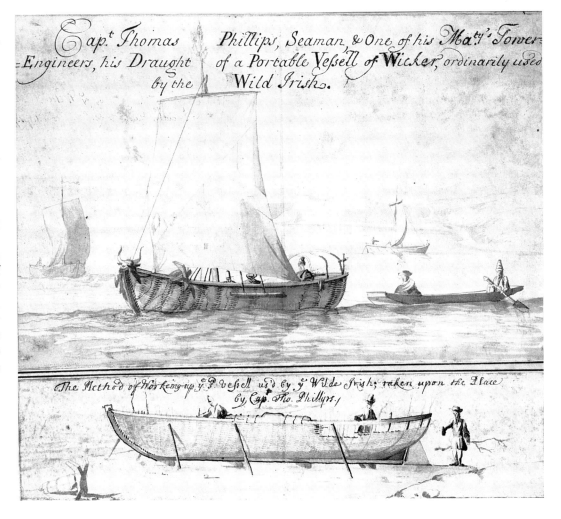

The stern of the Brigg logboat as excavated in 1886. The separate fitted transom has been removed and the additional thickness of bottom and sides at the stern can be seen. (National Maritime Museum)

practical viewpoint, to the hypothesis that hide boats could have been used in the seas off northwest Europe in the Bronze Age. It now remains for an early example of such a boat to be found and excavated.

Logboats

Logboats have been excavated in almost every country in northwest Europe.[13] Until relatively recently it had been assumed that all such finds were prehistoric, but of those that have been dated scientifically, more than half have proved to be post-Roman. Of the finds which are *pre-*Roman, most are either Stone Age or Iron Age, and only a few are from the Bronze Age. Five of these are from Britain: from Locharbriggs, Dumfriesshire, dated *c*2000 BC; Appleby, Lincolnshire of *c*1365 BC; Short Ferry, Lincolnshire of *c*1030 BC; Brigg, Lincolnshire of *c*1020 BC; and Peterborough, Northamptonshire of *c*700 BC .[14] All five boats are of oak (species *Quercus*).

Only about 2m of the oldest British logboat, that from Catherinefield, Locharbriggs, has survived. This boat had a flat bottom with flared sides and a rectangular end in plan. More survived of the other four boats and they have several features in common. First, they had all been converted from their parent logs so that they retained the log's taper in plan and in elevation, from stern to bow. They had a generally rectangular transverse section, with a rounded bow and a rectangular stern. The large slow-grown oaks from which these logboats were made were of great age and had developed heart rot at their butt end. Although this rot made it easier to hollow out the log, it also meant that the resulting open end, which, because it was broadest, invariably became the stern of the boat, had to be closed in some way to make it watertight. The Bronze Age solution to this problem was to leave the sides and the bottom of the stern thicker than the rest of the boat and to fit a separate transom board, some 60mm to 120mm thick, into a transverse groove worked into these thicker parts. Each

logboat also had some form of strengthening timber (beam tie), or possibly a lashing, across the stern to force the sides of this open end tight against the transom and thus keep the hull watertight.

Three of these boats had several holes bored through their bottom, along the centreline, which had been filled with wooden plugs; these are interpreted as gauges to estimate the bottom thickness during construction. In a small logboat the thickness of the bottom can be judged by eye or by feel, but this is not possible in larger boats. The Bronze Age solution was to remove the bark and sapwood, and then bore holes into the log, along the intended centreline, to a depth equivalent to the required bottom thickness. The log was then rolled over and hollowed out until daylight was seen. Subsequently, the holes were filled with tightly fitting wooden plugs.

Three of these boats had split longitudinally, either during manufacture or in service, and had been repaired. The sides of the split in the Short Ferry boat were held together by a timber within a transverse groove of dovetail cross section, underneath the stern. Splits in the Appleby boat were held together by two-stranded birch (species *Betula*) stitching and by flat wooden clamps of double-dovetail shape set into the inner face of the boat. In contrast,

splits in the Brigg logboat (Brigg 1) were filled with moss held in place by oak (species *Quercus*) patches stitched-on outboard. The largest of these patches, over 5ft (1.5m) in length, had three integral cleats which projected inboard through the split and were locked by wedges (keys or cotters).

The Brigg and Peterborough boats had a series of transverse ridges some 50mm to 100mm proud of the bottom. Such ridges have

The stern of the Short Ferry logboat. Note the dovetail groove under the stern for a timber designed to hold together the split halves of the hull. (National Maritime Museum)

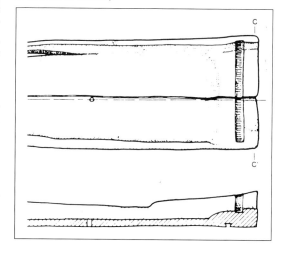

13. D Ellmers, 'Kultbarken, fahren, fischerboote Vergeschichtliche in Niedersachsen', *Die Kunde* NS24 (1973); Sean McGrail, *Logboats of England and Wales*, BAR 51 (Oxford 1978), pp4-13; F Rieck and O Crumlin-Pedersen, *Bade fra Danmarks Oldtid* (Roskilde 1988).

14. S McGrail, *Logboats of England and Wales*; Switsur, unpublished data.

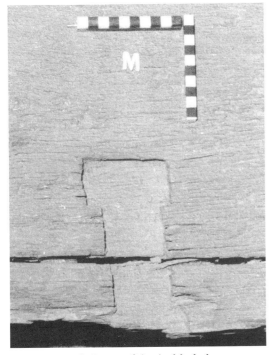

Recess cut into the bottom of the Appleby logboat to receive a wooden clamp intended to hold together the split sections of the hull. (National Maritime Museum)

been noted in many logboats, recent as well as archaeological specimens; some are spaced at regular intervals, but the majority seem to be haphazard. There is no single explanation for these ridges.[15] Some may be skeuomorphs, copied from the ribs of a plank boat, although, as they are integral with the logboat's hull and not separate timbers, they can contribute little, if any, transverse strength. Others may divide the boat into functional spaces, *eg* propulsion, cargo, command and steering. Ridges across the bottom may give a foothold for standing or kneeling paddlers; a ridge near the stern may similarly be used by a paddler/steersman sitting on the flat end. Where they extend up the sides they could well provide a seating for thwarts. Irregularly spaced ridges may have been used to support longitudinally-laid bottom boards thereby raising cargo above the bilge water. Other ridges may have been left in the solid as

dwarf bulkheads which would retain water along the length of the boat, thereby reducing drying-out problems when the boat was not in use.

The three ridges in the Brigg boat were all in the forward 40 per cent, spaced 1.40m and 1.85m apart, and did not extend up the sides of the boat. These may have been stations for paddlers, two at each ridge port and starboard, leaving the midships section clear for cargo. The five ridges across the bottom of the Peterborough boat were spread out along the length, yet still irregularly spaced at intervals ranging from 1.06m to 1.83m; possibly these supported bottom boards.

Large knot holes in each bow of the Brigg boat were filled with 0.30m diameter wooden plugs which protruded like bosses; these clearly had a secondary purpose as *oculi*, the eyes of the boat. Comparable 'eyes' are also found on the

15. S McGrail, *Logboats of England and Wales*; pp55-7; *Ancient Boats in NW Europe*, pp75-6.

The Brigg logboat as excavated. Engraving from Harold Dudley's Early Days in North-West Lincolnshire *after a contemporary photograph.* (By courtesy of Scunthorpe Central Library)

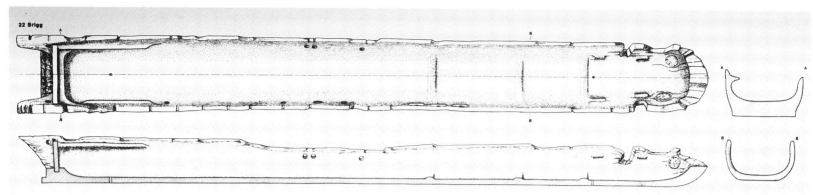

Plan, sectional elevation and sections of the Brigg logboat. Note the transverse ridges, and the sides and bottom left thickened aft to support the transom. (National Maritime Museum)

Hasholme logboat of *c*300 BC,[16] now in Hull museum; the first-century BC logboat from L Arthur/Lotus, Kirkcudbright, now in the National Museum in Edinburgh; logboat Holme Pierrepont 3 from the River Trent, probably of the second/third century BC; and on the 0.50m wooden model boat with warriors from Roos Carr, North Humberside, also in Hull museum, which has quartz eyes and has recently been dated to *c*600 BC.[17]

This Brigg boat has other features which its excavators in 1886 found difficult to interpret and the boat cannot now be re-examined as it was destroyed by fire during an air raid on Hull in 1942.[18] However, a logboat of comparable size was excavated at Hasholme near Holme on Spalding Moor, North Humberside in 1984[19] and research on this boat has thrown light on the Brigg find. The horizontal 'brackets' or 'shelves' left in the solid and extending along the sides of the Brigg boat from the stern for *c*6ft (2m) may now be confidently interpreted as supports for a platform or deck on which the steersman stood so that he could see over the heads of standing crew and heaped cargo. Similar 'brackets' or 'knees' in the forward part of the Brigg boat were probably for a deck for the lookout/bow steersman.

Several holes through the sides were found just below the sheerline of the Brigg logboat; descriptions of these from the late nineteenth/early twentieth century are not clear, but they appear to have been similar to holes in the Hasholme boat, which are most likely to have been where transverse lashings were temporarily fastened to hold the sides of the boat together during hollowing-out, until the transom

The Roos Carr ship model is thought to represent a logboat with a crew of warriors. The model has quartz eyes in what may be seen as a figurehead. (Hull City Museums and Galleries)

stern and transverse beam-tie timbers had been fastened in position. An alternative possibility is that these holes were fastening points for leather covers used to keep the cargo dry.[20]

Logboat function and performance

The diameter of the parent log inherently limits a logboat's waterline beam measurement, hence its transverse stability, and its depth of hull, hence its freeboard. In an unmodified form, therefore, logboats made from European trees are not suitable for seagoing except in unusually calm weather. There are, however, ways of overcoming these inherent handicaps. Freeboard may be increased by adding washstrakes to the sides, and stability may be improved by increasing the boat's effective

beam in one of four ways: forcing the sides apart after heat treatment; pairing two boats alongside one another; fastening stabilising timbers outboard along the waterline; or by booming out a timber float on one or two outriggers. Outriggers do not appear to have ever

16. M Millett and S McGrail, 'Archaeology of the Hasholme logboat', *Archaeological Journal* 144 (1987), pp96-155.

17. S McGrail, *Logboats of England and Wales*; figs 84 and 112; *Ancient Boats in NW Europe*, pp84-5.

18. S McGrail, *Logboats of England and Wales*; pp167-9.

19. M Millett and S McGrail, 'Archaeology of the Hasholme logboat', *Archaeological Journal* 144 (1987).

20. M Millett and S McGrail, 'Archaeology of the Hasholme logboat', pp122-4.

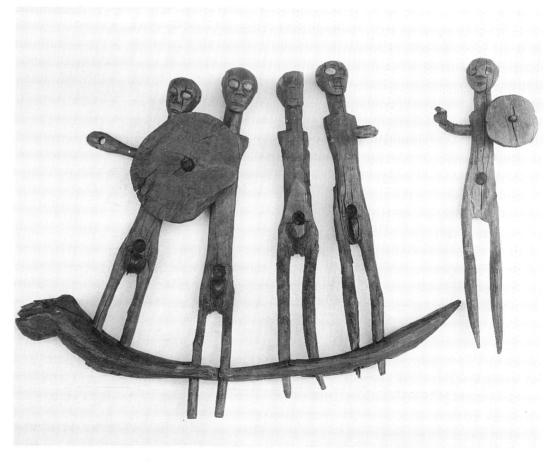

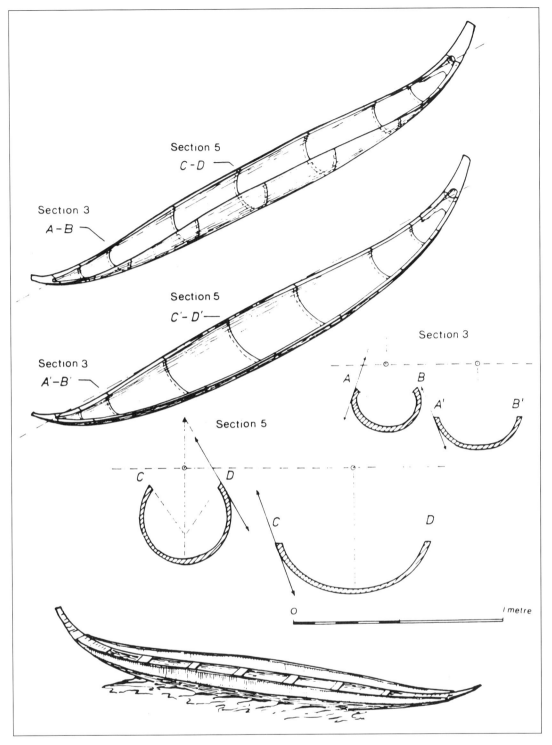

A logboat from Guiana showing the effects of expansion. After J Hurault, Africains de Guyane *(The Hague 1971).*

freeboard and is unlikely to have needed wash-strakes which would, in any case, have made paddling more difficult; and the holes through her sides are too high above the waterline for stabilisers. Theoretically, these holes might have been used to fasten another logboat alongside to form a pair, but to do this a tree of similar proportions to the Brigg parent log would have had to be found, and the result would have been a vessel which would undoubtedly have been stable but which would have been difficult to manoeuvre, probably suitable only for transporting a special load on a unique occasion. These holes, as described above, are best explained as temporary lashing points for use during construction or in service.

In summing up, then, there is no clear evidence for freeboard- or stability-enhancing modifications to the Brigg boat or to any other Bronze Age logboat so far known in Europe.[22] Indeed, it is not until the Roman period and later that there is clear evidence for any of these techniques in northwest Europe.

Logboats were used on inland waters, lakes, rivers, and possibly on the upper reaches of estuaries for hunting, fishing, fowling, reed-gathering and the like, as well as the more prosaic tasks of ferrying animals, cargo and people. At times they may also have been used by raiding parties – see, for example, the armed men associated with the late Bronze Age model logboat from Roos Carr, North Humberside. The Brigg logboat and her contemporaries were propelled by paddles, or by poles ('punted') in the shallows. They were also steered by paddles, with one steersman in the stern and, in the longer ones, a second steersman in the bows. Paddles suitable for propelling boats are known in northwest Europe from the late eighth millennium BC onwards.[23] The fourth-century BC Hjortspring plank boat had steering paddles that were larger versions of her propulsion paddles; these are also known ethnographically. Metal terminals for 'punting' poles have been found in Iron Age contexts.[24]

In order to deduce the capabilities of specific ancient boats, it is necessary to reconstruct

been used outside the Pacific and Indian Oceans and are thus unlikely to have been used in Bronze Age Britain. Only certain species of timber can be safely expanded and, notwithstanding Gifford's preliminary and incomplete experiment,[21] oak is one of the more intractable. Furthermore, the sides of the boat have to be made relatively thin and fashioned to a particular shape before expansion. The known Bronze Age logboats, of oak and with sides up to 60mm in thickness, are thus unlikely to have been expanded.

As no fittings have survived, the only evidence which might suggest that Bronze Age logboats had been modified so that their freeboard and stability were improved are the patterns of holes through their sides and ends where fittings may formerly have been fastened. None of these boats has holes which might have been where washstrakes or stabilisers were fitted or by which two boats were paired, except for the Brigg boat. However, hydrostatic calculations show that, when loaded, this boat (Brigg 1) has relatively good

21. E Gifford, 'Expanding oak logboats: is it possible?' in Coles, *et al*, *Spirit of Enquiry*, pp52-3.

22. S McGrail, *Ancient Boats in NW Europe*, pp66-75.

23. S McGrail, *Ancient Boats in NW Europe*, pp205-7; Rieck and Crumlin-Pedersen, *Bade fra Danmarks Oldtid*, p28.

24. S McGrail, *Ancient Boats in NW Europe*, pp204-5.

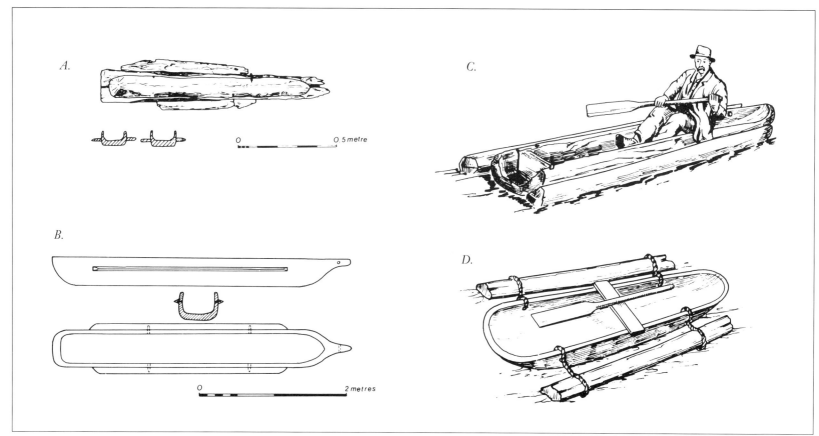

Table 2/1: Details of Bronze Age boats

Boat	Overall size (metres)	Load	Dwt (tonnes)	T (metres)	F (metres)	%	Dwt coef	Vol coef
Brigg 1	14.8 x 1.4 x 1.0	Max men 2 + 26	1.44	.35	.65	35	0.34	1.54
		5 men + 5.49t	5.79	.60	.40	60	0.67	–
Brigg 2	12.2 x 2.3 x 0.34	4 men + 26 sheep	1.54	.25	.09	74	0.23	–
	12.2 x 2.3 x 0.55	6 men + 17 cattle	7.16	.46	.09	84	0.57	6.70
Ferriby 1	15.4 x 2.6 x 0.70	men and goods	3.00	.30	.36	45	0.54	–
		men and goods	5.50	.40	.26	61	0.52	3.80
Ferriby 1*	15.9 x 2.5 x 0.98	2 + 18 men + 5.2t cargo	6.70	.58	.40	59	0.63	4.16
		2 + 18 men + 30 passengers + 2.9t cargo	6.70	.58	.40	59	0.63	4.16
Hjortspring	13.6 x 2.04 x 0.71	2 + 20 men	2.11	.31	.39	44	0.80	0.83

Notes:

Size = Overall length x maximum beam x depth from sheer to underside of keel at max beam station.

Dwt = Deadweight (weight of crew and entire load).

T = Draught.

F = Freeboard.

% = Ratio of draught to height of sides expressed as a percentage. 60 per cent is used for international comparisons of seagoing vessels.

Dwt coef = Deadweight coefficient (deadweight divided by displacement – the greater, the better the boat is for carrying high density loads).

Vol coef = Volumetric coefficient

$$= \frac{\text{displacement}}{(\text{waterline length})^3}$$

or: displacement divided by waterline-length-cubed. The given values should be multiplied by 10^{-3}. Values less than 2×10^{-3} suggest a hull with high speed potential.

Brigg 1 = Brigg logboat. Source: S McGrail, *Logboats of England and Wales* (1978).

Brigg 2 = 'raft'. The estimates are made at two different heights of side. Source: Coates in S McGrail, *Brigg 'Raft' and Her Prehistoric Environment* (1981).

Ferriby 1 = Minimum solution. Estimates made at two different waterlines for unspecified loads. Source: Coates, personal communication.

Ferriby 1* = Recent reconstruction by Wright, *Ferriby Boats* (1990) with rockered plank-keel, three instead of two side strakes and other changes.

Estimates by Coates at same waterline; (a) as a cargo carrier (b) as a passenger ferry.

Hjortspring. Overall size is without end extensions. Source: Rosenberg, *Hjortspring fundet* (1937).

Comparison of performance. Although general comparisons of these boats may be made, based on the data in this table, precise comparisons may not be valid as not all have been assessed at the standard waterline. Moreover, different reconstructors have used different values for parameters, such as the weight of a crewman.

One method of increasing beam, and hence stability, in logboats is to attach additional timbers to the outside of the hull. Four examples are shown here.

A. Logboat with stabilising timbers from North Småland, Sweden, now in the Göteborg Museum.

B. Logboat from Tappnäs, Sparreholm, Hyltinge, Södermanland, Sweden, with stabilising timbers. Now in Statens Historiska Museum.

C. Logboat from Gunnarskog, Värmland, Sweden, with stabilising timbers treenailed to the sides and a fitted transom.

D. Logboat from Mangskog, Värmland, Sweden with stabilising timbers fastened by withies.
(National Maritime Museum)

their original full shape and structure, in a theoretical way, by removing distortions, bringing together fragmented parts, and filling in the missing pieces. This process has proved possible only for Brigg 1 out of the known Bronze Age logboats. Data concerning this reconstruction are given in Table 2/1 where it can be seen that, as an armed raider or in a 'despatch boat' role, with a draught of just over 1ft (0.35m), she could carry a crew of two steersmen standing and twenty-six paddlers kneeling. With a low volumetric coefficient this boat had relatively good speed potential and therefore it is likely that, with this full complement and in fair conditions, she could have achieved a sprint speed of 6kts to 7kts for a short while, although her cruising speed is unlikely to have been greater than 3kts to 4kts. As a cargo carrier with a single steersman and four paddlers, at a draught of 2ft (0.60m), she could have carried loads of more than 5 tonnes, depending on the cargo density of the load.

Plank boats

There has been much debate about the origins of the plank boat, but without any generally agreed conclusions. It seems unlikely, however, that there was just one unique origin; the plank boat was probably conceived in different places at different times, and was probably developed from different bases: perhaps from the logboat in northwest Europe, the hide boat in northern Europe, and from other basic boats and rafts elsewhere. In Neolithic northwest Europe there were logs suitable for conversion into planks and the tools and technology needed to build simple plank boats were certainly used in that period to make other artifacts. There is, however, no evidence for such boats until the Bronze Age, not just in northwest Europe, but anywhere in the world.

The earliest plank boats to be excavated in northwest Europe had no metal fastenings, rather stitched or sewn planking. They have been found in four areas: four finds from the Humber estuary region in eastern England; two fragmentary finds from the northern shores of the Severn estuary in southeast Wales; one find from Dover in southeast England; and one find from the island of Als, Denmark. Chronologically, they can be divided into three groups: (A) mid-second millennium BC; (B) late second/early first millennium BC; and (C) the fourth century BC. So far it has proved possible to date only the Goldcliff fragments (one of the Severn finds) by dendrochronology; the others have been dated by radiocarbon assay which is a less precise method. The accuracy of both methods depends, in the last analysis, on estimates of the number of annual growth rings which were removed in antiquity when the parent logs or limbs were fashioned into boat timbers. For

25. E V Wright, *Ferriby Boats* (London 1990).

26. V R Switsur and E V Wright, 'Radiocarbon dates and calibrated dates for the boats from North Ferriby, Humberside: a reappraisal', *Archaeological Journal* 146 (1989), pp58-67.

27. E V Wright, G R Hutchinson and C W Gregson, 'Fourth boat-find at North Ferriby, Humberside', *Archaeological Journal* 146 (1989), pp44-57; E V Wright and V R Switsur, 'Ferriby 5 boat fragment', *Archaeological Journal* 150 (1993), pp46-56.

28. S McGrail, *Brigg 'Raft' and Her Prehistoric Environment*, BAR 89 (Oxford 1981), p242.

Ferriby 1 on the foreshore of the River Humber during excavation in 1946. Eventually parts of three stitched plank boats were discovered and these have been dated by C14 methods to about 1300 BC. (National Maritime Museum)

this reason, it should not be assumed that the Caldicot find (southeast Wales) is necessarily older than the Ferriby finds (Humber), nor Goldcliff older than Brigg (Humber), although, in both cases, the summary dates given below may appear to suggest that.

The Ferriby finds

The remains of a stitched plank boat were discovered by E V and C W Wright in 1937 on the foreshore, between the tides, on the northern bank of the River Humber at North Ferriby. Later, part of a second boat was found and both were excavated in 1946. A third fragment was excavated in 1963.[25] Samples from all three boats have been dated by radiocarbon and these boats are now thought to have been in use *c*1300 BC.[26]

Two further timber fragments have recently been recovered and dated: a plank fragment of alder (species *Alnus*) from 535 to 355 BC; and a fragment of oak (species *Quercus*) from 410 to 350 BC.[27] The latter timber resembles the top of a cleat from the Brigg plank boat (Brigg 2, below) and may therefore have come from a

stitched boat. The alder plank fragment, however, has neither cleats nor stitch holes and its relevance to sewn boat studies is therefore doubtful.

Although the first three Ferriby finds differ in detail (for example, boat 3 has no cleats on the surviving elements), they have many characteristics in common. Boat 1 had the most remains – the greater part of the bottom and part of one side strake – all of oak. The central bottom plank, the two parts of which were joined in a simple half-lap, was thicker than the other two and protruded below them as a plank-keel. The edges of all three bottom planks were cunningly shaped so that the planks interlocked; 'tongue-and-groove' generally describes this joinery, but that is not an accurate description; perhaps 'interlocked' is better. These planks were fastened together by individual lashings of yew (species *Taxus*) over a caulking of moss held in position within and over the seams by longitudinal laths. The yew lashings were passed two and a half times through opposing fastening holes and then wedged in position. These lashings were single withies which had been twisted to separate the fibres and thus make them sufficiently pliable for use in this manner. The three bottom planks of boats 1 and 2 were further linked by horizontal transverse timbers wedged within cleats which had been left proud of each plank at intervals along its length. These timbers, acting in some respects like framing, kept the bottom planking aligned, both longitudinally and vertically, and thus reduced the stresses on the lashings. They were also probably used to re-align the planking before it was fastened together after periodic dismantling for which there is much ethnographic evidence.[28]

The surviving end of boat 1 had been given an upward curve by externally shaping and

The method of fastening the lowest side strake to the outer bottom planking in the Ferriby boats. (Drawing by E V Wright)

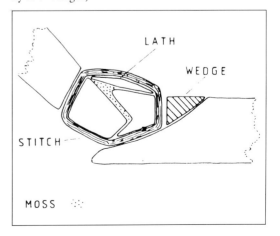

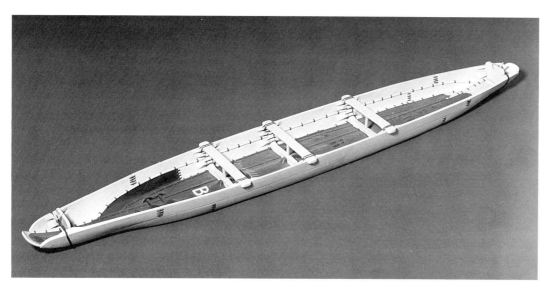

The 1/10th scale reconstruction model of Ferriby 1, the minimum compatible with the excavated remains (represented by the black part – the remainder is conjectural). (National Maritime Museum)

internally hollowing the plank-keel. The end of the lowest side strake had been worked to curves in two dimensions to form the turn of the bilge and to blend with the curve of the plank-keel to form the lower bow. The bevels worked along the lower edge of this strake clearly display the builder's mastery of woodworking techniques for they had varying cross sections so that this strake fitted *within* a rabbet in the edge of the outer bottom plank, yet *enveloped* the edge of the plank-keel towards the end of the boat. Having the lower seams interlocking in this manner ensured that the lashings did not protrude below the boat's bottom where they could have been damaged when the boat was beached or otherwise took the ground. Comparable precautions are taken by builders of stitched boats today. The upper edge of the Ferriby side strake was worked to a half-lap joint and fastening holes had been worked along its length to receive a second strake (see section on Caldicot finds below).

The minimum reconstruction compatible with the excavated remains is depicted in a 1:10 scale model on display in the National Maritime Museum at Greenwich; it is assumed that the missing end was similar to the surviving end. The rising part of the plank-keel and the two strakes each side which are fastened to it form a fairing to an inserted transom which is the true watertight end to the boat. Three composite frames lashed to the bottom and sides strengthen this shell of planking and conjectural crossbeams from sheer to sheer could have been used as thwarts by crew and passengers. The resulting vessel measures 15.4m x 2.6m x 0.70m.

E V Wright's most recent (1991) reconstruction of Ferriby 1, with three side strakes. (Drawing by E V Wright)

At a draught of 0.30m this minimum reconstruction could have carried crew and cargo up to a total of *c*3 tonnes; or at 0.40m, 5.5 tonnes (Table 2/1). She would have been used within the Humber estuary and in the many rivers that flow into it, as a ferry, primarily of men, but also of animals and goods. With a length-to-breadth ratio of *c*6 to 1 and a lowish volumetric coefficient, she had good speed potential and could have achieved speeds of, say, 6kts when carrying a full complement of paddlers (eighteen?) with correspondingly less space for cargo. Such speeds would have been necessary when crossing the tidal Humber at times other than slack water. In shallow waters she could readily have been propelled by poles, probably one on each bow and one on each quarter, leaving room for goods and passengers amidships.

Ted Wright has recently re-assessed his excavation records[29] and proposed a new and radically different reconstruction of Ferriby boat 1, with a longitudinally rockered bottom,

greater height of sides and other structural changes. A variant of this revised reconstruction has a mast and sail but, as the Ferriby boats were being used 1000 years before the earliest evidence for sail in northwest Europe, this possibility is purely conjectural.

This revised reconstruction, with three side strakes, would have measured 15.9m x 2.5m x 0.98m. In a cargo-carrying role, at a draught of 0.58m, this version could have carried about 5.2 tonnes of cargo, with a crew of two standing steersmen and eighteen sitting paddlers; alternatively, at the same draught and with the same crew, she could have carried thirty passengers and 2.9 tonnes of cargo.[30]

Finds from Caldicot, Gwent

Excavations in 1990 at Caldicot Castle, Gwent in a former bed of the River Nedern, a tributary of the Severn, revealed a large fragment of oak planking from a stitched boat.[31] This fragment was 3.55m long, broken in antiquity at one end and having a rounded point at the

29. E V Wright, *Ferriby Boats*, pp85-109; 'North Ferriby boats – a final report', in C Westerdahl (ed), *Crossroads in Ancient Shipbuilding*, Oxbow monograph 40 (Oxford 1994), pp29-34.

30. Wright, 'North Ferriby boats – a final report', pp113-5.

31. S Parry and S McGrail, 'Prehistoric plank boat fragment and a hard from Caldicot Castle Lake, Gwent, Wales', *International Journal of Nautical Archaeology* 20 (1991), pp 321-4; McGrail and Parry, 'Bronze Age sewn boat fragment from Caldicot, Gwent, Wales', in C Westerdahl (ed), *Crossroads in Ancient Shipbuilding* (1994), pp21-8.

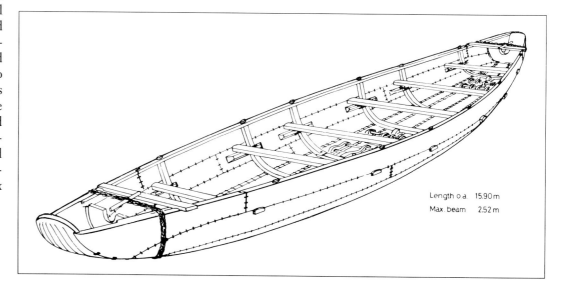

Length o.a. 15.90m
Max. beam   2.52 m

The substantial plank fragment found at Caldicot, Gwent in August 1990; remains of three cleats protrude from it and it is clearly from a stiched boat of the Ferriby type, even if different in detail. (Glamorgan Gwent Archaeological Trust)

other; its maximum breadth was 0.66m and its thickness varied from *c*60mm to 90mm.

Protruding from the inner surface of the plank are the remains of three cleats which originally were probably *c*100mm high. The find's outboard surface was curved in three dimensions, especially towards the surviving end. One edge (probably the upper one) was square; the other had a rabbet which was probably part of a half-lap joint. Along both edges L-shaped fastening holes had been worked from the inboard face to emerge within the plank edges. As in the Ferriby boats, lashings through these holes would not have been visible outboard. These holes were much bigger in section than the Ferriby fastening holes, being on average 134mm x 42mm compared with *c*35mm x 25mm. Why these Caldicot holes were so large is not clear, but possibly it had something to do with ease of manufacture; this great size does suggest, however, that the strake of which this was a fragment was fitted where it would normally have been above the waterline, probably a

The remains of the Dover boat in situ, *showing the main features of the construction: the longitudinal 'cleat rails' and the half-round cleats, both integral with the bottom planks; the yoke-shaped opening at the end is also apparent.* (By courtesy of Paul Bennet, Canterbury Archaeological Trust)

second or higher one. The rabbet cut on the lower edge of this fragment, near the broken end, is in fact the mirror image of the rabbet on the upper edge of the first side strake of Ferriby 1. The Caldicot find was most likely the end section of a second strake of a stitched boat which was generally, but not precisely, like Ferriby 1; the fragments' curved end and expanded rabbet would blend into a Ferriby-style bow or stern. This conjectural boat would have had a narrow third strake, more a capping, which would have been stitched on to the second strake in a butt joint. The cleats on the inboard face of the Caldicot strake would have housed elements of the boat's upper framing.

Found near the plank and similarly dated to *c*1600 BC were two fragments of yew withy which had each been twisted upon themselves to form a 'rope' similar to a Ferriby lashing but, in this case, only *c*30mm in girth (10mm diameter). It seems unlikely that, at this date, such insubstantial 'ropes' were used as plank fastenings; they may, however, have been used in other parts of a boat.

From another context and dated to *c*1100 BC came a minor and insubstantial fragment of planking with holes for stitched fastenings. The size of these holes and the general character of this fragment suggest that it came from the edge of a plank similar to a Brigg 2 bottom plank (see below).

All these nautical finds from Caldicot are being conserved for display in Newport Museum.

The Dover boat

In 1992, whilst monitoring construction work connected with improvements to the A20 trunk road in Dover, Canterbury Archaeological

Trust identified the remains of a stitched plank boat. Although some of the remains had to be left unexcavated, a large proportion of the boat was lifted, including much of the bottom planking, substantial portions of two side strakes and parts of one end. These remains are now under conservation and will subsequently be displayed in Dover.[32]

The boat is provisionally dated to *c*1300 BC. It is built of oak and the timber scantlings are comparable with those of Ferriby 1, as are the yew lashings and the cleats. The bottom consists of two thick planks which meet in a butt joint along the centreline of the boat. A lath overlies this seam, with moss caulking. Beside the seam are 'cleat rails', integral with each plank and running along its length. These two planks are not lashed together but linked by tapered timbers (keys/cotters) driven through holes in the cleat rail so that they become wedged in position; these linking timbers also firmly hold down the longitudinal lath on top of the seam. The bottom planks are further linked by occasional transverse timbers, similar to those in the Ferriby boats, which run through cleat rail holes and through Ferriby-style cleats proud of each plank.

The lowest side strakes have a hollow cross section and interlock at their lower edges with the outer edges of the bottom planks where there are moss/lath/lashing fastenings. A half-lap bevel on their upper edges would match the bevel on the lower edge of the Caldicot upper side strake fragment. There are occasional cleats on these Dover side strakes but these are not in line with the bottom plank cleats; as on

32. K Parfitt and V Fenwick, 'Rescue of Dover's Bronze Age boat', in Coles *et al*, *Spirit of Enquiry*, pp77-80.

An overhead view of the Brigg 'raft' (Brigg 2) during excavation. The main parts comprise five bottom planks and one side strake; the white dots indicate some of the holes for the stitching that held the planking together. (National Maritime Museum)

the Caldicot strake, these side cleats could have housed framing elements.

Towards the surviving end of this boat the two bottom planks and the side strakes were scarphed to a now-missing board which closed that end. This scarph was fastened together by tapered timbers wedged through a yoke-shaped cleat rail, and made watertight by moss caulking and a lath.

The post-excavation work on these remains will not be finished for some time and until that research is published the precise details of the boat's structure will not be clear. It is already evident, however, that the Dover boat has the general characteristics of the Ferriby boats but differs in specific features. As the Dover boat is keel-less whereas Ferriby has a plank-keel, and the two boats had different shapes in plan and different length-to-breadth ratios, different performance may be expected. How this boat was used depends not only on its form and structure but also on its contemporary environment, and research on this has also still to be completed.

The Brigg plank boat

The Brigg logboat (Brigg 1) was excavated in 1886. Two years earlier, part of a wooden causeway (known to archaeologists as a 'trackway') had been excavated some 400m northwest of the logboat find-spot, on an east/west alignment across the Ancholme valley. In 1888, two years after the logboat excavation, the so-called 'raft' (Brigg 2) was exposed by workmen digging for brick clay *c*120m north of the causeway.[33]

The Brigg 'raft' was re-excavated by the National Maritime Museum in 1974, when about three-fifths of the bottom planking and part of a lowest side strake were recovered. These timbers are now in the Museum at Greenwich, being conserved before display.

Brigg 2 was not a 'raft' but a flat-bottomed boat. The bottom of this boat consisted of five planks of equal thickness so, unlike the Ferriby boats, she had no keel. As in the Dover boat, the Brigg bottom planks were butted edge to edge; unlike Dover, however, these planks were fastened together by a continuous zig-zag stitching of a two-stranded 'rope' of willow

The method of fastening the bottom planking of the Brigg 'raft'. (National Maritime Museum)

(species *Salix*) over a moss caulking, capped by a longitudinal lath of hazel (species *Corylus*) along each seam. As these planks were significantly thinner at their edges, where the fastening holes were sited, than over their remaining breadth, the stitching was well above the bottom of the boat and therefore was unlikely to be damaged when the boat took the ground.

The Brigg bottom planking was also linked by transverse timbers wedged within cleats proud of each bottom plank, as in Ferriby 1 and 2, and Dover. The Brigg cleats were, however, bigger and more closely and regularly spaced than those in the other three boats. The outer edge of each outer bottom plank was not reduced in thickness and the fastening holes here were not vertical but angled so that they emerged within the outer edge of the plank. A side strake was fastened on here so that it partly

overlapped the bottom, with moss/lath/zig-zag stitching which was well above the bottom of the boat. There were also fastening holes along the upper edge of this strake where a second strake had formerly been fastened in a bevel-lap joint.

No signs of any framing timbers, other than transverse timbers, were found on excavation and both ends of the boat were incomplete. The minimum reconstruction therefore must be in the form of a lidless box, some 12.2m in length, slightly tapering in plan towards both ends from a maximum of *c*2.27m at a position *c*8m from one end. The minimum solution to the problem of making the ends watertight, and one that accords with the technology known to

33. S McGrail, *Brigg 'Raft' and Her Prehistoric Environment* BAR 89 (Oxford 1981), pp3-6.

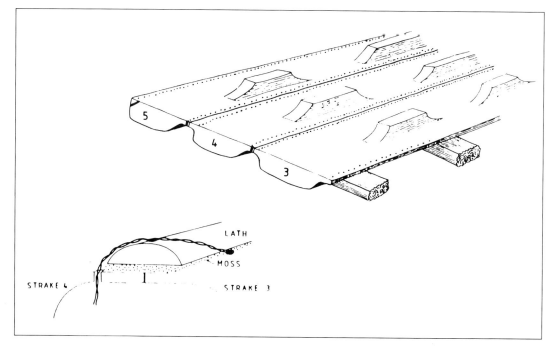

have been used in British logboats at that time or earlier, is to have a transom board set in a groove in the bottom and side planking. The minimum number of side strakes is two, the second one being of such a breadth that the total side height would be either 0.34m or 0.55m. Due to lack of evidence it is difficult to suggest suitable framing, additional to the system of transverse timbers and cleats, and it may be that none was necessary. However the suggestion by Sam Manning in *The Evolution of the Wooden Ship* (1988) that there could have been four crossbeams, hooked at their ends over the sides, has the virtue that not only would they brace the, otherwise unsupported, side strakes but would also serve to pen any animals being carried.

Owain Roberts[34] has recently proposed a more complex reconstruction as a round-hulled vessel with a longitudinally rockered bottom. These proposals are partly based on a misunderstanding of the excavated evidence[35] and, in any case, the reconstruction as a 'lidless box' (for which there are many ethnographic and some archaeological parallels) is a minimum solution: other solutions are theoretically possible–providing they are compatible with the evidence–but would involve more conjecture. A round hull is *not* compatible with the evidence, but some rocker is a possibility which requires further investigation.

The 'box-like' Brigg boat 2 was a poled or paddled ferry on the middle reaches of a tidal creek of the Humber estuary at a point in the Ancholme valley where the highlands to east and west were closest, thus restricting the water virtually to a permanent channel rather than the ever changing, transitory channels which are typical of many tidal creeks. The Brigg site was thus a nodal point on which east/west traffic converged, and Brigg 2 was a vital link as a ferry operating from mud flats on the margins of the channel, where animals, people and goods could be embarked. In this role she would have made a significant contribution to the economic and social well-being of the region immediately south of the Humber, from the east coast to the River Trent further west. Details of the carrying capacity of Brigg 2 are given in Table 2/1 where it can be seen that she could have carried loads varying from 26 sheep with 4 men, to 17 cattle with 6 men, depending on the height of sides of the original vessel.

High speed was not essential for this boat and she was not 'designed' with that in mind.

When no longer needed as a boat, Brigg 2 was moored in *c*800 BC, on the eastern approaches to the river, as a landing stage, with one end on relatively dry ground and the other end floating in the deep water channel where boats could be boarded. It seems likely that the Brigg causeway had been built for a similar purpose, some time earlier further upstream. As sea levels fell in the local region and the Ancholme creek became non-tidal at Brigg, the re-used Brigg 2 boat settled into a bed of reeds and was quickly covered by sediments.

The Goldcliff Find

During excavations on the foreshore, between the tides, at Goldcliff on the northern side of the Severn estuary, east of the mouth of the River Usk, two fragments of stitched planking were found to have been re-used in a small platform.[36] Along the centreline of each fragment was an integral cleat ridge, comparable in some respects to those on the bottom planking of the Dover boat. Along the edges of the fragments were fastening holes similar to those on Brigg 2. These timbers have been dated by dendrochronology to *c*1000 BC.

The Hjortspring Boat

The remains of a stitched plank boat were excavated in 1921-2 from a small bog, 50m x 50m, at Hjortspring, near the centre of the island of Als off the eastern coast of southern Denmark.[37] The boat had been broken and the parts ritually deposited along with numerous weapons, including swords, spears and shields, in what was then a pool or shallow lake. Recently the timbers of this boat have been re-conserved and re-assembled in the National Museum in Copenhagen.[38]

The shape of this boat resembles the outlines of boats depicted in some rock carvings and on

swords generally dated to the Bronze Age.[39] The weapons with the Hjortspring boat are, however, dated to the fourth century BC, and a radiocarbon date of timbers recently excavated from the original site has given a date of *c*350 to 300 BC. This date places the boat in a period known as the Pre-Roman Iron Age, nevertheless, it is appropriate to discuss the vessel here alongside earlier stitched boats, with which it has affinities, since, after Hjortspring, this method of fastening boat planking seems to have become restricted to the margins of Europe in northern Scandinavia and the eastern Baltic.[40]

The Hjortspring boat was built shell-first, with the shell consisting of seven main parts, all of them of lime (species *Tilia*): a bottom plank; two block stems; and four side strakes. There were ten frames *c*1m apart, each consisting of a rib, two crossbeams and one or two pillars. The bottom plank which was *c*15m long, was hollowed internally and externally to give a curved lower hull, *c*20mm thick. It is unclear whether the varying cross section was obtained entirely by hewing or by expansion after heating. Expansion could not only have produced appropriate cross sections, but could also have

34. O T P Roberts, 'Brigg "raft" re-assessed as a round bilge Bronze Age boat', *International Journal of Nautical Archaeology* 21 (1992), pp245-258.

35. S McGrail, 'Brigg "raft": a flat-bottomed boat', *International Journal of Nautical Archaeology* 23 (1994), pp283-8.

36. M Bell, 'Intertidal archaeology at Goldcliff in the Severn estuary,' in Coles *et al*, *Spirit of Enquiry*, pp9-13.

37. G Rosenberg, *Hjortspring fundet* (Copenhagen 1937).

38. J Jensen, 'Hjortspring boat reconstructed', *Antiquity* 63 (1989), pp531-5.

39. A E Christensen, 'Scandinavian ships from earliest times to the Vikings', in G F Bass (ed), *History of Seafaring* (1972), pp160-80

40. S McGrail and E Kentley (eds), *Sewn Plank Boats*, BAR S 276 (Oxford 1985), pp195-268.

The rather crude 1971 'replica' of the Hjortspring boat was too narrow and too shallow, but gives a fair overall impression of the appearance of this type of craft. (By courtesy of Basil Greenhill)

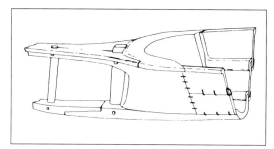

The bow structure of the Hjortspring boat as currently interpreted. (National Maritime Museum)

led to longitudinal rocker and a sheerline with significant sheer; however, Johannessen's drawing, published by Rosenberg, shows a nearly flat bottom, but the sheerline curves all the way. This bottom plank was extended at both ends by an upcurving timber. The block stems each had projections parallel to the bottom plank extensions; were fastened to the bottom plank by a vertical timber of oak held within mortises in the bottom plank and the base of the stem projection by treenails and resin. Another similar timber further joined the upper and lower projections towards the tips of these extensions.

At their lower edges stems were stitched to the edges of the bottom plank. The stems also had 'wings' of plank thickness to which the side planks were stitched in a bevelled lap. This side planking was also stitched together and to the bottom in bevelled lap. The fastenings were ropes or cord of lime bast, threaded through small holes outside the lap, which were then stopped with resin. Rosenburg's figure 55 shows how the fastenings were executed. The planking was generally *c*20mm thick, but the top edge of the upper strake was thickened to strengthen the 'rim'.

The ten ribs in this boat were light timbers

of hazel (species *Corylus*) bent to the shape of the boat and lashed to several cleats proud of each plank. This pre-stressing of the ribs helped to force the planking together. Upper and lower crossbeams were linked to each rib through holes near their ends. The lower of these, at lower strake level, was of ash (species *Fraxinus*); the upper one of lime (species *Tilia*) was fashioned so that it could be used as a thwart by two paddlers. A similar thwart of pine (species *Pinus sylvestris*) has recently been noted in a museum in Vasternorrland, Sweden and has been dated to *c*220 BC.[41] Further support is provided to each thwart of the Hjortspring boat by vertical timbers of ash (species *Fraxinus*) which run from mortises in the thwart, through the lower crossbeam to the lower sections of the ribs.

The Hjortspring boat was a keel-less, round-hulled, double-ended craft with (to our eyes) unusual stems, and planking that was stitched together over a bevelled overlap (edge splayed-lap). Her excavator, Rosenberg, published reconstruction drawings which give her size, without projections, as *c*13.61m x 2.04m x 0.71m. Several propulsion paddles were found with the boat as well as fragments of larger-bladed steering paddles, one at each end. Rosenberg therefore deduced that she had been propelled by twenty paddlers, two on each thwart, with a steersman standing at bow and stern. With such a crew and their weapons, this fourth-century BC warboat would have been carrying a load of *c*2.11 tonnes at a draught of 0.31m. Having a waterline length-to-breadth ratio of *c*10 to 1 and very low volumetric coefficient, she should have had a good turn of speed when propelled by a full crew in fair conditions.

In 1971, a group of Danish scouts used Rosenberg's drawings to build a 'replica' of the Hjortspring boat on the shores of Roskilde fjord. This twentieth-century boat was, however, less deep and significantly less broad than the original, as lime timber of the correct dimensions proved unobtainable. Ballast had to be embarked to achieve stability, but this must

have been due to the 'replica's' reduced water-line breadth rather than a reflection of the original boat's abilities.[42]

Rosenberg's account does not answer all the questions one could ask today. For example: was the bottom plank expanded? Were the side planks hewn or bent to shape and were they fastened by lashings or continuous stitching? And was caulking used as well as resin to make the seams watertight? These questions, as well as others about performance may be answered in the publication being prepared by the National Museum of Denmark's Centre for Maritime Archaeology at Roskilde, based on their recent detailed examination of the surviving fragments.

Stitched plank boat characteristics

The three chronological groups, mid second millennium BC; late second/early first millennium; and fourth century BC, whilst having general features in common and some individually distinctive characteristics (a polythetic group), may be differentiated from one another by reference to the details of plank fastenings. This can only be a provisional classification which will need to be revised after the publication of the Dover and Hjortspring boats and in the light of future finds.

Sub-group A. Ferriby 1, 2 and 3, Dover, Caldicot 1. These are dated to the period 1600 to 1300 BC. Edge to edge, 'interlocking' or half-lap planking is fastened by lashings through large holes, over moss capped by a lath along the seam. Dover also has wedges (keys/ cotters) through cleat rails.

Sub-group B. Brigg 2, Caldicot 2, Goldcliff. These are dated to the period 1100 to 800 BC. Edge to edge and bevel-lap planking is fastened by continuous stitching through small holes, over moss capped by a lath along the seam. Ferriby 5 of *c*380 BC may also belong to this sub-group.

Sub-group C. Hjortspring of 350 to 300 BC. Bevel-lap planking fastened with a resin sealant probably by continuous stitching through small holes.

Boats with stems and keels?

None of these Bronze Age plank boats had a conventional stem and although Ferriby 1 and 2 both had a keel, it was a plank-keel. There are suggestions, however, that plank boats with 'conventional' keels and stems may have been known in Bronze Age Britain. A 'boat-shaped'

41. S Jansson, 'Hjortspring boat from northern Sweden?' *Maritime Archaeological Newsletter from Roskilde* 2 (1994), pp16-7.

42. H Kahl, I Neilsen, F Terp and P Veje, *Roar Linde 71* (1971).

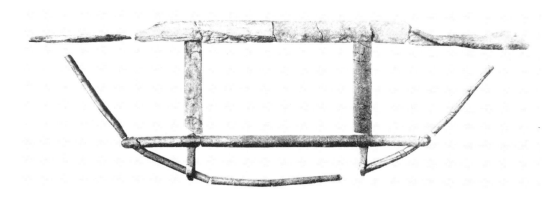

The midships frame of the Hjortspring boat showing the structure of crossbeams and struts. (National Maritime Museum)

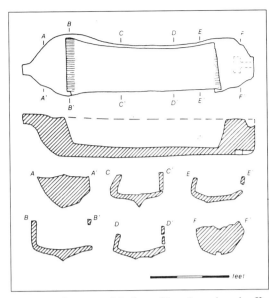

Measured drawings of the Loose Howe boat-shaped coffin showing what appears to be a keel and stem, but logboats do not need such features so the coffin is probably modelled on a plank boat or possibly a skin boat. (National Maritime Museum)

log coffin found in an Early Bronze Age round barrow at Loose Howe, northeast Yorkshire[43] had a prominent keel and stem worked in the solid; such features are unnecessary in a logboat and can only have been copied from a plank boat or possibly a hide boat. Two logboats from the Iron Age, Poole and Holme Pierrepont 3, also have stems in the solid showing that this feature was used in the third century BC, at a time when there is still no evidence for indigenous plank boats with stems. Scandinavian rock art includes representations which some have claimed may be plank boats with keels,[44] but the detailed interpretation of these 'diagrammatic silhouettes' is notoriously difficult and often very subjective.

The evidence for a northwest European plank boat tradition, other than the Ferriby/Brigg/Hjortspring style, is thus not substantial; the discussion can only be taken further if and when an early plank boat with 'conventional' keel and stems is excavated.

Bronze Age techniques

By the end of the Bronze Age (including the 'outlier' Hjortspring boat) we have evidence for a range of woodworking and boatbuilding techniques among which were, no doubt, the seeds of later developments. These techniques include the following:

The Iron Age Poole logboat has a solid stem, but there is no evidence for indigenous plank boats with such a feature at that time. (National Maritime Museum)

Large trees were felled and logs and branches transported to sites suitable for boatbuilding.

Whole or half logs were converted into logboats with rectangular, flared or rounded transverse sections.

Open ends were closed with a transom board or with block stems, and sides were held together with beam ties.

Treenails were used to plug holes and to fasten fittings; dovetail-shaped clamps were used to repair splits and dovetail-shaped joints to hold fittings in position.

Planks with integral cleats were fashioned from half logs. They were used to build boats with flat bottoms, with curved or vertical sides, with or without plank-keels. Hollowed planks were used to build round hull boats.

Planking was fastened together edge to edge, in a bevelled lap, in a half-lap, or using an ingenious form of 'interlocking'. Planking was lengthened by edge-halved scarves. Plank fastenings were (a) lashings over moss and lath, (b) continuous stitching over moss and lath, (c) continuous stitching with a resin sealant, or (d) wedges (keys or cotters) through cleat rails. Various techniques were used to protect the stitching.

Framing consisted of transverse timbers through integral cleats or flexible ribs lashed to integral cleats. Cleats with wedges (keys or cotters) were also used to repair splits.

Boats were built either entirely shell-first, or bottom-based with shell-first sides. *Oculi* or boat's eyes were depicted in the bows.

Features for which there is, as yet, *no* evi-dence in the Bronze Age but which appear in subsequent finds – in Iron Age logboats and in plank boats of the Romano-Celtic and the early Nordic traditions – include:

Logboats with composite bows; logboats with washstrakes; splayed scarves; planking converted radially; full overlap planking (clinker); iron fastenings, clenched by turning the point through 180 degrees or by deformation over a rove; nailed lead patches; treenails locked by wedges or by keys/cotters; framing with grown timbers; building skeleton-first; full stems; full keels; mast and sail; oars; steering oars; side rudders.

Bronze Age boat operations

The known boats of Bronze Age northwest Europe were used on lakes, rivers and estuaries. At certain times, in fair weather, they may have made short coastal voyages, but it does not seem, on present evidence, that they can be considered seaboats in the usual sense of that term.[45] It may be that some future reconstruction of one of the stitched plank boats may undergo sea trials to determine its capabilities at sea. However, without such an experiment –

43. H W and F Elgee, 'An EBA burial in a boat-shaped coffin from NE Yorkshire', *Proceedings of the Prehistoric Society* 15 (1949), pp87-106.

44. J M Coles, 'Boats on the rocks', in Coles *et al*, *Spirit of Enquiry*, pp23-31.

45. S McGrail, 'Prehistoric seafaring in the Channel', p204.

and experiments which can tell us anything worthwhile about the past are difficult and expensive to organise[46] – we may look to the hide boat, or possibly another type of plank boat, as the probable seagoing boat of Bronze Age northwest Europe.

Informal landing places on lake and river margins (eg as at North Ferriby and Brigg in the Humber region) and within natural harbours (as in Christchurch Harbour and in Plymouth Sound in later times) were used throughout northwest Europe until Roman times. These had little, if any, man-made facilities – on soft mud strands, possibly a hardstanding of light timbers and hurdles (as found close to the boats at Ferriby) or of gravel (as found on an Iron Age foreshore in Christ-

Timothy Severin's hide boat replica Brendan. *The hides were tanned in oak bark, oiled with cod oil and dressed with wool grease; there was no major problem with the leather during the translantic voyage, and a hole caused by ice was repaired by a patch sewn externally and backed with wool grease and fibre.* (Timothy Severin)

church Bay, Dorset). Boats were beached at these landing places, or they were anchored off and unloaded into smaller craft. They may also have been off-loaded into carts or wagons pulled by draught animals.[47] As found at Brigg, causeways and floating pontoons could be used at tidal landing places to give access to boats in the deep water channel.

In archipelagos (as in the western Baltic), within the coastal waters of continental western Europe protected by the chain of islands of which the Frisian Islands are now a remnant, and in the estuaries, rivers and lakes of Britain, Ireland and the other Atlantic lands of western Europe, these logboats and plank boats of the Bronze Age would have played a very important part in economic, social, and possibly political/military life. The rivers and streams were the natural routes for exploration, trade and exchange, social intercourse and invasion. Passages upstream, except in tidal sections, may have been arduous; and low water levels, rivers in spate and river beds encumbered by obsta-

cles could have made rivers impassable at times, especially seasonally. Nevertheless, travel and transport by river would often have been preferable to overland, if only because of the higher payload/man ratio. The boat and the raft were the means by which Bronze Age man explored and exploited his environment, socialised with his neighbours and interacted with his foes.

Sean McGrail

Acknowledgement

I am very grateful to Dr E V Wright, excavator of the Ferriby boats, who kindly read and commented on an earlier draft of this text. I am also grateful to Dr V R Switsur of the Godwin Laboratory, University of Cambridge, for permission to refer to recently calibrated radiocarbon dates before their publication. Dr P Marsden kindly made available information from his current work on the Dover boat.

46. S McGrail, 'Experimental Archaeology and the Trireme', in T Shaw (ed), *Trireme Project*, Oxbow Monograph 31 (Oxford 1993), pp4-10.

47. S McGrail, 'Celtic seafaring and transport'.

3

Sailing Ships of the Ancient Mediterranean

THE INVENTION of the boat – *ie* of a floating structure that, unlike a log or a bundle of reeds or similar materials, would not only carry people across water but keep them dry in the process – goes far back in time. By the eleventh millennium BC, for example, men had boats in which they were able to get from the Greek mainland to the island of Melos to bring home the distinctive obsidian that was to be found there.[1]

The obsidian-seekers paddled themselves over the waters they crossed, and for many thousands of years thereafter muscle continued to be the sole force available to make a boat move. Then, some time in the fourth millennium BC came the breakthrough that revolutionised maritime history and determined its course right up to the last century – the invention of the sail. The earliest evidence for it is a picture on an Egyptian vase of *c*3500 BC that shows a long and slender vessel with a square sail mounted on a pole mast stepped forward in the bows.

The invention, then, probably took place in Egypt, and this is not surprising. Egypt boasts a unique waterway, a great river that, running the length of the country, provides the easiest and quickest and most convenient way of getting from one place to another. What is more, its prevailing wind accommodatingly blows opposite to the direction of its flow. Once Nile boatmen had the sail available to them, they could travel without having to rely on muscle in either direction: the current would carry them downstream and the wind propel them upstream.

Thanks to the unique and rich archaeological finds that Egypt furnishes, a good deal is known about the craft its boatmen used, for they are pictured in paintings on the walls of tombs and reproduced in miniature models that were placed in tombs. By 2600 BC the Egyptians were building big vessels and fitting them with a sizable spread of canvas, a single

square sail that – and this is a feature typically Egyptian – was spread by two spars, a boom along the foot as well as a yard along the head. The boom was heavy, on larger ships heavy enough to support the weight of a man, and hence required a line of lifts to hold it up; they run from points all along the boom to the top of the mast. The presence of a boom meant that sail could not be shortened, but this may not have been a major consideration for craft whose use was limited to a river. For steering the Egyptians used the mechanism that was to be standard on ships of all places throughout antiquity, steering oars mounted on each quarter.

The Egyptians not only rigged but built their craft in a special way. In Europe and other parts of the West the traditional procedure for assembling a wooden hull is to start with a skeleton of keel and frames and wrap a skin of planks about this, fastening the planks to the frames. In the East, from the eastern coast of

Africa to India and even further, the traditional procedure has been just the opposite: shipwrights start by building up the skin of planks, creating, as it were, a shell of planking; since there are no frames to fasten the planks to, they make each fast to its neighbours by means of pegs or joints or nails or – a favoured method among the Arabs and Persians – by sewing the planks together with twine. After the shell has been partially or completely built up in this fashion they then insert a set of frames. Through the discovery and examination in recent years of numbers of ancient wrecks by marine archaeologists, we have learned that this was the procedure the ancients used for assembling a hull, the creation of a shell of planks and then the insertion of framing.

Circumstances, however, forced the Egyptians to adopt a variation. In their country

---

1. See *The Age of the Galley*, chapter 1 (in this series) for further details.

The earliest representation of a sail, on an Egyptian vase of c3500 BC. (The British Museum)

Egyptian sailing ship: wall-painting from a tomb of c1350 BC. The lower horizontal spar is the boom that runs along the foot when sail is spread; a network of lifts supports it. After N Davies and A Gardiner, Ancient Egyptian Paintings *(Chicago 1936), Vol II, p82. (By courtesy of the author)*

timber has always been in short supply; the one species locally available was acacia, and its wood is hard and brittle and comes only in short lengths. Therefore Egyptian builders in creating their shell of planking used short pieces of wood, piecing them together with mortises and tenons or dovetails or both. Herodotus, the keen-eyed Greek traveller who visited the land in the fifth century BC, likens Egyptian boatbuilders putting a hull together

to masons laying bricks. And he notes that they dispensed with frames.

The Egyptians, who needed watercraft chiefly to ply the relatively quiet waters of a river, were not in the mainstream of the development of ancient shipbuilding. For that we must turn to the Mediterranean: it was there that a rig was devised to handle its often violent winds and hulls were built to stand up to its often violent waters.

The lands about and in the Mediterranean do not offer anywhere near the archaeological riches of Egypt; as a consequence, little is known about the early stages of the ships that plied it. Indeed the first sure clue to what Mediterranean ships were like is owing to a

picture found in Egypt, a huge relief illustrating a battle fought around 1200 BC between the Egyptian navy and a fleet of Mediterranean invaders. The ships of both sides are rigged in the same way, with a single broad square sail – but the sails are loose-footed, *ie* they have no boom along the foot as was typical of Egyptian sails hitherto. In addition, they are furled by means of lines that run from points along the yard. These are brails, the ancients' unique device for shortening sail; more will be said about them below. The new features, the loose foot and the system of brails, must have arisen in the Mediterranean, where it was vital to be able to shorten sail, and proven so useful that the Egyptians adopted them.

How the hulls of Mediterranean ships were put together at this early date is also known thanks to the fortunate discovery just a few years ago off the southern coast of Turkey of a wreck of the fourteenth century BC. As in Egypt, it had been built shell-first with the planks made fast to each other. But unlike Egyptian ships, whose planks were fastened with casual joinery, on this ship they are locked together with closely set mortise and tenon joints that are transfixed by pegs to keep them from coming apart. Then, into this tightly knit structure was inserted a set of frames for stiff-

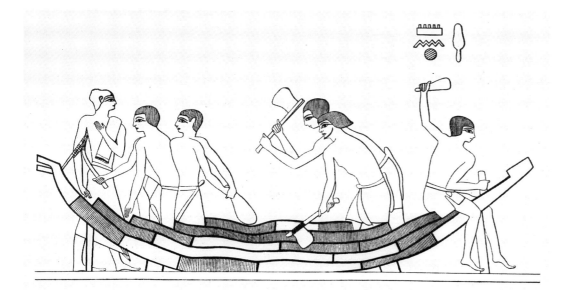

Egyptian shipwrights put together a hull; relief from a tomb of c2000 BC. A shell of planking is being built up of short lengths of wood. After A Köster, Das antike Seewesen *(Berlin 1923), fig 1. (By courtesy of the author)*

Egyptian men-of-war fight off Mediterranean invaders; relief on a temple erected by Ramses III (1198–1166 BC). The ships of both sides are rigged with loose-footed square sails furled by means of brails. After Journal of Near Eastern Studies *2 (1943), pp40–55, fig 4. (By courtesy of the author)*

ening. Wrecks of later centuries reveal that this, by and large, was to continue to be the ancients' standard method for assembling a hull.

The Egyptian relief and the wreck off Turkey provide a glimpse at an early stage in the development of the Mediterranean sailing ship. There is no further information until after the passage of hundreds of years.

During the early part of this span of time, the opening centuries of the first millennium BC, the Phoenicians and the Greeks emerge as the foremost maritime peoples of the Mediterranean, carrying out voyages along trade routes that traversed its length and breadth. Little is known about the sailing craft the Phoenicians used, since not much of their art has survived, and what has rarely includes representations of ships. But of Greek art much has survived, particularly in the form of decoration on vases, and among Greek vase-painters ships were a favoured motif. Though they much preferred to depict the slender and shapely men-of-war, ordinary sailing ships now and then make an appearance. An outstanding example is a cup dating about 510 BC which is adorned with two dramatic scenes showing an attack by a pirate vessel on a merchantman. The difference between the two types of craft is manifest: the pirates are aboard a man-of-war, a long and narrow galley driven by a line of oarsmen, while their prey, moved by sail alone, is beamy and well-rounded, as one would expect in a vessel designed for carrying cargo. Despite its bulky lines, it is not unhandsome; the prow, concave like those of American

clipper ships, is particularly pleasing. The rig of both ships is the same, a loose-footed square sail that is far wider than tall – so wide, in fact, that the yard along the head was usually of two spars fished together – and that is fitted with brails. In the first scene the pirate galley, under oars and full sail, comes up on the freighter

which, since a strong wind is blowing and it is unaware of danger, is proceeding under closely reefed sail. In the second scene, the freighter, now aware of the danger, has spread full sail in an effort to escape, while the galley is in the act of taking in sail as a preparation for boarding.

The scenes demonstrate how effective were the brails as a system for shortening sail, much more convenient and flexible than the reef-points of later ages. They were made fast at regular intervals along the foot of the sail, carried up the forward surface and over the yard, and brought down to the deck aft. For shortening sail the deck hands merely hauled on them, thereby bunching the canvas up much in the manner of a venetian blind. To let the canvas out they simply slacked them off. This is what the crew of the merchantman in the picture presumably did, switching from closely

Two scenes showing a pirate craft first chasing and then preparing to board a merchantman; on a Greek cup of c510 BC. (The British Museum)

Shipwrights assemble the hull of the replica of the Kyrenia wreck. Each plank is bound to its neighbours by closely set mortise and tenon joints. (Ira Bloch)

certain that the procedures the wreck reveals had been followed by shipwrights for centuries.

The remains consist mostly of the lower part of the hull, the part that was underneath the vessel's cargo of millstones and clay jars of wine; it owes its survival to these, for, being of materials well-nigh impervious to seawater, they protected what they lay over from erosion. This is true of almost all ancient wrecks: what is left is that portion of the hull saved from destruction by an overlay of cargo, usually of clay shipping jars. In the case of the Kyrenia wreck, the state of preservation of what remains is good enough to yield a wealth of detail. The ship was about 15m long and 4m to 5m broad; its capacity was about 30 tons. As in the much earlier vessel found off Turkey, the planks were fastened to each other by mortise and tenon joints, and the excavators were able to determine that there were over four thousand such joints. They were no more than 7-8cm apart and they went that deep into the planks. Above and below the seam they were transfixed by pegs so that the tenons would never come out of the sockets. There was no driven caulking; indeed, with each seam crossed by a multitude of tenons, it would have been impossible to drive in any. The only caulking was a coat of black pitch over the exterior of the hull; the planks were so carefully fitted to each other that, once the ship was launched and the wood swelled up, the seams were watertight. Into the hull was inserted a full set of frames placed some 25cm apart. The framing provided a certain amount of stiffening but the vessel's basic strength lay in the tightly knit shell of planking.

The excavators were even able to determine the size of the crew: four. In the forward area, where it was customary to put the cask holding the water supply, they found four identical cups, and, in the after area, where gear was usually stored, they recovered four wooden spoons and four jugs of olive oil. There were no signs of a galley or even a firebox; the little ship probably stayed so close to land that, when it came time for a meal, it could put in to let the men cook and eat on shore.

So much of the Kyrenia wreck survived and in such good condition that it was possible to create a full-scale replica. The sails and lines, to be sure, had all been lost, so the replica was fitted with the standard rig, a broad loose-footed square sail fitted with brails. This functioned perfectly. Over a number of voyages, the

reefed to full sail in a twinkling; had this been an attack in, say, the eighteenth century, the hands would have lost vital time undoing one by one the knots in the lines of reef-points. Yet another advantage of the system of brails was that it permitted the shortening of any part of the canvas to any amount; the hands merely hauled on selected brails a certain distance. To be sure, brails could not be used on ships with tiers of canvas, the rig par excellence of the

West from the end of the fifteenth century onward, but this limitation did not affect ancient seamen; brails perfectly suited their basically one-tier rigs.

The cup, then, shows what the standard rig of a small Mediterranean merchantman was like; the discovery of a well-preserved wreck off Kyrenia on the north coast of Cyprus shows how its hull would have been built. The date happens to be somewhat later, *c*300 BC, but it is

The replica of the Kyrenia wreck under sail. The rig is hypothetical but reproduces the predominent ancient rig, a broad loose-footed square sail furled by means of brails. (Susan Womer Katzev)

From mention in ancient writings it is apparent that, already by the fifth century BC, Mediterranean merchantmen had attained considerable size. Those that worked between coastal points commonly had a capacity of 100 tons or so, while bigger ships, sometimes much bigger, were used for hauling over long distances the ancient world's chief commodities – grain, wine, and olive oil. The Greeks referred to particularly large carriers as *myriophoroi*, 'ten-thousanders', *ie* vessels able to hold that many shipping jars, which could well amount to 400 tons in weight.

Toward the end of the fourth century BC the Mediterranean world changed radically. Till then it had been dominated by city states, small political entities made up of a city and the land immediately surrounding it. Even the greatest of these, Athens or Corinth or Syracuse, boasted no more than a few hundred thousand inhabitants. The spectacular achievements of Alexander the Great changed all that. He ushered in what historians have named the Hellenistic Age, an age in which the city states were swept up into large-scale empires ruled by autocratic kings. Then, by the end of the first

ship achieved remarkable speeds and weathered some severe storms with no trouble.

Such a rig was sufficient for the smaller merchantmen that tramped along the coasts; larger craft were given a bigger spread of canvas, as can be seen from a painting on the wall of an Etruscan tomb that dates *c*480 BC. A freighter is depicted whose hull, beamy and well-rounded, looks much like the hull of the ship on the cup. It too has, stepped amidships, a main mast with a broad loose-footed square sail. But this vessel, being larger, is a two-master: it has a fore mast, which is a bit shorter than the main mast and has a slight forward rake; on it is a somewhat smaller version of the main sail. A fore sail, the *artemon* as the Greeks called it, becomes a standard feature on ancient seagoing ships. Most often it is not nearly as big as here, being a fraction of the size of the main, and its mast has so strong a forward rake that the sail hangs over the bows, like the bow spritsail of later ages. The purpose seems to have been to aid steering rather than contribute to drive.

Greek merchantman with large artemon *(fore sail); wall-painting in an Etruscan tomb of c480 BC.* (By courtesy of Mario Moretti)

over to cabins – thirty in all, including a master's cabin three times the size of the others – as well as a galley, salons, gymnasium, chapel, bath complex, and several promenades, all made of expensive materials and decorated in elegant style. Floors were of mosaic or stone, bulkheads of expensive woods; there were paintings and statuary, and the promenades were lined with beds of plants in boxes and vines in pots. The top deck was given over to a unit of marines and armaments that were state of the art; the VIPs who sailed in this ship were to be perfectly safe as well as perfectly comfortable. The description does not include the vessel's dimensions but it does list the cargo it carried on its maiden voyage, and this works out to at least 1700 tons. It was so gigantic a vessel that launching the hull, getting it to slide down the ways into the water, presented an almost insurmountable challenge; fortunately the foremost engineer of antiquity, Archimedes, was a native of Syracuse, and Hiero was able to call on his unique expertise to get the job done.

The ship was a three-master, with a mizzen on the afterdeck as well as a main amidships and an *artemon* forward; in fact, the three-masted rig may have been invented for this vessel. The main mast it required was of such size that it was only 'located with great difficulty in the mountains of Bruttium [the toe of the Italian boot] . . . ; Phileas of Tauromenium

century BC, this age came to a close when these were themselves swept up into the Roman Empire; from that time on, the Mediterranean world was a single great political entity ruled from Rome.

From its very beginning this new world was marked by largeness of scale: the empires that made it up maintained big armies and bureaucracies, they spent big amounts of money on big projects and the volume of their commerce was bigger by far than what the city states had carried on. Tens of thousands of tons of grain were now annually exported by Egypt, tens of thousands of heavy jars of wine and olive oil were now annually exported from Greece and the Greek islands. All this called for bigger freighters.

The advance in the size of merchantmen took place so rapidly that by the middle of the third century BC, c240 BC to be more precise, the largest ship ever built in antiquity was launched. It is known to history because its fame was so great that an ancient writer, considering it one of man's great achievements, drew up a detailed account of it, and this has fortunately survived.

The vessel was the brainchild of King Hiero of Syracuse, who intended it not only to haul the massive amounts of grain his land exported but also to accommodate himself, his family, members of his court, his agents or other such highly placed folk when they needed overseas transportation. Consequently, it can claim a double distinction: not only was it the biggest ship of the ancient world but it was the ancestor of the luxury cruise ship. It towered three decks high, of which only the lowest was for cargo. The middle was for passengers: it was given

A modern Swedish shipwright at work; photo taken in 1929. He uses, as was customary, the shell-first technique for building his clinker-built craft; he has reached the same point as the Roman shipwright in the illustration above. (Gothenburg Historical Museum)

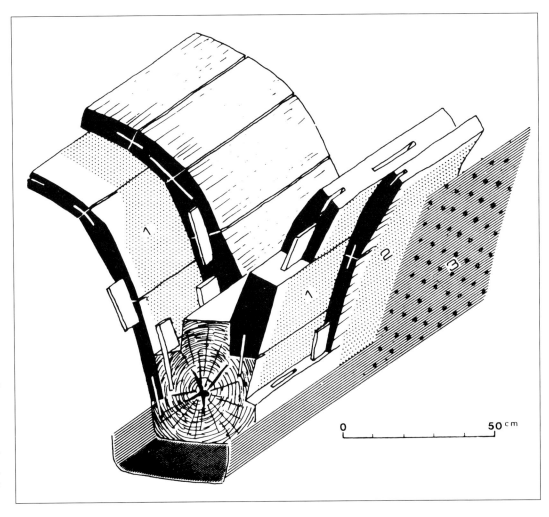

Sketch illustrating the construction of the keel and adjacent planking of the wreck of a big Roman merchantman, dating from about 50 BC, found off Madrague de Giens near Toulon. Built with notable care, it had two layers of planking (1, 2), each mortised and tenonned, plus a sheathing of lead sheets laid over tarred fabric (3). After A Tchernia et al, L'épave romaine de la Madrague de Giens *(Paris 1978), p86, fig 12. (By courtesy of the author)*

[Taormina], the engineer, had it brought down to the shore.' In other words, even after a tree of the appropriate height had been found, there still remained the formidable task of hauling the immense piece of timber to a point where it could be put aboard a ship and sailed to Syracuse; this was so memorable a feat that the name of the man who carried it off was inscribed in the record.

The amount of information that survives about Hiero's ship portends, in a way, what is to come: information about sailing ships in general becomes much more plentiful from this time on, thanks to the greater number of wrecks that have been found and the greater number of representations of ships that have survived. Wrecks dating from 200 BC to 200 AD and pictures of ships dating from the early centuries of the Roman Empire, a time when overseas commerce flourished, outnumber by far those from any other period.

Let us turn first to the wrecks. They reveal that the method of shipbuilding gradually underwent some change. Hulls were still assembled shell-first, with planks made fast to each other by means of mortise and tenon joints, and down to the first century BC they were still built as strongly as ever: the mortises are wide and deep, are set closely together, and are carefully transfixed by pegs. Some vessels were even double-planked, with both layers, inner as well as outer, mortised and tenonned. Some vessels were given, as protection against marine borers, a sheathing of thin lead sheets laid over a lining of fabric impregnated with pitch or resin. This practice did not outlive ancient times, and it was not reinvented until the eighteenth century, with copper being used for the sheathing instead of lead.

The hulls so produced were admirably sound and durable – but they were expensive. They required a lot of timber because many of the planks, especially those where the surfaces were curved, virtually had to be carved out of a log, with the rest of the log abandoned as waste. And they required a great deal of labour for the measuring, cutting, and fitting of thousands of joints and pegs. The wrecks reveal that, from the first century AD on, efforts were made to

cut down on these costs. The joints become smaller, looser in fit, and, by being placed further apart, reduced in number. In a wreck of the mid first century BC, for example, which was found off Toulon, the joinery was as careful as in the Kyrenia wreck: this ship, a big freighter *c*40m long and 9m in beam, had a double layer of planking, both layers of planks fastened with mortise and tenon joints transfixed by pegs; in the inner layer the mortises were 10cm to 12cm deep, the tenons fitted snugly, and the joints were 6.5cm to 7.5cm apart. In a wreck of the fourth century AD, found at Yassi Ada off the southwest coast of Asia Minor, the mortises were 5.5cm deep, the tenons fitted loosely, and the joints were in places almost 30cm apart. Apparently shipwrights no longer expended the care they once had in creating a tightly knit shell, no longer joined plank to plank with such close-set perfectly fitting joinery. This must have affected the vessel's basic strength, which hitherto had been almost wholly provided by the tightly knit shell of planking; to compensate, shipwrights probably increased the strength of certain interior members, but there is no way of knowing since such members rarely survive.

Inasmuch as the information provided by wrecks with very few exceptions is limited to the lower parts of the hull, for the topsides, fittings, rig, handling, and all such matters we must turn to other sources, notably pictures that have survived and passages in ancient writings that happen to deal with ships.

The pictures, in mosaics and reliefs, though not big enough or of good enough workmanship to offer much detail, are invaluable for showing hull shapes. They reveal a basic difference in the shape of the prow. On most craft it was more or less straight or had a rounded convex curve, as is commonly the case today. But some, running the gamut from mere rowboats to seagoing freighters, had a prow that was concave in profile and at the waterline ended in a projecting forefoot. A mosaic of *c*200 AD found at Ostia, the port of Rome, where it marked the office of the 'Shippers of Sullecthum', a port on the eastern coast of Tunisia, shows two big freighters sailing on opposite courses past the lighthouse at the entrance to Rome's harbour; the one to the right has the rounded convex prow, the one to the left the concave prow with projecting forefoot. Ships with the concave prow generally

Two big Roman freighters at the entrance to Rome's harbour; mosaic of about AD 200. The ship to the left has the concave prow with projecting forefoot and stempost capped by a volute. Both carry the small artemon. (Author)

had a stempost capped by a volute, while the other type had its stempost capped by a massive block-shaped adornment. The sternpost on both types, indeed on most sailing ships, ended in a goose-headed adornment. Aft of the sternpost was a statuette of the vessel's guardian deity; on safe arrival or similar occasions, a portable altar was brought out and set up on the afterdeck to use in making thank-offerings to the deity. On either quarter was an oversize oar, the steering oars, the standard mechanism

for steering from the days of ancient Egypt to the end of the ancient world and for all craft, from the smallest to the very largest. Tiller bars led from the top of each loom inboard and the helmsman, stationed just forward of the sternpost, gripped one in each hand and directed the vessel by pushing or pulling them.

Seagoing sailing ships had roomy and capacious hulls to provide plenty of cargo space. There were no passenger ships as such. Travellers who were headed for destinations

overseas booked passage on freighters that happened to be going their way, and they expected, and got, little in the way of accommodation. There was on all ships of any size a deckhouse, usually on the afterdeck, but the limited space in this was reserved for VIPs – the skipper, the owner of the ship or of the cargo, or their agents. Other passengers slept on the open deck. They came aboard with their own bedding which their servants – people who could afford to travel were always accompanied by personal servants – spread out for them at night. They also brought their own food, which the servants prepared for them. On big ships an overhanging gallery girdled the stern, and sometimes the overhang was great enough to leave room for a small shelter suspended over open water behind the sternpost; to judge from the location, this probably was a latrine, the only one aboard. Pieces of cork were carried as lifebuoys, but there were no lifeboats, only a ship's boat, which was usually towed astern with a hand stationed in it; if the ship ran into trouble it could, of course, serve as a lifeboat, but only for the few lucky enough to cram into it.

As noted above, by the fifth century BC merchantmen had attained respectable size, not uncommonly with a capacity as high as 400 tons. The increased volume of trade that took place under the Roman Empire, particularly during its golden age, the first and second century AD, called for bigger ships than that. For the transport of government grain, for example, the Roman authorities considered vessels with a capacity of 340 tons as standard, while for carrying the 135,000 tons of grain annually imported by the city of Rome from Egypt, a haul of some 1200 nautical miles that took at least a month and often twice that or more, there was a fleet of oversize freighters, of which some could handle over a thousand tons. The exact dimensions of one have survived, thanks to an accident: it had run into a spell of foul weather and was blown so far off course that it ended up in Piraeus, the port of Athens;

A Roman merchantman prepares to moor; relief on a tombstone of around AD 50. A hand furls the sail by hauling on the brails while other hands go aloft to make the furled canvas secure. The domed shelter overhanging the water behind the sternpost is probably a latrine. (Author)

Stern of a Roman merchantman moored alongside a quay; relief on Trajan's Column in Rome, early first century AD. The sail is fully brailed up and the starboard steering oar is raised almost free of the water. Ancient vessels carried anchors aft as well as forward. (German Archaelogical Museum, Athens)

Athens by this time was no longer a commercial centre but a sleepy university town, and it created such a sensation there that people flocked to see it, including by good fortune Lucian, a famed writer of the second century AD, who was so impressed that he wrote up a description of it:

> What a size the ship was! One hundred and eighty feet in length, the ship's carpenter told me, the beam more than a quarter of that, and forty-four feet from the deck to the bottom, the deepest point in the bilge. What a mast it had, what a yard it carried, what a forestay held it up! The way the sternpost rose in a gradual curve with a gilded goose-head set on the tip of it, matched at the opposite end by the forward, more flattened, rise of the prow with the figure of Isis, the goddess the ship was named after, on each side! And the rest of the decoration, the paintings, the red pennant on the main yard, the anchors and capstans and winches on the foredeck, the accommodations toward the stern–it all seemed like marvels to me! The crew must have been as big as an army.

To judge from the dimensions cited, the ship had a capacity of 1200 to 1300 tons; it was, in other words, as big as the biggest British East Indiamen of the eighteenth century. And this was no unique craft, such as Hiero's vessel was, but just one unit of the Alexandria – Rome grain fleet. The ship St Paul boarded at Myra for his voyage to Rome and that came to grief off Malta was another, and it can be assumed that it was big from his remark that 'We were in all in the ship two hundred three score and sixteen souls'–and this for a voyage taking place in September, dangerously near the end of the sailing season and hence a time when travellers thought twice about making a long crossing; normally the ship would have had more aboard.

Nor were these the biggest ships afloat: special needs brought into being some that were still bigger. The Roman emperors had a predilection for decorating the city of Rome with obelisks from Egypt. Even the great grain

Big Roman merchantman sails into a harbour; mosaic of the third century AD. The ship's boat is towed astern. The shelter behind the sternpost is probably a latrine. (Author)

The most detailed representation of an ancient sailing ship extant. It pictures a big freighter passing the lighthouse at the entrance to Rome's harbour and then tied up, prow to, to a quay; relief of about AD 200. Three persons on the afterdeck sacrifice over a small altar in thanksgiving for a safe arrival. The rig includes a triangular topsail. The artemon *has been secured, the main sail is being braled up, and the hand in the ship's boat towed astern pulls it up to the quarter to secure it.* (Gabinetto Fotografico Nazionale, Rome)

carriers could not handle these mammoth chunks of ponderous stone; vessels had to be designed and built for the purpose. The obelisk now in front of St Peter's together with its pedestal stands about 40m high and weighs just under 500 tons. The Emperor Caligula had it brought over about AD 40 and the vessel he constructed to carry it was ballasted with 800 tons of lentils – a total load of 1300 tons. Pope Sixtus V's architect, Domenico Fontana, in 1585 moved the obelisk from its original location in Nero's circus to the spot where it is now, a distance of less than a mile, and the whole contemporary world broke into applause

at the feat. But Caligula's seamen and engineers had taken the monument from Heliopolis near Cairo, barged it down the Nile, loaded it on its ship, and sailed it against foul winds all the way from Alexandria to Rome.

Lucian exclaims in admiration about 'the anchors and capstans and winches on the foredeck' of the ship he saw. The discoveries of marine archaeology make clear why he was so impressed. The artefact the divers most com-

Sailing ship with large artemon; *relief of about AD 200.* (The British Museum)

squared projected so far beyond the sides that weights could be fitted to the yardarms to drop on any attackers who came alongside; multiple lifts were required to support a yard of such length. Sometimes above it was a main topsail, a small bit of canvas shaped like a broad isosceles triangle; the base ran along the yard and the apex reached to the tip of the mast. The mast was stayed forward by a massive fore stay and laterally by shrouds that were fitted with tackles so that they could be adjusted; since ratlines cannot be fitted to such shrouds, there was a rope ladder abaft the mast for getting aloft.

Three masts were for the very biggest vessels. Most merchantmen had only main sail and *artemon*. On some the *artemon*, as on the Etruscan ship of five or more centuries earlier, was a proper fore sail, being almost the size of the main and hung on a mast that was not much shorter than the main mast and had but a slight forward rake.

Ancient sailing ships, with their single tier of sails (the main topsail, to be sure, was a superimposed sail but it was too small to have any great effect on a vessel's drive), were rigged for safety and not speed. Safety was always the major consideration, so much so that, in order to avoid the perils of winter travel, voyaging was by and large limited to a sailing season which opened in April at the earliest and went to the end of October at the latest. A safe rig is inevitably a slow rig: the fastest ancient voyages on record, done with favourable winds all the way, averaged 6 knots; the clipper ships of the nineteenth century could almost treble that figure.

The representations show square sails so predominantly that until quite recently naval historians thought they were the only type the ancients used; the prevailing opinion was that fore-and-aft sails–those set, not across the ship, but in a direction parallel to the keel, in other words, from fore to aft–were unknown. Not so: certain representations that have been overlooked reveal that Greek and Roman sailors actually knew two types of fore-and-aft sail: the lateen, more or less triangular in shape and secured to a yard all along the hypotenuse,

Lateen rigged craft; relief on a tombstone of the second century AD. (National Archaeological Museum, Athens)

monly come across are anchor stocks, for, while the shanks and arms were of wood, the stocks were of stone or lead, materials that withstand exposure on the sea floor, and so the stocks survive even when not only the rest of the anchor but the rest of the ship has totally vanished through erosion. They run the gamut of size, depending on the size of the boat they came from–and those from big ships are gigantic. One behemoth found off Malta is almost 4.2m long and weighs over two tons; Lucian's ship could well have had anchors this heavy, along with the massive capstans required for handling them.

So far as rig is concerned, the representations that have survived accommodatingly illustrate various types carried by ships of varying size. The square rig predominates. The biggest vessels, like Hiero's giant, carried three square sails on three masts, of which the mizzen generally was relatively small, the *artemon* was even smaller and set over the bows like the spritsails of later ages, and the main, dwarfing the other two, was the chief contributor to the vessel's drive. It was a huge broad spread of canvas, often so broad that the yard it hung from was nearly as long as the ship, and when

Sprit rigged craft: relief on a tombstone of the second or third century AD. It has the concave prow with projecting forefoot. (Author)

Three vessels, two square rigged and one sprit rigged, at the entrance to Rome's harbour; relief on a sarcophagus of the third century AD. (Alinarini)

and the sprit, more or less rectangular in shape and supported by a spar – the sprit – that runs from a point near the base of the mast diagonally to the peak of the sail. Both were used on small craft, but the sprit appears in at least one instance on a larger vessel. A relief carved on the side of a sarcophagus, a stone coffin, done some time in the third century AD, pictures three ships that neatly illustrate different types afloat at the time. The two on the outside are square rigged: the one on the left has the rounded prow, that on the right the prow with projecting forefoot. The ship in the centre, with a rounded prow, is the same size as the other two but carries a sprit rig: the mast is stepped far up in the bows and the sail made fast to it by the luff, very loosely, as was the practice on occasion centuries later; the sprit runs diagonally across the windward side of the sail to the peak, and a double-ended vang made fast to its tip permits trimming of the peak. Brails are conspicuously absent; they cannot be fitted to such a rig.

The relief is of particular interest since it is the earliest surviving detailed representation of a crisis at sea. The coffin held the remains of a boy – or man – who had drowned, and the coffin-maker decorated it with the dramatic story of how he met his end. The scene is the mouth of the harbour at Rome. Here, on a windy day when the waves were running high, the boy had fallen out of a tiny skiff in which he had been rowing, pehaps in the very sight of his parents standing at the end of a mole. Two vessels race to the rescue from inside the port, one slightly ahead of the other. At the critical

Detail showing the sprit of the sprit rigged vessel pictured on the sarcophagus. (Author)

moment the one in the lead finds itself in imminent peril of colliding with a ship heading into the harbour. It is this moment that the artist chose to portray, and his portrayal is detailed enough to enable us to work out precisely what happened. The two rescue ships, facing right, are travelling with the wind on the port quarter. The one heading in, facing left, is on the starboard tack. Clearly there is a strong wind blowing, for the square-riggers have shortened sail by taking up on the brails, and the sprit-rigger by tricing up the tack of the main sail. This vessel, though in the lead, has had to give up all thought of making the rescue, for it suddenly finds itself in danger of colliding with the ship sailing in from the left. The one behind has taken over that task, and a member of its crew is leaning anxiously over the bow ready to reach out a hand to the boy in the water. He apparently is unaware of help from this quarter: his attention is riveted despairingly on the ship nearest him which, confronted by its own peril, can no longer bother with him. The two vessels in the collision zone are manoeuvring to avoid disaster – and are doing precisely what is called for. On the square-

Diagram illustrating the manoeuvres of the three vessels pictured on the sarcophagus. (Author)

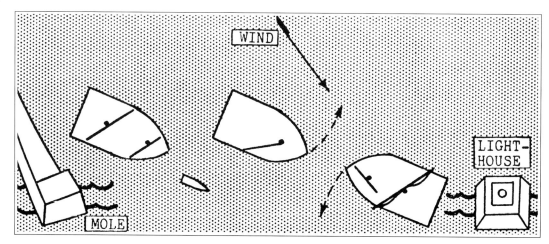

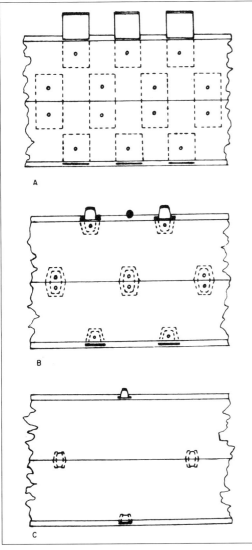

Diagram illustrating the development of mortise and tenon joinery on ancient Greek and Roman hulls: (A) joinery typical of wrecks dating through the first century AD; (B) joinery in a wreck of the fourth century AD; (C) joinery in a wreck of around AD 625. After International Journal of Nautical Archaeology 5 (1976), p122, fig 7.

rigger the skipper has backed the main sail. This will slow his forward motion. The *artemon* is still drawing, which will throw his bow to port and carry him past on the outside of the other ship. Very likely he wants the *artemon* trimmed, but he cannot call on the hand nearest it, since this man has given up in fright, rushed amidships, and settled down to pray. On the other vessel the skipper is working to swing his bow to port and pass on the inside. This will bring him from a broad to a close reach, and his hands accordingly are busy trimming sail: the

An early representation of skeleton-first construction; detail from the Building of St Ursula's Boat *by Paolo da Venezia (1310–1358). After A Munro,* Paolo da Venezia *(University Park, Pennsylvania 1970), fig 84.*

one aft has grabbed the leech to get the sail inboard in a hurry.

In the final period in the history of the ancient sailing ship a significant development in the technique of shipbuilding took place, the completion of a transition from the ancients' long practised shell-first method of assembling a hull toward the skeleton-first method that was to become dominant in the western world from the Middle Ages onwards.

As noted above, a wreck found off Yassi Ada dating to the fourth century AD exhibited a distinct weakening in the way the shipwright knit the shell of planking together, which, it is surmised, must have been accompanied by a strengthening of the inner structure to compensate. A wreck also found at Yassi Ada that dates from about AD 625 demonstrates how far along this path shipwrights had moved in the intervening two centuries. In this vessel the planks were joined to each other only up to the waterline, and by the feeblest possible joinery: the mortises were only 3.5cm deep, the tenons fitted very loosely in them, the joints were spaced from half a metre to almost a full metre apart, and none was pinned by pegs. Their purpose was simply to hold the planking in place until some framing could be inserted, to which the planks were then made fast by iron nails. What is more, even this minimal joinery went only as far as the waterline: above that point wales and planking were fastened directly to framing that was already in place. The shipwright, in short, was well on the way toward skeleton-first construction.

And just a little further south from Yassi Ada,

at Serçe Liman, a wreck was found that illustrates the last step. It was a small coastal freighter, about the same size as the Kyrenia wreck–and it was built with no joinery between the planks whatsoever. The shipwright laid the keel, made fast to it a certain number of frames, and nailed the bottom planking to this partial skeleton. He then erected the rest of the framing and nailed up the rest of the planking. The skin of planks, in a word, was all made fast to an inner skeleton. He was but a step away from the final stage, the setting up of a total skeleton of keel and frames.

The vessel illustrates another advantage in building a hull in this way beyond the savings in time and money that were mentioned earlier: it allowed more flexibility in the shaping of the hull. The Serçe Liman wreck had a boxlike hold, which would have been very hard to achieve in shell-first construction. This enabled the vessel, although it had just about the same dimensions as the Kyrenia ship, to carry almost one-third more cargo.

Not only in construction but in rig as well the Serçe Liman vessel had, as it were, left the ancient world: enough clues survived to reveal that it was a lateener, a two-masted lateener at that–it had, in other words, a form of the rig that predominated in the Mediterranean from the end of antiquity on. Only in its steering mechanism, a steering oar on each quarter, did it still carry on an ancient system. But so did all its sisters, for the stern rudder was not to reach the Mediterranean until several more centuries had passed.

Lionel Casson

4

Celtic Plank Boats and Ships, 500 BC–AD 1000

SHIPBUILDING in the cultural realm of the Celts, and the capabilities of those peoples in terms of sea travel, have long been considered virtually impossible subjects for scientific research, because of the lack of uniformity in source material rather than any lack of such material. It seemed extremely difficult to establish a common denominator from these sources, which consisted of reports by ancient writers, graphic representations in the form of model ships, images on coins and relief pictures on Roman graves, and also the archaeological ship finds, which do exist but tend to be fragmentary, and are certainly strewn over a very wide region.

In 1962 the English archaeologist Peter Marsden excavated a coastal sailing boat of the Roman period in the Blackfriars area of London. It was only when he realised that this vessel corresponded precisely with a description of Celtic ships in Brittany which Caesar had written around 50 BC that the crucial breakthrough was achieved. Suddenly it became clear that Celtic shipbuilders on the Continent and in the British Isles continued to build vessels based on the shipbuilding traditions developed by their forefathers even after the Roman occupation. Since that time numerous further examples have added weight to these assertions.

In order to understand the various Celtic ship types and their continuous development, the first stage is to consider briefly the navigable inland waters of southern central Europe, France and the British Isles, *ie* those regions which were settled by Celts. As far back as the middle of the first century BC geographers of the time wrote reports of a system of transport in Gaul (present-day France) which amazed everyone who was familiar with Mediterranean transport arrangements. In the Mediterranean sphere long-distance communications could only be maintained with the help of sea travel. By contrast, to the Celts rivers were clearly much more important as a means of long-distance transport. To illustrate this, the naturalist Poseidonius, who died in Rome in 51 BC,

wrote the following about Gaul:

> Rivers flowing from the Alps, the Cevennes and the Pyrennees cross the entire country, ending in the ocean or the Mediterranean. The regions traversed by the rivers are flat or only slightly hilly and the waterways are navigable. The natural conditions are so advantageous that goods can easily be transported from one sea to another, with only short overland stretches to be negotiated.

In terms of natural vegetation the regions settled by the Celts constituted forest land, where rivers represent the only natural routes of communication. In contrast to Mediterranean rivers, those in the Celtic regions featured relatively shallow gradients and flowed at relatively constant speed, enabling the Celts to travel far upstream by boat. In conjunction with the large number of navigable tributaries these rivers formed a fairly closely woven network of waterways with connections to the Mediterranean and the Black Sea via the Rhône and Danube. At the upper reaches of the rivers there were short, relatively easily negotiated land routes over the watersheds to the upper reaches of the adjacent rivers, which in turn could be travelled right down to their estuaries in the Atlantic, the Channel and the North Sea. This network of natural transcontinental waterways with their short link routes over low watersheds constituted the vital means of goods transport for the Celtic peoples.

For several millennia – from the beginning of the Neolithic period to the end of the Bronze Age – this providential waterway network was used by the prehistoric cultures north of the Alps, who in turn communicated with the cultures of the eastern Mediterranean region via the Danube. It was not until around 600 BC, when Greeks from Phocaea founded the colony of Massalia (present-day Marseille) close to the Rhône estuary, that the western link of the waterway network quickly began to gain preference over the older eastern route. The extent

to which Greek traders exploited this new gateway to dispose of Greek products amongst the Celts of Gaul and its neighbouring regions is shown by the map, which shows the distribution of large Greek transport amphorae, Greek bronze vessels and black-figure ceramics from Athens (sixth to early fifth centuries). No less than 24,000 sherds of Italian wine amphorae were found at the Celtic trading site of Chalons-sur-Saone, and although these date from a later period the quantities give an idea of the extent of the ship traffic, since these heavy amphorae were typical shipping freight, easily transported by inland vessel on the Rhône and Saône.

The Greeks' motive for their trade with the Celts was twofold: their desire to increase the turnover of their own products, and their need for raw materials which were not available in sufficient quantity in the Mediterranean region. One indispensable material was the tin produced in Cornwall, which the Greeks needed to make bronze in conjunction with Mediterranean copper. The bronze was used to manufacture numerous finished articles (jewellery, vessels, implements of all kinds, works of art etc). Around 330 BC the Greek long-distance merchant Pytheas of Massalia described the tin trade, and in so doing gave us the oldest surviving description of Celtic inland ship travel, even though the ships themselves are not mentioned at all:

> The natives of Britain in the region of the Belerion foothills [Cornwall] are extremely hospitable and their dealings with foreign merchants have given them quite a civilised mode of living. They produce the tin by a sophisticated method of processing the rock which contains the ore . . . they bring it in astragal-shaped ingots and carry it to an island off the British coast named Ictis [St Michael's Mount, Cornwall]. If the sand flats are dry at ebb tide, they transport the tin in large quantities by cart . . . there the merchants trade the inhabitants' tin and bring it over to Gaul. Finally they transport it by pack horse through Gaul over the

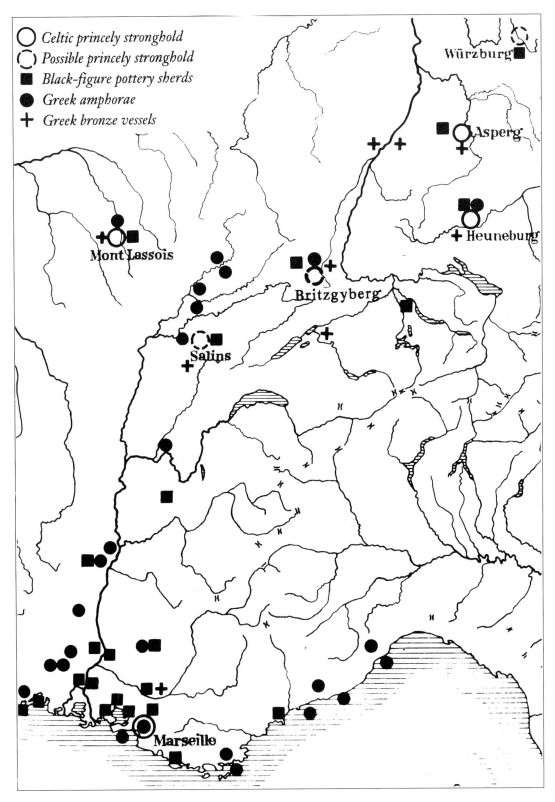

A distribution map of Greek merchandise shipped into Gaul in the sixth and fifth centuries BC along the river Rhône.

the coastal shipping route to the river Seine as described by Pytheas. Another typical feature of Celtic merchant shipping pointed out in Pytheas's text is the market located on a water-side bank, where foreign merchants could land their ships directly. Further evidence of Celtic bankside markets is provided by the numerous Roman place names which end in -*magus*, the Celtic word for market. These places are all located on navigable waters, *eg* on the Rhine (from south to north): Noviomagus (= Speyer), Borbetomagus (= Worms), Rigomagus (= Remagen), Durnomagus (= Dormagen), Ulpia Noviomagus (= Nijmegen); and also: Brucomagus (= Brumath on the Zern, tributary of the upper Rhine), Contiomagus (= Pachten on the Saar), Noviomagus (= Neumagen on the Mosel), Rotomagus (= Rouen on the Seine).

Pytheas states definitely that the inhabitants of the immediate vicinity used carts solely to transport goods to the bankside market; in this case carrying tin ingots from the smelting sites to the waterside. The foreign merchants arrived by ship from Gaul and traded the tin ingots for unnamed goods. It is reasonable to assume that the carts carrying the tin ingots were run directly on to the merchants' ships, left high and dry at low water, so that the ingots could be moved from cart to ship without major difficulty. At flood tide the ships would refloat and could start the return voyage to Gaul if they had shipped a sufficient load. The first stage of the return trip would have been eastward, staying within sight of the south coast of Britain, until the vessels were able to cross the Channel by the shortest route towards Normandy, where the 180m high Cap de la Hague provided a navigation point which was visible from a great distance. From there the voyage continued along the northeast coast and into the Seine.

If the merchants used for the Channel crossing the lightweight hide boats which Pytheas mentioned in a different context, they would

land routes to the Rhône estuary, which they reach in 30 days.

This brief report contains more information on the characteristics of Celtic trading and mar-itime activities than is obvious at first sight. Among all the excavated tin ingots of various shapes there is only one that fits Pytheas's description: as long ago as 1810 an astragal-shaped ingot of 99.9% pure tin was dredged up at St Mawes near the harbour entrance of Falmouth, Cornwall. Unfortunately this ingot itself cannot be dated, but it fits Pytheas's text very closely, not only in its shape but also in its weight of about 80kg, approximately half the load of a pack horse. Furthermore the 89cm long ingot was found on the shore a relatively short distance east of St Michael's Mount, along

Tin ingot found near Falmouth, Cornwall, United Kingdom (around fourth century BC).

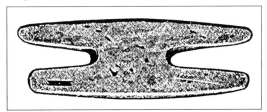

also have been able to travel a very long distance up the Seine in them. On the other hand, if they had used seagoing ships of deeper draught, they would have had to load the tin ingots onto smaller inland ships which could also navigate the upper reaches of the Seine. Only when the waterway became too constricted for even small boats did it become necessary to unload again. Pytheas writes that pack horses were used for this purpose. In fact the tin ingots were so shaped that a load of about 160kg for one horse could be made without great difficulty from two ingots and a rope sling, with one ingot suspended on each side of the pack saddle. The weight corresponds exactly to the load which a pack horse could carry. The watershed would then be crossed by the shortest route, after which the tin would be loaded on to an inland ship at the first practical location on a tributary of the Saône. From there it was an easy journey downstream as far as the Rhône estuary, which was reached 30 days after leaving Cornwall.

The quoted time for this journey is extraordinarily fast, and should be considered as the best that could be achieved. Average journey times must have been much longer, for the first towpaths were constructed by the Romans, and therefore would not have been in place in the Celtic period. Celtic inland ships had to be poled upstream, and on the meandering Seine this would have been highly time-consuming. Pytheas did not mention the use of inland ships at all, as he and his contemporary readers would have assumed that this was the only possible means of travel. All he mentions is the unusual application of the pack horse. The pack horse was the most expensive of all means of goods transport, and as a result this method was used only where there was absolutely no alternative, namely on the short mountain stretches between the upper river reaches, as Pytheas described in the text quoted earlier. Pack horses were certainly not used for entire land-based journeys right across Gaul, as is suggested even today by certain writers. However, the whole system of transcontinental inland water transport could only function if the essential means of land transportation was available at the crucial land routes over the watersheds. In this case it is pack horses, although at other watersheds, where the terrain was easier, carts would have been preferred. Certain watershed paths would have been in regular use, and it can be assumed that the people who lived close to them specialised in keeping sufficient numbers of pack horses or covered vehicles available to transport the goods belonging to long-distance merchants – together with the people travelling

with them – from one river network to the other, for which service they would naturally collect corresponding dues. To date little archaeological research has been directed at these critical points in the overall transport network. Nevertheless, certain structures of Celtic culture are already apparent.

In the sixth century BC Celtic princes (of the later Hallstatt Culture) established fortified hill strongholds at the most important transitional points between two river regions, and these forts were maintained by those dynasties until well into the fifth century BC. The strongholds were Mont Lassois, located above a navigable stretch of the Seine, the Britzgyberg at the Burgundian Gate, with the navigable Ill at its foot, flowing into the Rhine, and the Heuneburg on the upper Danube, where the river is already fully navigable; this was the point where the most convenient route from Lake Constance meets the river. From the Mediterranean point of view, all three princely seats are located where travel by ship to the distant trading destinations could be resumed after completing the overland route over the watersheds. As such these locations had a function akin to a bridgehead for this trading activity. It is easy to imagine the wide variety of imported Greek items and the wealth of gold articles in these forts and their grave mounds as evidence of active participation in the organisation of this trade. Evidently the means of transport over the short land routes were prepared at these princely forts, and fort personnel must have provided protection from attack at these particularly dangerous points. In return taxes were demanded at such levels that they maintained a noble court. Clearly the same long-distance trading which promoted Massalia as a trading colony also helped these princely seats to thrive, even if their prosperity was short-lived. Other princely seats of the time such as the Asperg on the Neckar were sited in such a location that they could control the river traffic as it passed through.

In order to obtain an accurate overall impression of this trading activity, the most important question to be answered is how far the Greek merchants extended their trading journeys using the organisation described here. The foundation of the trading colony at Massalia only makes sense if it was seen as the starting point for Greek trading journeys into Gaul, rather than as a destination for trading in itself. Archaeological methods can easily prove that Greek goods were imported into Gaul, but these methods cannot show whether the imported goods were carried by Greeks or by Celts. In only a few cases special circumstances

suggest the presence of Greeks in the land of the Celts. For example, the grave of the Vix princess at the base of Mont Lassois, which was prepared around 525 BC, contained a 1.64m tall bronze *krater* (a Greek vessel for mixing wine with water) which could hold 1100 litres of liquid. This beautifully decorated vessel weighs more than four hundredweight, and was specially made in Greece in several parts, then transported to the princely seat and assembled on site. Code marks in the form of Greek letters on the component parts were intended to facilitate their assembly, and suggest that Greek specialists made the journey to carry out this work.

Other Greek specialists were in charge of the erection of the great mud-brick wall at the Heuneburg on the upper Danube around 550 BC.[1] This is significant, because the Heuneburg, unlike Mont Lassois, could not be reached from Massalia simply by ship along the Rhône and its tributaries followed by a short ride over the watershed. The journey to the Heuneburg involved several changes of transport, namely over the Rhône, Saône and Doubs to the Burgundian Gate, through the Gate to the upper Rhine overland, and from there eventually to the Danube, although it is not known how travellers negotiated the difficult upper stretch of the Rhine with its waterfalls. Yet the Greeks, in spite of tough travelling conditions, showed considerable determination in seeking out the seats of the princes.

The same applies to the Asperg on the Neckar, at the foot of which, at Hochdorf, the bronze beam of a pair of fine Greek scales was found (dating from around 550 BC). The scales were used to determine the level of payment for traded goods against Greek precious metal coins, a form of transaction which first evolved in the sixth century BC. These scales show that a Greek long-distance merchant had penetrated as far as the Asperg at that time. Obviously one swallow does not make a summer, but as the two other examples show, it is no longer reasonable to consider the presence of Greek merchants and other specialists at the distant destinations of Greek trading activities as entirely exceptional. It is more logical to assume that at least a few Greeks pursued their economic objectives deep into the Celtic region. One further example of this is Pytheas

1. The construction technique of the excavated wall is undoubtedly Mediterranean and the objects found on site include many of Greek provenance. The distribution pattern suggests they came to the Heuneburg via Massilia, not directly up the Danube, so there is the strongest possibility that the wall was built by, or under the supervision of, Greek specialists.

of Massalia's journey around 330 BC, which took him at least as far as the northernmost islands of Scotland, although by then the political structures had changed completely.

The long-distance merchants travelling along the Rhône from Massalia were able to navigate the river region using their own vessels – assuming that they could survive the coastal voyage from Massalia to the nearest branch of the Rhône estuary in an inland ship. The map showing the distribution of archaeological finds in this area indicates that a large number of merchants only went so far by water, and left their boats under guard at the upper reaches of the river. They would then carry their goods over the watershed to the next navigable river, where they would offer them to the native merchants and exchange them for coveted raw materials, such as the tin already mentioned. However, as demonstrated by the examples quoted above, there were quite obviously other Greeks who went further. They had to rely upon those means of transport which the native Celts could provide for them on their protracted journeys, not only for the short overland routes, but also for the long river and coastal journeys – ie they were dependent on Celtic inland and coastal ships.

Before turning to these ships, it is necessary to point out that no definitive statements can be made about the organisation of transport for the land crossings over the watersheds after the end of the princely forts in the sixth/fifth

Cargo-carrying dugout found near Hasholme, North Humberside, United Kingdom (c300 BC). A. upper bow with treenails; B. lower bow; C. transverse timbers with wedges; D. washstrakes with treenails and keys; E. repairs with treenails and keys; F. shelves; G. beam-ties with treenails; H. transom with wedges; I. hypothetical deck. (National Maritime Museum)

century BC, because for a period of several centuries archaeological evidence is notable by its absence. It was not until the second century BC that Celtic *oppida* were established at other sites on the transit routes. The *oppida* were fortified town-like mountain settlements such as Alesia, situated between the Seine and the Saône, with which we are familiar as a result of Caesar's siege of the place. The *oppida* catered for the short-range overland transport requirements as a form of organised service, and also carried out the essential protective functions.

Once the Romans had occupied Gaul and the lower Alpine regions, an unheard-of period of peace settled on the territories within the Empire. The frontier army assumed the role of protective shield against external enemies, and as a direct result the towns were able to abandon their defensive positions up on the mountains. They were re-established in valley locations where communications were easier; one example was Epomanduodurum (today Mandeure) at the Burgundian Gate. On the bank of the Dubis (Doubs) we even know the position of the riverside quays where, during the Roman period, goods were loaded from inland ships onto carts travelling to the river Ill, and vice versa. The towns promoted free trade as a sort of industrial service, a system which had evolved in the late Celtic period. The only military organisation employed for transport purposes was that used for military supplies, which of course also used the routes provided by nature. Neither of these activities are discussed in detail here. For the purposes of this chapter, the only point to note is that by the late Celtic period the decisive innovation in terms of transport had already been introduced, and moreover it survived past the end of the Roman occupation: from late Celtic times

it was the towns which carried out the task of organising the technicalities of long-distance transport over the short watershed routes.

Inland craft

Because the rivers and the lakes through which they flowed were so important to their transportation system, the Celts developed a wide variety of inland ship types. However, they were not the first people to exploit the network of transcontinental inland waterways, and as a result the roots of Celtic shipbuilding extend far back into prehistory. With the present state of research this is best illustrated by the cargo-carrying dugout found at Hasholme, North Humberside, in England which was almost 13m long and 1.40m in beam. It was built around 300 BC, *ie* approximately at the time of Pytheas of Massalia, and was cut from the trunk of an oak tree that was about 800 years old. The vessel was capable of transporting no less than 5.6 tons of freight, which means that it could carry 70 tin ingots of the type mentioned above. The load had to be arranged on the bottom of the boat along its length in a double layer about 10m long, in order to distribute the load evenly in the hull. This would have left sufficient space for the small crew to carry out all the essential work, including poling the vessel upstream. With a freeboard of 50cm the dugout would have drawn 75cm, and would have been very stable in the water.

A draught of this magnitude would have been too much for the upper reaches of the smaller rivers, however, which means that the vessel would only have been suitable for certain stretches of the tin's journey across Gaul. As a result it would have been necessary to transship the freight into boats of smaller draught, *ie*

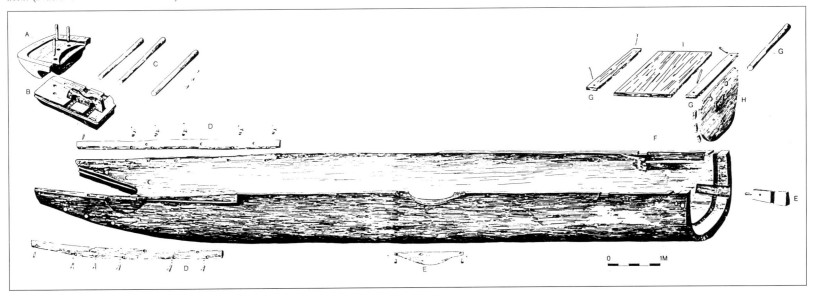

vessels of much inferior carrying capacity. A crew of 3–5 men could pole this dugout upstream carrying 70 tin ingots. Even when transferred to a number of shallower-draught vessels only a few more men would have been required for poling, since eight men were sufficient for four vessels. However, once it became necessary to use land tracks over the watersheds no less than 35 pack horses would have been required for the load of tin, with a correspondingly large number of handlers. Unfortunately too little is known about Celtic freight carts to be able to calculate their load-bearing capacity, and for this reason it is impossible to ascertain how many cart loads a dugout of this type could accept. Nevertheless, what calculations can be made do provide a very clear idea of the efficiency and capacity of Celtic water transport on transcontinental waterways.

The Hasholme dugout is a key to the understanding of the stage of development in shipbuilding technology achieved by the Celts, and its significance cannot easily be overestimated. It belongs to that species of dugout which took the form of an open-ended channel, a design which had been developed since the earlier Neolithic Age (see illustration on page 22). In large dugouts the short-grain timber at each end always presented problems, but in this variant the ends had not been cut transversely in some way, but omitted or cut away entirely. As a result it became possible to use old oaks of very large girth, which are often hollow by nature in any case. The open ends were sealed with semi-circular boards set transversely and provided with watertight joints. At the stern of the Hasholme boat, dating from around 300 BC, this characteristic Neolithic design feature was still evident, with the vertical stern board fitted in a prepared rebate just short of the aft end, and held in place by wedges. In the Neolithic Age the bow was formed in exactly the same way. However, the Hasholme boat's bow board was not set vertical, but at an angle, which bestowed two advantages: the vessel was more streamlined, and it could also be beached simply by running it up onto land where the bank sloped into the water. The angled bow board was cut to fit in a sort of rebate at the lower front edges of the side walls and the bottom, and held by two dowels which passed through a double cleat carved from the solid wood of the bow board and into corresponding through-holes in the side walls.

This cleat construction is familiar from the early Bronze Age North Ferriby boat (illustration on page 31) and the early Iron Age boat bottom found at Brigg (illustration on page 34). Thus in terms of its basic constructional features the Hasholme dugout is a very traditional boat. This is underlined by the fact that no iron nails or other metal parts were used in its construction. Even the narrow washboards in the foreship, which were less than 4m long, were attached using wooden dowels. A wedge was pushed into the narrow end of each dowel in order to obtain a very secure joint. Small pieces fitted to the stern and the port side as repairs were also held in place by this method. As pointed out later, the Celts were to lay equal stress on obtaining really secure joints when they adopted iron nails.

The top section of the bow was formed by a thick wooden block which was cut accurately to fit the narrow hull sides and the angled bow board. This block was fixed to the bow board by means of three wooden spikes. There are certain types of boat used on the Rhine to this day which have their roots in Celtic boats, and they still feature this bow block, now termed the *Maulklotz* (mouth block). At the stern three cross-bars were used to secure the transom when it was pushed in place. The timber on the inside top edge of the side walls between the two upper cross-bars is rabetted, presumably to support a quarterdeck. This part did not survive, but would have been highly advantageous to the helmsman. The two holes at the top of the transom must have been the support points for the long steering paddle.

A bas-relief found on an early Roman gravestone shows a freight boat of broadly the same shape. The gravestone was found at the *vicus* (commercial settlement) of Mainz-Weisenau,

opposite the confluence of the Main and Rhine, and dates from the middle of the first century AD, *ie* about 350 years later than the Hasholme boat. The overall shape and the inset, angled bow board are generally similar, although the curved top edge is depicted in slightly clumsy perspective. One difference is that the narrow washboard battens in the relief picture extend over the whole length of the boat. The only area of the vessel which differed markedly was the stern, which had been fundamentally redesigned and no longer exhibited the typical Neolithic construction. Nevertheless the raised platform for the helmsman, as seen on the Hasholme boat, is still a feature. A fragment of a relief picture dating from about 90 AD, found only a few years ago in Cologne, provides clearer evidence of the stern construction. Here the helmsman stands on a platform consisting of a horizontal board, corresponding to the hypothetical quarterdeck on the Hasholme vessel. Aft of the platform the transom rises to the height of the helmsman's hip, where it is supported by relatively narrow cross-timbers. In the position where the Hasholme boat had two holes in the transom, this vessel features a semi-circular component held in place by two (wood or iron) nails, which encloses the oar shaft. The top end of the shaft is linked to the inside of the transom with a loop of rope. Two additional ropes run from both upper corners of the oar blade to the top edge of the transom, and prevent the steering oar slipping down. As on the Mainz relief the tiller runs downward, and the helmsman is handling it in a very relaxed manner.

The Cologne relief shows at least three pairs of rowers standing at the oars, which were supported in rope loops; on the Mainz relief only

Skipper Blussus at the tiller of his river craft. Relief on an early Roman tombstone found near Mainz-Weisenau, Germany (about AD 50).

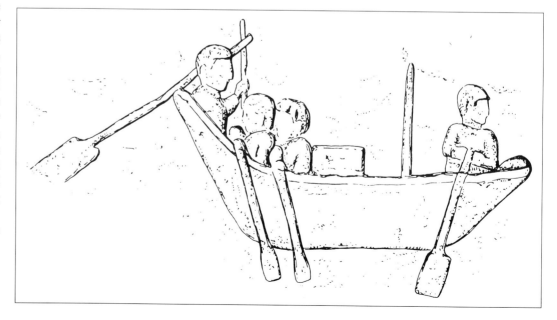

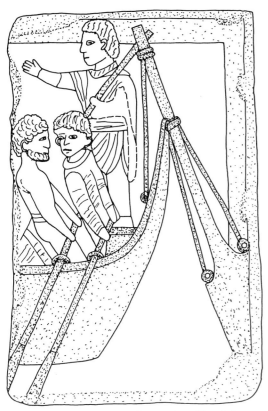

Standing oarsman in a riverboat with rudder of the Blussus type. Fragment of a relief found near the Roman harbour of Köln, Germany (about AD 90).

two pairs of oarsmen can be seen, although an extra man is working a second steering oar at the bow. This arrangement was essential for the type of valley journey depicted here, where the ship was running downstream with the current. Even though there were four men at the oars the flow of water around the long stern oar was not very strong, with the result that the ship was sluggish in responding to the helm. The supplementary bow rudder had to be used to effect sudden changes in direction to avoid shallows or other obstacles. The short mast indicates that for the journey upstream the boat could be towed, and the bow helmsman had to work in conjunction with the stern helmsman to steer the boat on a course parallel to the riverside, so that the tow line did not pull the ship against the bank.

It is known that during the final phase of towed ship transport one man could pull about 2 tons of cargo up the Rhine. The owner of the Mainz boat could therefore transport about 8 tons of goods with his own crew, and the vessel must have been substantially larger than the Hasholme dugout. This assumption is rein-

Skipper Blussus with his wife Menimane and their son Primus. The parents have Celtic names, their son a Roman one. Blussus is wearing a Celtic hooded cloak, the cuculus. *Principal side of the tombstone from Mainz-Weisenau, Germany.*

forced by the small shelter between the mast and the oarsmen. The barrel shape of its roof is clearly to be seen, even in shallow relief. We have no means of knowing whether this was a shelter for delicate freight or for travellers.

The Mainz gravestone provides very accurate information on the socio-economic conditions in which the cargo carrier operated, thanks to its inscription, the picture and the location of the find. The inscription is particularly helpful, as it says that the gravestone was a memorial to an inland boatman (*nauta*) who died at the age of 75 years. He bore the Celtic name Blussus; his wife, who survived him, and both their fathers also had Celtic names, but in contrast they gave their son the Roman name Primus. Thus the gravestone indicates the period when the native Celts were in the midst of the Romanisation process.

Blussus must have been born between 30 and 20 BC, and therefore learned his trade around the last decade BC. He settled close to the banks of the Rhine, where conditions were good for landing his ship, but his estate was part of the commercial settlement (*vicus*) outside the gates of the Roman military camp of Mainz-Weisenau. His wife may well have been younger than him, and her clothing followed the latest Roman fashion, which is familiar from grave finds dating from around 50 BC. Blussus and his wife are seated on a Roman couch, have adopted the Roman custom of a gravestone, had mastered the Roman language (Latin) and – not least – had given their son a Roman name. The gravestone also shows a very prominent purse, indicating that Blussus was doing quite well at this period; for this was a time of prosperity, when the frontier army

Helmsman with hooded cloak on board a medieval cog. Town seal of Kiel, Germany (1365).

stationed in the Roman Rhineland and paid from Rome helped all sections of the area's economy to thrive.

However, in two particulars the adaptable Blussus relied on the inheritance of his own people within the new provincial Roman culture, rather than bending before the Roman wind: for the whole of his life he earned his livelihood with the type of native Celtic ship whose predecessor was the English Hasholme dugout dating from around 300 BC. In this respect Blussus should not be considered particularly conservative, as all his fellow Celtic tradespeople did the same. In fact, Celtic shipbuilding technology had reached a very high level of refinement over the protracted period of its development, and Celtic vessels were so well tuned to the conditions encountered on local waters that there was absolutely no reason to adopt Mediterranean shipbuilding technology for native use, even though the Roman army had brought such vessels (in the form of its warships) to the Rhine. In summary, Celtic merchant ships became (provincial) Roman ships by dint of the fact that the Celts themselves became Romanised. Even so, the Celtic ship's carpenters were prepared to absorb technical advance to the extent that they fitted their ships with towing masts once the first towpaths had been constructed.

The second legacy of Celtic tradition is the hooded cloak which Blussus is wearing, in contrast to his wife's fashionable Roman garb. In the provinces of Gaul this garment retained its

Model of the riverboat of the Oberländer *type found in a former bed of the Rhine near Krefeld-Gellep, Germany. (seventh – eighth century AD).* (Deutsches Schiffahrtsmuseum)

Celtic name of *cuculus*. Like the *lodenmantel* – a waterproof overcoat still familiar in Germany today – the *cuculus* was a foul-weather cloak which was popular amongst river travellers and others because it provided the best protection available at that time against cold, rainy conditions. Ship crews continued to wear this effective garment until the end of the Middle Ages, by which time it was known as a *gugel* – a corruption of the Latin *cuculus*. It was in widespread use in regions which were never settled by Celts, such as the Baltic Sea coasts.

Like the Celtic hooded cloak, Blussus' Celtic ship type also survived untouched through the Roman occupation of Gaul, the stormy periods of tribal migration and the end of the Western Roman Empire, and persisted on the Rhine and other rivers throughout the Middle Ages. Towards the end of the Middle Ages the type was known as the *Oberländer* in the Cologne region, in order to differentiate it from other ship types which arrived in Cologne from the Netherlands. Nevertheless the *Oberländer* were still found far south of Cologne.

In 1973 a fairly small *Oberländer* was excavated at Krefeld-Gellep, and, using the radiocarbon method, the date of origin of this vessel was established as the seventh – eighth century AD. It was found on the western side of the lower Rhine in a dredging pit, and so many fragments were found that it proved possible to reconstruct most of its shape with considerable certainty. This *Oberländer* was clearly a development of the Hasholme style of dugout: first the oak trunk selected for hollowing was split along its length, and from the log were cut two identical semi-circular dugout shells as a mirror-image pair, destined to form the two

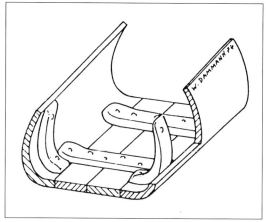

Construction of the midship section of the Krefeld Oberländer.

sides of the vessel. Like the Hasholme dugout the shells were cut off perfectly 'square' aft and at an angle forward. Two parallel floor planks were fitted between these two dugout shells, extended forward by three angled bow boards. The components were then joined together by means of cross-timbers laid over the hull bottom. Curved timbers, following exactly the rounded shape of the two dugout shells, provided support to the side timbers. These timbers also carried a narrow washboard, attached to the top edge of the dugout shells by means of dowels. The outer skin was only linked to the internal timbers by dowels, which were split at the narrow end. A small wooden wedge driven into the split would have provided a very firm joint.

The open, square-cut stern of the *Oberländer* was completed by a broad transom which was set against the outside end of the boat and then attached using wooden dowels fitted into holes

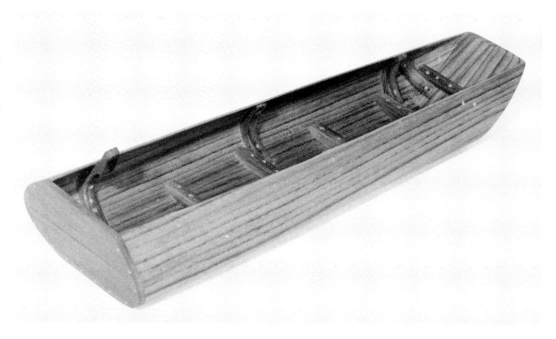

At the end of the Middle Ages the Oberländer was the biggest cargo vessel on the Rhine. Woodcut by A Woensam, Köln 1531.

bored in the end-grain. The transom and dowels have not survived, but the dowel holes are clearly visible. Evidently the boat sank when its transom was torn off. It is only possible to reconstruct the exact shape of the lower part of the transom, where it ended exactly flush with the outside edge of the hull; how the component continued higher up is unknown. The lack of any iron parts is characteristic of early medieval inland ships.

The flat bottom of this boat type, derived from the dugout typified by the Hasholme find, represented an important advantage for inland ships, as it could not flex even when the boat was quite long because the two longitudinal dugout shells provided great strength to the hull. This example was very squat at only 5.75m long and 1.77m maximum beam (at the stern), but in spite of its small size it could transport a load of about 2 tons.

Armed with the detailed information on the Krefeld-Gellep *Oberländer*, it is possible to make more of Blussus' ship on the Mainz-Weisenau gravestone. Even in its side elevation the bow transom and the covered semi-circular superstructure indicate clearly that the boat's beam was greater than that of the Hasholme dugout. A load-bearing capacity of around 8 tons can be assumed, and this is further evidence that Blussus' ship was more than a simple dugout. Most likely it was an *Oberländer* assembled from two dugout shells and more than one floor plank. This proposition gains greater credence if Blussus' vessel is compared with a large *Oberländer* dating from the late Middle Ages.

In the period around 1500 *Oberländers* up to 30m long were in use, and these represented the largest cargo vessels on the Rhine south of

Cologne. The most accurate surviving picture of such a vessel is on a woodcut of the town of Cologne produced in 1531 by Anton Woensam. The illustration clearly shows that the longitudinal dugout shells, with the thicker root end at the stern, dictated the characteristic trapezoidal shape of this ship type. Two gunwales are attached to the top edge of the shells. The angled bow transom is clearly recognisable. The stern transom curves forward at the top, as is familiar from the early Roman relief found at Cologne, but in this case it forms the rear wall of a relatively narrow, tapered stern superstructure. The superstructure makes it impossible to route the long steering oar over the centre of the transom, so it was shifted slightly further forward on the starboard side, where it was supported by various rope loops and a hoop-shaped support, so that the helmsman could vary the steering oar's angle of incidence – a system which was just as complex as that used in the Roman period. The tiller could now no longer hang down vertically; instead it projected into the ship almost horizontally.

Even though this *Oberländer* dates from 1500 years after the Blussus ship, it was still necessary to use a bow rudder for the valley journey depicted in the woodcut. In fact, the size and clumsiness of the later ship necessitated a much

larger bow rudder which required no fewer than five men to operate it, whereas Blussus had managed with one. As a result the method of hanging the rudder also had to be altered. Furthermore, the ship's large size meant that a ten-man rowing crew had replaced Blussus' four oarsmen. One notable point is that the oarsmen still stood to operate their heavy oars, as depicted in the early Roman relief from Cologne. The only difference is that in the period around 1500 they were located on the rounded roof of the long, low superstructure between helmsman and towing mast, *ie* they were not stationed as low in the ship as in the Roman period. The Blussus ship of Mainz also featured the rounded, covered superstructure located in the same position, and a towing mast with similar rigging, and one can only marvel at how little had changed in the originally Celtic ship type between Blussus' gravestone and the woodcut of 1531. The only fundamental difference is the completely enclosed cargo hold formed by a superstructure aft of the mast, and a deck, most of it forward of the mast. On Blussus' ship the crew stands so low in the vessel that a full-length deck fore and aft of the superstructure could not have been present.

Finally it can also be shown that certain details of the constructional technology used on *Oberländers* changed in the course of the Middle Ages without affecting the vessel's overall shape. In 1976 the forward part of an *Oberländer* dating from the twelfth/thirteenth century was found close to Meinerswijk on the Rhine opposite Arnheim in the Netherlands. This vessel is generally similar to the Krefeld-Gellep boat, but larger. For this reason a detailed description of it is not necessary, but it is worth looking more closely at the wood joint technology: in both *Oberländers* the frame components (floor timbers and side brackets) were fixed to the outer skin using dowels, whose

Forward part of an Oberländer *found in the Rhine near Meinerswijk, Netherlands (thirteenth – fourteenth century AD).*

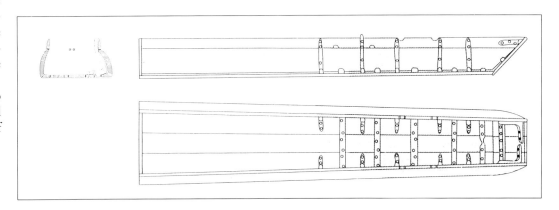

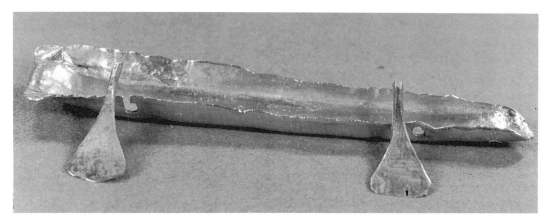

Small gold model of a cargo boat with open bow port, found in a grave high up the Duerrnberg near Hallein, Austria (c370 BC).

ends were each secured with a wedge. At the crucial area of the outer skin – where the angled bow transom meets the flat bottom – the joints were secured using iron nails whose tips were bent back into the wood, so that there was no possibility of the joints coming loose. All the seams in the outer skin were caulked using moss, held in place by narrow battens secured with iron caulking clamps similar to cleats.

The development of one very closely defined ship type over a period of nearly two thousand years, illustrated here using the Celtic dugout of the Hasholme type and its progressive development into the Rhine *Oberländer* of the late Middle Ages, reveals the clear pattern of development which applied to other types of Celtic inland ship. Initially they were integrated into the Roman civilisation, then after the end of Roman rule they continued in existence amongst the changing circumstances of the medieval economy. The next section will follow other Celtic ship types down through the ages, as far as the fragmentary archaeological evidence permits, taking as examples vessels whose characteristics are as unambiguous as possible. This will concentrate on the Celtic cultures of the pre-Christian centuries, but a brief account of how these ship types continued in later periods will also be included.

Roll-on, roll-off – a Celtic invention

The dugout was based on a tree trunk, with the broad root end forming the stern. This vessel, with its square cut ends and trapezoidal plan-form, evolved into the inland ship type discussed above. It also spawned another variant which eventually resulted in a new inland ship type. Once again a Celtic archaeological discovery forms the starting point for description.

In 1959 a burial site was excavated on the Duerrnberg, above Hallein on the Salzach river in Austria, near to a Celtic salt mine. Two men, members of a local noble dynasty, had been interred in the grave, although not at the same

time. The younger of the dead men had been buried around 370 BC, and he was accompanied by artefacts including a model boat only 6.6cm long, made of sheet gold. At first glance the model's trapezoidal plan-form appears to fit exactly into the series of vessels previously discussed.

The rowing equipment also fits neatly into the pattern of the propulsion techniques described above, although it represents an earlier stage before the influence of the Romans becomes apparent. The model featured two short, broad-bladed oars, both of them on the starboard side only as two holes in this side of the hull prove beyond doubt. The model was on display in the Hallein museum with the oar shafts fitted through these holes, but this is obviously incorrect since the oars do not have sufficient freedom of movement for single-sided application. The oars in question are in fact 'thrust oars', which are still in use to this day on small boats on Alpine lakes and on Venetian gondolas. The thrust oars were operated above the gunwale, suspended in slings. A loop of this type would have been passed through each of the holes of the gold model, and the oar shaft fitted through the loop above the gunwale, as illustrated on the Cologne relief dating from around 90 AD. However, in contrast to the relief picture the man at the thrust oar would stand in the boat facing forward. To produce forward thrust the oarsman had to hold the oar at a fairly steep angle and push the shaft forward. The blade stayed in the water when he pulled it back, but had to be swivelled through 90 degrees so that its narrow face cut through the water. The broad side would then be used for the next working thrust. At the same time the oarsman could direct the boat to one side or the other by varying the amount of rotation he applied to the oar whilst making the working thrust. In this way a single process produced thrust and steering.

In principle a single thrust oar was sufficient

for a fairly small boat, as is clear by watching present-day Venetian gondolas. The Duerrnberg model's second thrust oar provides extra forward thrust and supplementary steering for the valley journey. From this it is clear that the model represents something larger than a very small barge. Using the method of propulsion described here it makes no difference whether the forward thrust oar was carried to starboard or to port. In fact the forward oar in the Blussus ship was also on the starboard side, with the oarsman looking forward and holding it like a thrust oar at a steep angle, which means that by around 50 AD nothing had changed compared with the Duerrnberg model, which was approximately 400 years older. In contrast both the Blussus ship and the (slightly more recent) Cologne relief show that the function of the thrust oar at the stern had been divided into its two components: the long steering oar projecting over the stern had assumed the function of steering alone, while propelling oars, now necessarily arranged on both sides of the vessel, provided the forward thrust. This layout meant that the oarsmen had to face backwards but could use pulling power, which is more effective than pushing. However, they did remain standing, and the oars were still supported in loops. This was true in the early Roman period and continued right to the end of the Middle Ages (see top figure on page 59).

In contrast to the series of *Oberländer* ship types the Duerrnberg model does not feature a truly horizontal hull bottom. Certainly the midships section of the bottom is flat, but it curves up relatively steeply to the stern, and rises in a very shallow curve forward to a point only slightly above water level, with an open bow port between the timbers of the hull sides. For a long time this detail was ignored by all researchers, including the author, until the excavation of a medieval cargo boat at Krefeld-Gellep in 1972. This vessel featured an open bow port of exactly the same type. Boats with a bow port were designed for load-carrying, and for landing on gently sloping banks in the same way as a ferry. This design made it possible to load heavy barrels on board without the necessity of lifting apparatus, as they could simply be rolled along a trackway of wooden planks which could be laid out quickly. We know that the Romans considered the transport barrel to be a Celtic invention. The Mediterranean equivalent (*ie* the primary container for ship transport) was the pottery amphora. There the ships were designed to allow the amphorae to be stacked up inside, with consequent maximum exploitation of space and minimal risk of breakage. In contrast, the Celts clearly developed the ship type appropriate to 'their' barrel, and their means of transport – the rivers. This was the inland ship with an open bow port, through which heavy barrels could be rolled in and out.

Barrels were certainly used for fluids, but also for any goods which would be damaged by moisture. This was evidently the reason why the Celts transported the rock salt mined at Duerrnberg in barrels. It is known that this was true of longer journeys, as they used a ship type developed specifically for the purpose. Once again the location of the archaeological evidence and the contents of the grave provide extremely valuable information on the socio-economic background to this form of ship transport, at a time when Celtic culture had a well established nobility, but had not yet established commercial settlements typified by the later Celtic *oppida*.

Characteristically the burial site of the Duerrnberg noble dynasty was not located by the Salzach river, on the banks of which the salt ships were loaded, but high up on the mountain near the salt caverns, *ie* where the salt was mined. Of course, this does not mean that the princes themselves worked in the caverns, took part in the loading activities, or actually rowed the transport ships represented by the model. What it does indicate is that the nobles controlled the salt mining business, and had claimed the prospecting rights. The weapons found in the graves of the noblemen make it clear that this dynasty was ready to defend its prospecting rights, and a fortified wall had been erected close by for this purpose. There is no explanation why a valuable gold model of what is undoubtedly a freight vessel, made specifically for the individual in question, was placed in a prince's grave, but presumably there were religious reasons which can only be imagined. All that is certain is that the bare fact of the model in the grave indicates that the prince was at the top of the hierarchy which organised the mining, shipping and final sale of the salt. It was he who organised the mining of the salt by his people and its overland transport to the nearest port – using the scheme described earlier in this discussion – where it would be loaded on to ships. It was he who had the

barrels made and the salt packed, and his was the responsibility for building, maintaining and loading the special ships and organising the freight voyages.

In conclusion, it can be assumed that members of the nobility accompanied the salt journeys themselves, at least for particularly important occasions, *eg* when new trading links were being forged. This type of commerce was known as sovereign trading, in which economic interests were indissolubly intermixed with social respectability, pomp and show. The nearby early Celtic salt mine at Hallstatt in Upper Austria has provided indisputable archaeological proof of the existence of sovereign trade. A member of the warrior aristocracy of Lower Kraina (in former Yugoslavia) travelled to Hallstatt in his full finery together with several of his landsmen. He died unexpectedly during the visit, and was buried there with all the rites, ceremonies and artefacts customary in his Lower Kraina home. Numerous other objects from Lower Kraina have been found at Hallstatt, which tells us that this grave is evidence of more than a single (*eg* diplomatic) visit. In fact it is an indication of regular, long-term trade connections between Lower Kraina and the Hallstatt salt mine. Clearly the salt could not be transported over the Alps by inland ship, and pack animals would have been required. However, the fact that members of the nobility in full regalia participated in at least some of these caravan journeys raises this type of trade out of the purely commercial profit-and-loss variety, and transforms it into a major society event.

Even the Duerrnberg dynasty allowed the economic side of its mining and transport enterprise to be overshadowed almost completely by the aristocratic ostentation which

was only made possible by that enterprise, as is evident from the artefacts buried in the grave. It is important to realise that even at times before a currency-based economy existed it was only the nobility that could afford the significant investment required before a financial return could be expected. The investment was needed to feed, clothe and accommodate the people working in the mines over a period of many years of privation during which the arduous development work was carried out. Eventually the return came when the first salt ships were able to transport their freight to the nearest market. The profits which were achieved after many years were not bad, as is implied, albeit indirectly, by the artefacts discovered in the grave. The gold objects, the exceptional bronze items and the iron weapons had to be procured through general trade connections, either in the form of metal ingots or as finished objects, although it is impossible to determine their provenance. The extent of this mainly ship-borne trade activity is suggested by an amber gemstone from the north, a slate ring from the Schwäbisch Alb and a drinking bowl from Athens, which were found in the two graves of the noblemen.

The noblemen themselves quite obviously considered these economic activities merely as a means of achieving their actual aim: gaining the highest possible rank in society and maintaining it even beyond death. Even in their graves they were supplied with everything they needed to celebrate great festivals, with ceremonial clothing and generous supplies of food and drink, including the vessels and implements required to enjoy them, often in exquisite form. From pictorial evidence it is known that the splendid weapons found in the graves were used in contests and chariot racing,

Riverboat with open bow port and Celtic leather sail on a mosaic from Bad Kreuznach, Germany (third century AD).

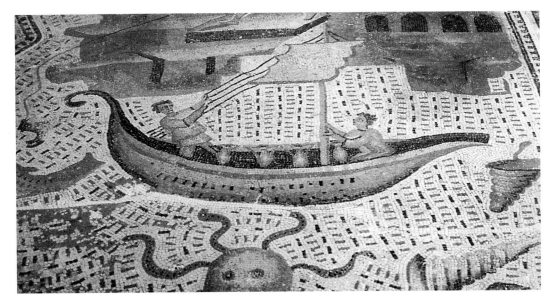

Celtic leather sail on a grave monument of Jünkerath, Germany (second – third century AD). (Deutsches Schiffahrtsmuseum)

which gave the men a chance to display publicly their capabilities in the use of weapons, even in times of peace. The costly material of which the gold model of the freight ship is made suggests that it had a role to play in these activities, and it is a reasonable assumption that it must have fulfilled an important function corresponding to the dead man's position in society. It seems very likely that this man had participated in a number of salt transport journeys using this type of vessel, within the framework of sovereign trade. At each destination he would have expected a magnificent reception.

Model of a riverboat with open bow port. The boat was found near Krefeld-Gellep (thirteenth – fourteenth century AD). (Deutsches Schiffahrtsmuseum)

If the boat was the key to the enhancement of his position in society, then even after death he would certainly not wish to be without it.

The tiny gold model provides relatively little information on constructional details. Even so, the trapezoidal shape shows that this boat was also developed from the dugout type, like the *Oberländer*. Although the Hasholme dugout would have been broad enough to contain small barrels stowed transversely, the bottom of a vessel with a bow port cannot be flat, as it has to curve gently up to and above the waterline, so that even in its loaded state the vessel would not take in water. This in turn would require that the wood fibres were cut at an angle at this point. The action of rolling salt barrels in and out of the bow port might have caused the boat's bottom to fail in this area, since they represented a heavy point load. For this reason it is probable that the entire bottom consisted of individual planks which curved up towards the bow port. This would have necessitated shaped dugout side components to give the whole structure the necessary stiffness. This type of construction was not unknown amongst the Celts of the eastern Alpine area; the evidence is a ship excavated at Laibach (present-day Ljubljana) in the upper Save valley. It is also known that the cargo vessel with open bow port was introduced into the Roman world by the Celts, as a similar vessel is depicted on the mosaic floor of a great Roman villa (*villa rustica*) dating from around 250 AD, found near Bad Kreuznach, Rheinland-Pfalz and excavated in 1966. The picture clearly shows the open bow port, and its purpose is beyond all doubt. This vessel therefore represents another of the inland waterway cargo ships being discussed here, although in this case

its load is amphorae, and not the barrels for which it was specifically designed.

Unfortunately the picture was evidently designed by a mosaic artist who was used to the appearance of typical Mediterranean ships, and he shows the boat's flat bottom rising to an exaggerated height forward where it curves gently up and beyond the waterline. Until a vessel from this period is discovered by archaeology, it is impossible to determine the extent to which the long extended volute at the stern is a figment of the artist's imagination. The only certainty is that the stern of the Duerrnberg cargo vessel is different. However, many details in the picture agree with established facts concerning Celtic ships during the Roman period: information gained from excavations, such as the iron nails indicated by rows of large, exposed nail heads and the forward position of the mast. It may just be a coincidence that the two-man crew is exactly the same as that of the Duerrnberg cargo vessel.

The sail of this boat is almost entirely without parallel amongst the hundreds of Mediterranean sailing ships shown in extant pictures. The only other sail of a similar type is shown on a Roman stone relief picture found at Jünkerath in the Eifel (Rheinland-Pfalz), which is only about 110km away. In contrast to the Roman *velum* and present-day square sails, all of which are suspended from a horizontal yard, this native Celtic type of sail featured two horizontal spars and a lower boom in addition to the yard, *ie* the sail consisted of three horizontal sections, each clearly inflated by the wind, and each suspended between horizontal spars. This is the Celtic leather sail which Caesar described in the middle of the first century BC. The Celtic term for this was the *sagulum*, and

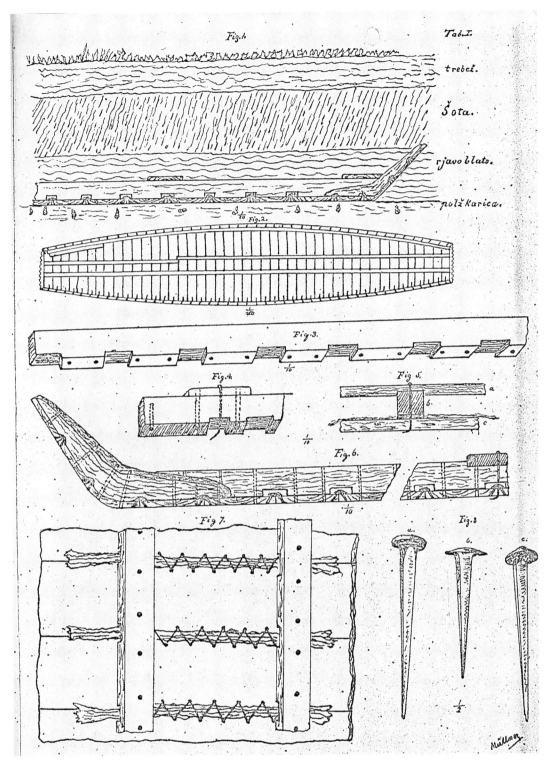

Celtic riverboat found near Laibach (today Ljubljana), Slovenia (sixth – fourth century BC). The drawing by the excavator and his short description is all that is known about the vessel.

Planks subject to severe stresses were held in place by means of short iron nails; the caulking was held in place by caulking clamps, which were used in the late Middle Ages as already mentioned. There was a mast socket a long way forward, so that the mast could easily be removed for loading freight. The clear width of the bow port was 1.50m, which means that about six to seven large wine barrels could be rolled on board. These barrels, termed *Tonnen* (or *tuns* in medieval English), were the origin of the modern unit of weight the 'ton' or 'tonne' (1 tonne = 1000kg). Calculations show that this ship was built to a very ingenious design. If the vessel was positioned with its bow port resting on the slope of the bank for loading, the first barrels would be rolled right to the stern. The boat's reaction would be to sink lower at the stern, and also to pitch towards the stern. The boat was designed in such a way that these two movements cancelled themselves out at the threshold of the bow port, which meant that the downward pressure which the bow port exerted on the bank remained constant, whether the boat was empty or fully laden. As a result the boatman always needed the same effort to pole the boat free of the bank, or position it for loading.

Ships with side gangways

The most exciting Celtic ship find was excavated as long ago as 1890 near Laibach in Slovenia, the present-day Ljubljana. The first step in this case is to attempt to establish that it was indeed a product of Celtic culture, since this is under dispute. Nothing of the ship has survived, and all that remains is the contemporary report of the excavation (including a few drawings), now over a hundred years old. The dating of the vessel is based on observations concerning the find strata at the moorland site. At another location a Roman road runs over the old turf (*sota*) layer, and it is known that this road was constructed around 50 AD. However, the ship sank before this, when the moor was still an open lake, as reeds grew over it after it had sunk. In amongst the roots of the reeds a layer of soil (*rjavo blato*) 30cm thick had been

the Germanic word *Segel* is derived from the Celtic rather than the Latin *velum*; the first indication that the Germanic peoples also adopted what is now known as the sail from the Celts. There is evidence for the existence of the lower boom on square sails of Germanic boats as late as the ninth century AD.[2]

The practical load-carrying barge with its open bow port continued to be built and used for barrel transport well into the Middle Ages. The fragmentary remains of just such a vessel

were dredged up near Krefeld-Gellep in 1972, and as the bow section survived in its entirety the find produced an understanding of the special features of this ship type for the first time. This was a cargo vessel, around 15m long and up to 3.36m in beam, and the shape of its wide stern corresponds broadly to the Duerrnberg model boat, even though the two vessels were separated by about 1700 years. It was constructed entirely of planks, held together by means of knees and wooden dowels.

2. Examples are to be found on picture stones in the island of Gotland and on the Hedeby coins found at Birka in Sweden. See D Ellmers, 'Antriebstechniken germanischer Schiffe im 1. Jahrtausend nach Chr', *Deutsches Schiffahrtsarchiv* 1 (Hamburg 1975), pp79-90.

deposited, and over this a layer of turf 45cm thick. This indicates that the ship might have sunk several centuries before the start of the Roman period, although not earlier than the pre-Roman Iron Age, since a small number of iron nails had been used in its construction. At this time the area was part of the East Hallstatt region, and later – after about 480 BC – it belonged to the La Téne culture, both of which are regarded as Celtic today.

This extraordinarily shallow vessel was about 30m long with a maximum beam of about 5.30m, and was built using planks only 3.5cm thick. As such it was much more lightly built than the heavy *Oberländer* and the dugouts of

the Hasholme type. None of the side planks had survived to their full height, but the dimensions of the knees which supported them indicate a side height of about 50cm (measured vertically above the bottom edge of the floor). The vessel's sides were angled outward steeply, with the result that it had a carrying capacity of about 25 tons whilst drawing only 30cm. This figure is unexpectedly high for the Hallstatt or early La Téne period, and suggests that the transport system in place at the find location had to cope with quite large freight loads.

The communications situation at the find site fits the scene described earlier in this text, namely ship transport over the Celtic waterway

network combined with short overland routes crossing the watersheds. In the early first century the geographer Strabo wrote the following description:

> The Okra [Birnbaumer Wald] is the lowest part of the Alps . . . . freight goods are carried by cart from Aquileia through this region as far as Nauportus [Oberlaibach, present-day Vrhnika], a journey of a little more than 40 stadia; from there the freight is carried by river to the Ister [Danube] and the surrounding regions. A navigable river from Illyria flows past Nauportus and later joins the Savus [Save], which allows the goods to be carried down . . . to the Pannonias [Hungary and former northern Yugoslavia].

Rome established the sea port of Aquileia in the year 183 BC at the northernmost point of the Adriatic, to form the starting point for communications with the eastern Alpine countries. Strabo states the distance to Nauportus by road very accurately at a good 80km. This overland route would therefore require no more than three days' travelling. From Nauportus the Laibach river was navigable for shallow-draught boats as far as its confluence with the Save.

The route across the Okra was easy and low in altitude, and even before the foundation of Aquileia it formed the most important link route between the Adriatic and the Danube. At this time the Celtic valley princes in Lower Kraina (Slovenia) had already set up active connections with the northern Italian Adriatic coast during the Hallstatt and early La Téne periods. Since the seventh century BC it was iron mining that formed the basis on which Krainan culture blossomed, although early glass production was also carried out there. Extensive hillforts, such as the Magdalenska Gora near Laibach, and burial mounds associated with the noble dynasties can also be considered in conjunction with transport organisation, which often took the form of sovereign trade at this time.

A more illuminating insight into the communications of the economic region of Kraina is provided by the distribution map of bowl helmets dating from the early Hallstatt period, in which the centre of distribution is definitely Lower Kraina. As already discussed, communications extended from there across the eastern

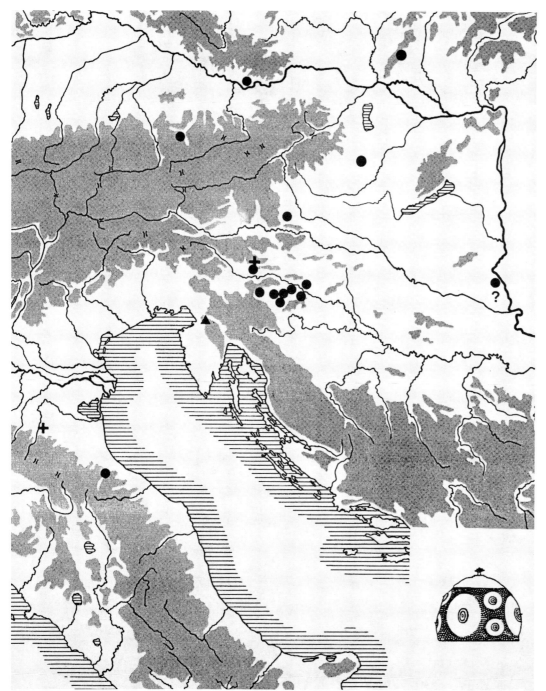

The distribution map of a special type of helmet from Kraina in Slovenia demonstrates the connection from Kraina to northern Italy in the early Celtic period (sixth century BC).

Alps to Hallstatt, but also stretched out to cover the entire central Danube region by land and water routes (often using combined transport methods). Everything which had to be transported from this large region to the Adriatic – including the three bowl helmets found southwest of Kraina – had to be taken by the one convenient route via Lower Kraina and the Okra. In the Hallstatt and early La Téne periods the shallow lake (now silted up) upstream of present-day Ljubljana could be used for water transport as far as Nauportus (or its predecessor) using shallow-draught boats. It was on this last stage of the water journey, before the start of the overland route, that the Laibach boat sank. The people accompanying the vessel were able to rescue its entire load and equipment, and only the boat itself, probably very old and weak, had to be abandoned. It is clear enough why this boat was built to bear a load as high as 25 tons: it was designed to be used on a waterway which carried valuable iron and iron products from Kraina, as well as all the goods from the eastern Alps and the central Danube region destined to be carried across the Adriatic.

The vessel itself was a masterpiece of the art of shipbuilding. At first sight the ship appears to belong to the small number of early European vessels which were built entirely of individual planks sewn together. This initial impression is deceptive in several respects. The supporting structural elements of the boat are located at the transition from the flat bottom to the side walls, and are not flat planks, but long dugout flanges worked from a tree trunk. They fulfil the function of angle irons on each side, and ensure that the long vessel does not flex when laden in spite of its low side height. This method of construction made it possible to build a keel-less boat (as required by shallow inland waters) with the minimum possible draught, which was still capable of carrying around 25 tons of goods.

The two lateral angle timbers were probably cut from spruce, and between them were set planks up to 20m long but only 3.5cm thick. These planks were of lightweight spruce, and each strake consisted of two planks 30 to 35cm wide, although nothing is known of the method by which they were joined. Holes were drilled at an angle into the side edges of the planks, through which lime bast cords were threaded, but these would not have been strong enough to hold the planks together securely. The purpose of the cords was only to press bundles of lime bast firmly onto the seams, in order to make them watertight. The strength of the structure as a whole came from the floor

timbers which were arranged transversely across the planks at intervals of 60cm. These cross-timbers were of elm wood, 12 x 10cm in cross-section, and were notched over the seams. The attachment to the planks and angle timbers consisted of two dowels made of thornwood (*rhamnus cathartica*) at each location. Knee pieces of naturally bent oak were located between the cross-timbers, exactly central in the gaps, and the knees supported the side walls which consisted of two strakes fitted to the top of the angle timbers. The additional planks projected outward at a steep angle. The bottom part of the knees only extended over the two outermost floor planks. In other respects these timbers were joined using exactly the same techniques employed on the bottom. The internal timbers of the *Oberländer* were arranged in exactly this way until well into the late Middle Ages. The bast caulking was hauled tight after the boat had been completed, then clamped in the holes using small thornwood dowels. All the planks of this boat fit edge to edge, and as such the vessel constitutes the oldest known boat of pure carvel construction. The only difference between this vessel's construction and the carvel-built boats of the late Middle Ages is the alternative method used to caulk the joints.

The construction of the bow and stern of the boat is not clear from the report's text or drawings, and at no point does it specify how much of these parts survived. It is only possible to say in very general terms that the boat had an elongated oval plan-form. In addition to the two angle timbers at the sides, the boat featured two parallel fore-and-aft timbers made of elm, fitted on top of the bottom cross-timbers and rabetted slightly where they crossed each one. These longitudinal components had been installed to provide additional stiffening over the entire length of the vessel. If only one timber had been fitted along the centreline, it could have been regarded as the forerunner of the later keelson. According to the drawing yet another internal timber was fitted along one hull side together with a short timber to provide a platform for the helmsman. However, the text also clearly mentions 'two gangways . . . along the sides', which corresponds more closely to the supposed purpose of these timbers – at least two men were stationed each on one of these gangways in order to pole the boat along. Starting from the bow, each man pushed the end of his pole down into the bottom of the shallow lake or river and jammed the T-shaped part of the other end of the pole under his armpit. This gave him a secure hold in the middle of the current, against which he

could lean to move the ship forwards. With his back facing the direction of travel he would then walk along the hull side towards the stern, thereby effectively pushing the ship away beneath him. Once at the stern he would pull the pole out, carry it as quickly as possible back to the bow and push it into the river bottom again. Each stroke would then propel the vessel forward by one ship's length. When the man with the loose pole was running to the bow, his colleague had to keep his pole firmly stuck in the ground and push forwards, otherwise the current would have driven the vessel back again.

A single 'working' poleman seems far too little to propel a ship carrying 25 tons of freight, but if several men were stationed on each side they would have to run back to the starting point at the bow along the centre planks, and it is possible that they were laid just for this purpose. As a result that would have required that the load be very carefully stacked between the lateral and central gangways, and to distribute the load evenly this would have been necessary over the entire length of the vessel. The available space would certainly have sufficed for stacking the load in this manner. If these planks represent gangways, the shallow freight boat from the Laibach moor at once becomes the earliest direct evidence for the application of the poling technique in Europe.

In the harbour area of the Roman *vicus* of Pommeroeul, Belgium, archaeologists excavated a smaller flat-bottomed boat built using native Celtic shipbuilding technology of the same type, based on two lateral angle timbers, and also featuring gangplanks along the sides. In this case the gangway was fitted with numerous cross-battens to give the feet of the poling men a more secure hold. In spite of its heavier construction (compared with the Laibach boat), this vessel was designed for goods transport on the small river Haine, which joins the Schelde a little below Pommeroeul. This river apparently had no towpath, and even in the Roman period it seems that boats had to be poled along using the old Celtic technique.

Illustrated documents from the Roman period, the Middle Ages and the early modern period show that this poling technique remained in continuous use at least into the seventeenth century on the upper reaches of rivers and smaller tributaries where towpaths were never built. In contrast, by the end of the Roman period the side gangways had disappeared from boats intended for use on large rivers (on which towpaths had been constructed in the early Roman period) and on the larger lakes, which were traversed using sailing boats.

However, it is not necessary to describe each individual example of the numerous post-Celtic shallow-water inland ships which have been excavated (primarily in the Rhine region). The aim of this chapter is to document the gradual changes which were introduced into shipbuilding technology over the centuries, with the aid of cross-sectional drawings showing the stage of development at various points in time. By this means it is possible to follow in detail how the technology developed step by step from the relatively early Celtic boat found on the Laibach moor to the late medieval Rhineland boats.

Stage 1

To begin once more with the Laibach boat, great understanding is evident in the selection of the various materials used in its construction: light but resinous spruce for the planking, oak hardwood for the 'grown' bent knees, which had to withstand the water pressure when the ship was fully laden, tough but flexible elm for the bottom timbers and gangways and very hard thornwood for the dowels. Finally the lime tree had to give up its bast to provide the caulking for the ship's seams. No example of such a variety of selected timbers for the construction of open boats has been found in later periods.

In contrast, iron nails were used extremely sparingly: only about twenty were found in the 30m long vessel, although these few exhibited a quite excellent standard of smithing. They had flat, rounded heads and shafts of rectangular cross-section like ship's nails employed later in the Roman period and the Middle Ages, although they had not yet developed the chisel-shaped cutting ends at the nail tips as used after the Roman period; instead they ran to a point. Nail lengths had evidently not yet been standardised, as the pieces measured varied in length between 6.5cm and 21.5cm. The longest were hammered through the gangway, the bottom timber and the bottom plank and bent over underneath, so that the point dug into the timber slightly. This represents the first recognisable version of the nailing technique which subsequently served to differentiate the native Celtic from the Mediterranean shipbuilding tradition in the northwestern provinces of the Roman Empire.

Stage 2

Unfortunately there have been no archaeological finds which might shed further light on this pre-Roman shipbuilding tradition. As a result the only available means of assessing the state of Celtic shipbuilding technology immediately before the Roman occupation of Gaul is to study Caesar's description of the coastal ships he encountered in the Brittany region during the campaign which he waged in the year 56 BC. In his description he restricted himself primarily to those features which differentiated the ships from the Mediterranean vessels famil-iar to his readers in Rome. Amongst these features he mentions the 'one foot thick transverse timbers secured using iron nails as thick as a man's thumb' (confixa clavis ferreis digiti pollicis crassitudine); the timbers being secured to the planking. Thus in contrast to the Laibach moor ship, the internal timbers are no longer fixed to the planking using wooden dowels and a small number of supplementary iron nails; by this time iron nails were the crucial linking element between these components. The nails were as thick as a thumb, and must have been substantially more than a foot long, otherwise they would not have been able to fasten beams one foot thick to the planking.

In archaeological terms large quantities of big iron nails are by no means unknown in Celtic cultures. They are found in the woodwork of the murus Gallicus, the ringwork fortifications around the late Celtic oppida (second–first century BC). The first time that smaller iron nails and clamps are seen in general use is in the wooden houses which the oppida contained. Caesar's description of the regular use of iron nails in shipbuilding therefore fits neatly into the overall view of the late Celtic oppida culture, in whose harbours these ships were based. The Hasholme dugout, whose date is known accurately, falls at the other end of the time-scale being considered here. It was built around 300 BC, ie about 150 years before the start of the oppida culture, and featured no iron parts at all. Overall, then, there are several good reasons for making a firm connection between the intensive use of iron nails in Celtic shipbuilding and the economic, technical and social changes which came to pass with the development of the Celtic oppida after the middle of the second century BC.

The most thoroughly researched flat-bottomed inland ship built in the Celtic shipbuilding tradition but within the Roman period is that found at Bevaix on the Neuenburger See in western Switzerland. This boat was 19.35m long, 2.80m wide and 0.85–0.95m high, and the oaks from which it was made were felled in the year 182 AD. Compared with the older Laibach boat the vessel's midship section exhibits the following changes, most of which can be seen as advances in the art of the shipbuilder:

– The hull sides are vertical, ie they no longer project outwards. This shape gives the longitudinal angle timbers, which are still in evidence, much greater strength in the chine region.

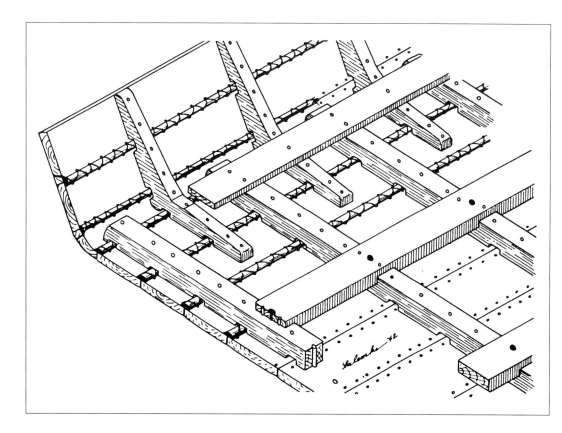

Construction of the midship section of the Celtic Laibach boat (sixth–fourth century BC).

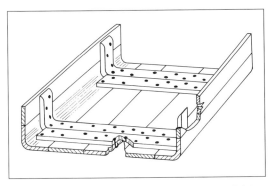

Construction of the midship section of a Romano-Celtic cargo boat, found in Lake Geneva near Bevaix, Switzerland (AD 183).

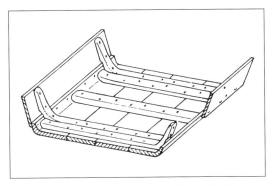

Construction of the midship section of a Frankish cargo boat, found in the Rhine near Krefeld-Gellep, Germany (eighth century AD).

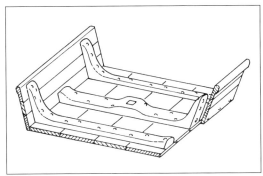

Construction of the midship section of the medieval German boat with open bow port, found in the Rhine near Krefeld-Gellep (thirteenth–fourteenth century AD).

– Of the internal timbers the knees and bottom cross-timbers are no longer separate and made of different materials; each composite component now consists of a single naturally bent timber which was cut from a tree junction–main trunk as floor support, branch junction as side support. In each case these timbers were installed in pairs: both components covering the whole width of the bottom, but alternately supporting one hull side only.

– Different varieties of wood are no longer used in the boat–oak is the only material.

– Transverse timbers, planks and angle timbers are no longer joined using wooden dowels, but exclusively using iron nails which are bent over twice under the bottom, so that their points project into the wood. On other boats of the same period some of the nails are hammered in from the outside, with their tips bent back into the transverse timbers.

– The caulking no longer consists of bast, nor is it held in place by bast cords. Now the basis of the caulking is a cord made from twisted grass stems, covered with layers of moss. The whole is secured using strips of osier fixed to the side edges of the planks with thousands of small, flat-headed iron nails. The different method of caulking makes it very clear that this boat was of pure carvel construction, *ie* it is even more obvious than in the case of the Laibach ship.

Stage 3

The best source of information on the state of boatbuilding technology in the early Middle Ages is the boat shaped like the later *nachen* excavated at Krefeld-Gellep in 1973. This vessel dates from the eighth century AD, and was approximately 16m long and 2.80m in beam. The vessel underlines the basic argument of this chapter that, after the end of Roman rule, boatbuilding continued with the construction of vessels retaining the basic features typical of original Celtic boats, but

smaller in size and incorporating few if any iron components. The features of this boat are:

– The hull sides are angled outward slightly. The longitudinal angle timbers are still present, but the upper flange is very low: just high enough to allow side planks to be fixed to it using dowels.

– As in the Roman period, the internal timbers consist of grown cross-timbers installed in pairs, with a supplementary bottom timber between each pair.

– All the transverse timbers are fixed to the planking by means of dowels. Iron components are entirely absent.

– There is no information on the method of caulking employed.

Stage 4

At present the most useful information relating to the state of shipbuilding technology in the late Middle Ages is another ship find made at Krefeld-Gellep, this time in 1972. This is a cargo barge dating from the thirteenth/fourteenth century AD, about 15m long with an open bow port.

– The gentle slope of the hull sides has not changed significantly, but the longitudinal angle timbers are no longer sections of a dugout cut from the full trunk. Instead this component is assembled from two sawn strakes, with the lowest side plank set against the outside edge of the outermost floor plank, and fixed to it with wooden dowels.

– The grown cross-timbers are still a feature, but in this case they are evenly distributed over the area of the boat, instead of being arranged in pairs. The side supports still alternate from one hull side to the other, however.

– The cross-timbers are still attached to the planks using wooden dowels.

– Iron nails are used to fix certain components and for joints between planks.

– The moss caulking is secured by means of osier strips held by iron caulking clamp bands.

The continuity of Celtic inland ships can now be seen clearly, in terms of the survival of recognisable ship types (*Oberländer*, cargo boat with bow port, cargo boat with fore-and-aft gangways), as well as the retention of proven shipbuilding techniques (longitudinal angle timbers, flat-bottomed carvel construction). This continuous line can be followed for a period of more than two millennia, starting in the early Celtic period and in some cases stretching beyond the end of the Middle Ages. Considering the subject in greater detail, it is possible to define four separate periods of shipbuilding technology, each representing a fairly logical development of the preceding stage, and each retaining certain elements unchanged (*eg* the longitudinal angle timbers in Stages 1–3, the grown cross-timbers in Stages 2–4). Other elements were developed rationally (*eg* separate knees and bottom timbers evolved into composite grown cross-timbers from Stage 1 to Stage 2), while other elements were changed fundamentally (*eg* wooden dowels superseded by iron nails between Stage 1 and Stage 2, and the reversion to dowels in the transition from Stage 2 to Stage 3).

Undoubtedly the most interesting feature of this development is the realisation that Stage 2 did not begin with the Roman occupation of Gaul, but with the establishment of the Celtic *oppida* culture. Unfortunately there is a dearth of archaeological evidence from this period, and details of shipbuilding developments are unknown; all that can be proved is that iron nails were used extensively. According to the evidence gained from the late Roman ships found at Mainz, iron nails were eventually abandoned as the means of securing the grown cross-timbers to the hull planks at the earliest in the course of the fifth century. The probable reason for this reversion is the economic depression which set in after the end of Roman rule.

Celtic coins, struck in Normandy, France, show model ships as the victor's prize in a chariot race (c100 BC).

Seagoing sailing ships

The oldest unequivocal evidence of Celtic sea-going ships is from pictures on coins, some of which were found as long ago as the eighteenth century. However, the interpretation of the numismatic images has been unsatisfactory until recently because the ship appears to be of only secondary interests: around 100 BC the Gauls (Celts who had settled on the coasts of Normandy) minted coins which show, in common with many Celtic coins, racing or war chariots. However, in this case the driver is shown in a particular position which does not occur on other coins – in an unmistakable victory pose he raises one hand up high holding his prize, a model ship. In studying the coin pictures care must be taken not to be misled by any shortcomings in the artist's skills. For example, the chariot is pulled by two horses, but only one is shown; there was not enough space for the racing chariot in the small area behind the horse, and it is indicated on one coin simply by the rear chariot rod and on another by a single wheel under the horse's tail. With this in mind, the ship is all the more unambiguous: it is a model of a high-sided sea-going ship with mast and yard, featuring animal heads at stem and stern.

Silver models of sailing ships are still presented as prizes at sailing regattas, but the idea that a model ship was presented as the victor's prize in a chariot race seems at first sight to defy all logic. Until recently research has been unable to suggest any explanation, but it is now possible to put forward a rational interpretation for the first time. Studying the coin pictures closely makes it clear that the artist considered not only the race and the trophy as important features, but also a sword, which appears below the horse. This indicates that the picture does not show pure 'sportsmen', but warriors. They are warriors who are practising with their war chariots, preparing for the serious business.

The nature of this serious business is indicated by the model ship. The reader should bear in mind that the route of the tin-bearing ships from Cornwall to the Seine took them along the coast of Normandy. Naturally the inhabi-

tants of the coastal regions profited from this through-traffic, both by participating in it and by exacting dues from the traders. However, on both sides of the Channel there were stretches of coast which were not directly involved in the tin trade, and the inhabitants of those areas would have become envious, and keen to cream off some of the wealth of the rich coastal settlements of Normandy. This they did by attacking from the sea. At that time it was possible to transport large bands of warriors by ship, and land them on any gently sloping beach for a surprise attack. For the attackers these assaults were low-risk enterprises, since they could load the booty on their ships and sail away as quickly as they had arrived.

For the inhabitants of the coastal regions it was no easy matter to set up effective defensive measures against such attacks. The only fact which aided them was the attackers' need to keep within sight of the coast, as this was the only reliable method of navigation. To exploit this advantage, the inhabitants initially had to organise coastal lookouts and a means of communication to inland sites, so that information of enemy approaches was passed on without delay. It was then up to the defence forces to head off the invaders as quickly as possible and confront them. On the Normandy coast these mobile attack troops took the form of war chariots and their drivers, since no other type of troops had the speed and stamina to intercept the attackers and drive them back to their ships. The defenders in turn had to be able to use their own high-speed ships to pursue the invaders and carry out their own attacks on enemy coastal settlements.

Thus it was that war chariots and military operations formed the sole means by which a coastal population could survive in this situation. Fighting men had to be skilled in the use of defensive and offensive weapons, and also be able to carry out all the necessary manoeuvres when driving a war chariot and sailing a ship. All of this demanded constant practice. The chariot races represented the climax of the warriors' protracted and arduous training, and were acknowledged as important events by the rest of society.[3] The purpose of the training –

coastal defence – was made self-evident by offering model ships as the victor's prize. Including this scene on coins intended for long-range trading purposes was also a deliberate propaganda measure, as the inhabitants of the coastal regions demonstrated thereby that they were capable of defending themselves against attack from the sea. At the same time traders with peaceful intent were shown that the coasts of Normandy could offer a high level of security. This demonstration of defensive awareness and readiness produced an impressive image which everyone would have understood immediately at this time, and which represented an initial preventative measure to ward off potential attackers. This was by no means an idle threat: real battle forces could be deployed at any time if a serious threat arose.

There is reliable written evidence that individual Celtic tribes and ambitious members of the Celtic nobility and their followers regularly made war upon each other. It was not for nothing that Celtic towns were located high up on hilltops, protected behind thick ramparts. Unfortunately there is only indirect information concerning Celtic attacks from the sea, as the surviving written evidence is sparse indeed, and researchers have not even acknowledged it as relevant until recently. However, the evidence in question is very welcome, as it confirms this writer's interpretation of the coin images. No less a person than the Roman general Julius Caesar himself became conversant with the organisation of coastal defence by the Celtic inhabitants of the Kent coastal region during his first British campaign in late August 55 BC, and he personally wrote a description of the events. Caesar was stationed at the narrowest part of the Channel, engaged in assembling the many ships required for the crossing, when the Britons learned of his planned invasion from merchants. This prior knowledge gave them the chance to prepare themselves. For his part, Caesar attempted to obtain information on harbour locations, methods of battle and numbers of warriors from the merchants whom he summoned from all sides, but they did not tell him what he needed to know, and he was forced to send out

3. Bronze Age rock carvings in Scandinavia indicate a similar system. See D Ellmers, 'Wagenrennen und Bootsparaden im bronzezeitlichen Skandinavien. Zum Gebrauch von Renn-und Streitwagen bei einer vorgeschichtlichen Küstenbevölkerung', *Achse, Rad und Wagen. Beiträge zur Geschichte der Landfahrzeuge*, Vol 2 (Gummersbach 1992), pp3-10

at least one ship to reconnoitre the coast. This ship triggered the first 'alarm stage' of the coastal defence system. This took the form of a well trained communications network, which simultaneously placed a blockade on information travelling in the opposite direction.

When Caesar approached the coast of Kent with his first wave of ships, he tripped the second 'alarm stage': all the high points of the coast were occupied by enemy troops, deployed in an impressive display of organised power. This performance was a deliberate attempt to convince anyone arriving by sea that they were facing well-armed opposition, and that any attempt at landing was pointless. One glance at this exhibition would have persuaded the commander of any Celtic fleet that his mission was bound to fail. However, Caesar was unimpressed. He waited until his fleet had assembled at a sensible distance from the coast, then, with a fair wind and a favourable current set sail for a more promising landing site.

Naturally the defenders saw through Caesar's plan and switched to 'alarm stage 3'. The chariot warriors – the principal defensive weapon – were sent out in advance together with horsemen, with orders to frustrate the landing wherever it might occur; for chariots and riders were faster than any ship. The remaining troops followed immediately. In view of the strength of this defensive effort, the Britons must have been incredulous when Caesar attempted to force a landing. Using specially trained horses they ran in amongst the Roman foot solders as they jumped into the water from their ships. The Romans were very severely impeded by the water, and the Britons pressed them very hard, but Caesar's warships were equipped with bows and catapults, and he now positioned the ships so that their artillery could fire into the right-hand flank of the defending troops. Had he not done so, and had the legionaries not been so disciplined and present in such great numbers, the difficult landing manoeuvre could not have succeeded. The chariot warriors and horsemen of the Celts' fast attack troops were not prepared for the ship's artillery, which could be brought easily into any position. They had never had to face such an opponent, and had no reply to Caesar's game-plan. The Celtic tactics were to destroy the Roman troops while they were still in the water, but they were prevented from doing this, and they had to admit defeat and concede the landing.

This report of the failure of the defensive system provides the detailed information required on the effectiveness of a coastal defence system. The system obeyed all the

rules of the art of war, and was successful along the Channel coasts for centuries, until the advent of ship-borne artillery. Hitherto the only chance for pirates was to mount a surprise attack on the coastal settlement and withdraw quickly before the battle chariots could gather.

Caesar also mentions attacks by the Celts on coastal settlements, and for this purpose and other military operations the Celts had not developed warships specifically. Instead they manned their ordinary, seagoing merchant ships with armed warriors. In the year 56 BC Caesar learned to his own cost how effective his mobile opponents could be when they had virtually unlimited numbers of these ships available to them. The event in question was the suppression of the uprising of the Veneti on the coasts of Brittany. At that time the basis of the maritime power exercised by individual Celtic tribes was a series of stoutly fortified sea ports which Caesar describes as follows:

> most of the towns of the Veneti were located on the tip of a peninsula or a coastal promontory. They were not accessible from the land because the flood tide rolled in from the open sea, . . . neither from the sea, because at ebb tide the ships (of the Romans) were at risk from the shallow waters . . . If we once succeeded in overcoming these obstacles by force of siege, *ie* by holding back the sea with masses of rubble and stone, . . . then the besieged people loaded all their belongings onto the large number of ships which they had available, and withdrew to neighbouring towns. Here they would defend themselves again, using the same advantageous position.

If a land-based siege was implemented, the best the besieged could hope for would be to be taken prisoner once the fortifications had been overcome. In their fortified sea ports they could always escape from their opponents by fleeing across the sea.

Caesar realised that he could only get the better of this flexible method of waging war if his own fleet was sufficiently large. When, after many months, he had finally assembled the fleet he needed, the Veneti did not respond by fleeing. Instead they attempted to avert the threat to their freedom of the seas – until that time unimpeded – by waging a sea battle. They confronted Caesar with a fleet of about 220 ships, fully battle-ready and well equipped in every respect. It seems likely that the Veneti intended a boarding battle, setting man against man. However, Caesar's fleet was able to gain the upper hand by immobilising the Celts' sailing ships. He did this by cutting the halyard

of the single square sail using sickle blades on long poles, with the result that the sail fell down onto the ship. The Romans were then able to defeat one Celtic ship after another, overpowering them by using several oared ships at a time. Around this time the wind abated, thus preventing the major part of the Veneti fleet escaping, and since all the remaining merchant ships and their warrior crews had gathered together, Caesar's victory was complete. He himself now had all the ships he needed to exercise maritime power.

Caesar's report on this campaign also contains important information relating to merchant shipping in the Brittany area: 'the tribe of the Veneti enjoys by far the greatest esteem amongst all the coastal populations. They have the greatest number of ships, and they regularly undertake journeys to Britain in them.' As noted above, the Veneti and their allies possessed more than 220 of these seagoing merchant ships, so the volume of trade which the Gallic peoples carried out with their coastal ships before the Roman occupation must have been extensive.

Caesar also said of the Veneti: 'They are also superior to all others in their knowledge and experience of things pertaining to the sea.' This undoubtedly implies an accurate knowledge of coastal conditions, but also experience in open-water navigation, since the inhabitants of Brittany were capable of crossing the 80 nautical miles of open sea to the Lizard Point on Cornwall's coast, without the benefit of a compass or other direction-finding instrument. To some extent they only dared to do this on clear nights, when some or all of the stars were visible, as the pole star clearly indicated North to them in such conditions. However, they also needed a good wind for sailing, so that they could cover the long stretch in a single night. By dawn they would then be able to make out the coast of Cornwall on the horizon when the pole star faded away. They also had to be able to make allowance for the currents at the western entrance to the Channel, which could be quite powerful.[4]

Finally Caesar points out two further important points pertaining to maritime travel along the coasts in the hands of the Veneti: 'the open ocean strikes the coast with immense and unchecked force, and the few harbours which offer protection from its onslaught are in the hands of the Veneti. As a result almost every-

4. D Ellmers, 'Der Nachtsprung an eine hinter dem Horizont Liegende Gegenküste. Die älteste astronomische Navigations methode', *Deutsches Schiffahrtsarchiv* 4 (Hamburg 1981), pp153-167.

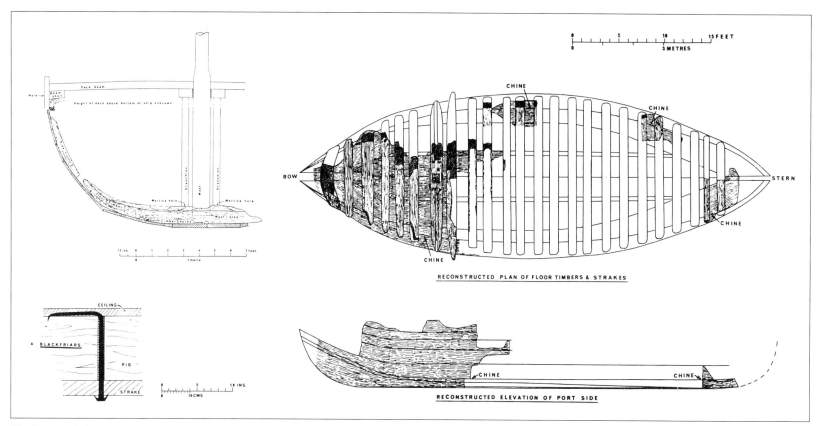

RECONSTRUCTED PLAN OF FLOOR TIMBERS & STRAKES

RECONSTRUCTED ELEVATION OF PORT SIDE

The Romano-Celtic coastal vessel, found at Blackfriars in London, United Kingdom (around AD 130).

one who travels the seas in that area must pay tolls to them.' On the stormy Biscay coast in particular an accurate knowledge of the position of all the sheltered harbours, where ships could lie up safe from storm and waves and wait for better weather, was crucial to survival. Anyone without the knowledge of these harbours would never have dared to attempt a voyage along the coast under any circumstances. The fact that the occupants of these harbours exploited the situation to raise money is understandable, and it is reasonable to assume that the same applied in earlier times. However, Caesar's report is the oldest definitive evidence for the historian, and it represents a vitally important reference point.

However, the most important part of Caesar's report as far as maritime history is concerned is his accurate description of the Veneti merchant ships.

Their ships were constructed and equipped as follows: the keels were considerably shallower than on our ships, making them less vulnerable to damage in shallow waters and at the ebb tide. The decks forward and aft were set high up in deference to the high waves and the force of the storms. The ships were built entirely of oak and as such could cope with all sorts of weather and other circumstance. The transverse timbers

were one foot [30cm] thick and were attached using iron nails as thick as a man's thumb. The anchors were suspended on iron chains rather than on ropes. For the sails the Veneti used hides and soft leather instead of linen . . . if our fleet met these ships in battle, our sole advantage lay in our vessels' speed and oar propulsion . . . for their ships were built too strongly to be damaged by the ram prow, their height made it difficult for us to fire at them, and for the same reason they were difficult to board. Moreover . . . they could run aground in the shallows without danger and had . . . nothing to fear from the ebbing tide.

The next section of text also makes it clear that these were purely sailing ships, with one mast and a single square sail, and had no oars of any kind.

This highly detailed description corresponds in all its general characteristics to the ships seen on the coins from Normandy: they are high-sided seagoing vessels with one mast and a yard for the sail. The coin images also reveal that these ships featured animal heads at stem and stern, probably carved from wood.

Had the Celts not continued building their traditional ships in the provincial Roman period, this would be all that could be said about their seagoing ships. To date extensive remains of two such vessels have been found: one in London in 1962, built no later than

around 130 AD, and one at Guernsey (Channel Islands) in 1984-86, which sank shortly after 285 AD. While he was excavating the Blackfriars ship the archaeologist Peter Marsden realised for the first time that it exactly fitted Caesar's description. It had no keel, but instead featured two extremely thick and wide bottom planks along the centreline of its relatively flat bottom, which would have allowed it to be beached on the ebb tide without suffering damage. All the surviving ship's timbers were of oak, and some of the transverse timbers (floor timbers and side supports) were even more than one foot thick, *viz* up to 44cm x 33cm in section. The nails, 'as thick as a man's thumb', were of corresponding length, *ie* up to 55.5cm. The longest nails had round shafts, while the smaller ones were rectangular. They were driven through holes in the planking and inner timbers and bent over twice into the bottom timbers and side supports, so that their points were forced back into the wood. Bearing in mind the thickness of the planks, this would have produced such strong carvel joints that a ram prow would probably have done little harm. Unfortunately the full height of the hull sides did not survive, but they must have been more than 2m above the bottom edge of the hull bottom, which cannot be considered as particularly high sides for a ship's length of 18.3m. This side height and a separately discovered knee piece indicate that the ship had a deck, at least over part of its area; Caesar mentioned that the ships had decks forward and aft. The mast step indicates that the single mast was located relatively far forward. Since traces of both stem- and stern-posts survived, this can also confirm the coin images, which depict stem and stern rising in an even curve from the horizontal bottom to the vertical.

Caesar described the Celtic seagoing ships of 56 BC with such evident technical knowledge and such a keen eye for the essential that even today it is possible to categorise a provincial Roman ship built about 200 years later as a member of the self-same shipbuilding tradition. This classification is underlined by certain details of the archaeological remains which agree with the extant pictorial evidence (stem/stern form; mast markedly forward of centre). Finally, the clear evidence that Celtic shipbuilding continued under Roman rule fits in precisely with what is known about the construction and use of inland ships. The vessel's carvel construction and identical nail technology add further reinforcement to these ideas.

The fragments of the ship found at St Peter Port, Guernsey belonged to a ship more than 25m long, but of narrower design, although the mast was also set far forward. In this case the extremely thick bottom section consisted of three parallel planks, but the remains give no indication of the height of the hull sides.

The load-bearing capacity of the Blackfriars ship cannot be calculated accurately, as not enough of the vessel has survived. The most reliable guide is the height of the attack by the teredo worm (*teredo navalis*) in the surviving fragments of the hull sides. The worm can only survive in salt water, and the height of its infestation therefore indicates the vessel's immersion depth over a long voyage. From this information it can be estimated that the ship would have been able to transport a load of 37.2 tons whilst drawing 1.30m. The vessel had a load of about 26 tons of ragstone in its hold when it sank in London, a load which it had shipped on the river Medway in the Thames estuary. Thus its last voyage was not very long, although the degree of teredo worm infestation indicates that it had undertaken much longer passages in salt water.

Conclusions

How the inland ships of the Celtic shipbuilding tradition survived beyond the end of the Middle Ages on the continent of Europe has been demonstrated above. The Germanic tribes who invaded the continent did not arrive by ship, and were not seafarers, so were likely to adopt the native style of vessel. However, in Britain every trace of the continued existence of seagoing ships built to the Celtic shipbuilding tradition disappears after the end of Roman rule. The likely reason for this is that the Anglo-Saxons migrated to England in their own ships and subsequently continued to use them for their sea journeys, as the post-Roman ships excavated in London show very clearly.

It is probable that this reasoning does not hold true for Brittany and the adjacent Atlantic coastal regions, for no Germanic tribes migrated to those areas in their own ships. How long people in that region continued to build ocean-going ships based on the Celtic pattern is an open question, as archaeological research has produced no evidence to date. However, the writer suspects that the carvel construction which, in the late Middle Ages, spread out from this region towards the east can be traced back to Celtic carvel construction, which was the standard method in that area even before the advent of Caesar and the Romans.

Detlev Ellmers

The Romano-Celtic coastal vessel, found at St Peter Port, Guernsey, Channel Islands (around AD 285).

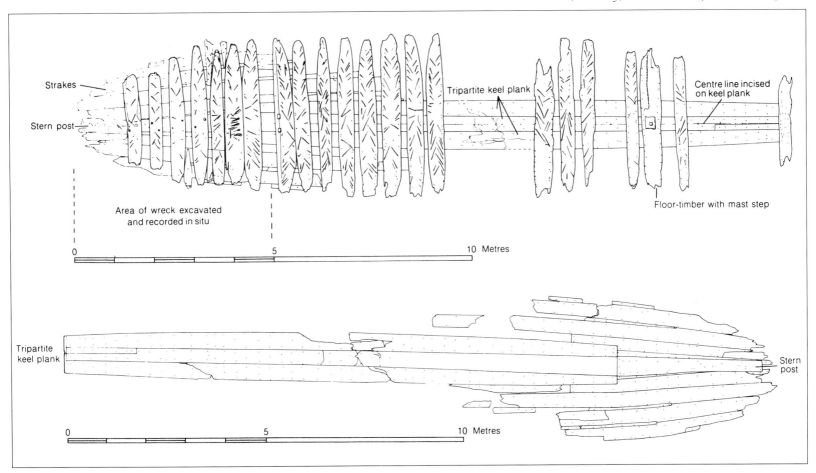

5

Proto-Viking, Viking and Norse Craft

THE MEREST glance at the map makes it evident that ships and boats must have been important to people living in Denmark, Sweden and Norway since they first arrived. All the countries have long coastlines, Denmark is composed of numerous islands, and Sweden has extensive inland waterways.

The spectacular finds of ancient vessels – the Nydam ship in Denmark in 1864, the Tune, Gokstad and Oseberg Viking ships in Norway in 1867, 1880 and 1904 – forced archaeologists to take the maritime past into consideration, and there is an extensive literature on ship archaeology in the three countries. The interest has centred on two main themes: what were the earliest boats like, and how did shipbuilding develop during the Iron Age? Most of the debate has been carried on in Scandinavian journals, but a number of publications have been in foreign languages, and scholars outside Scandinavia have taken part in the debate and widened the geographical territory to include much of northern Europe.

In more recent years, ship finds have multiplied thanks to underwater archaeology, and discoveries outside Scandinavia have widened our knowledge of the earliest ships of northern Europe. It is possible to see how different traditions existed side by side, but the material is still too limited for a full survey of how ships developed in all parts of northern Europe.

The first boats

The scholars debating what the first boats looked like have been divided into two camps. One sees the logboat as the start of boat building in the north, with an evolution where planks were added and ribs inserted in the logboat, at last reducing the original logboat to

the keel in a true plank-built boat. The other school maintains that the earliest boats were of hides stretched over a framework, with the Eskimo *umiak* as the best ethnographic parallel. At some stage, thin wooden planks came into use instead of the hides, but the wood was sewn together – the outer planking of the boat is still known as the skin, which may be seen as an indication of ancestry. Ships and boats depicted on rock carvings have been claimed as evidence by both camps.

No skinboat remains have ever been found, while logboats as old as about 4000 BC have

been found in Denmark. Other logboats of various dates have been excavated all over northern Europe, and this type of boat was in use well into this century in remote freshwater lakes. Only rarely can the logboats be dated by the usual archaeological techniques of how they look or were made, so systematic dating by the C14 method or tree-ring analysis should be undertaken on all new finds.

In a paper published in 1972, Ole Crumlin-Pedersen argued convincingly that the ancestor of Scandinavian boatbuilding is the expanded dugout. Expanded dugouts, extended with a

Seals, whales and boats on a Stone Age carving from Evenhus, Trøndelag, Norway. The combination indicates a society where fishing and hunting at sea was important, but the boats are too sketchy to indicate much about their construction. (Tracing by G Gjessing)

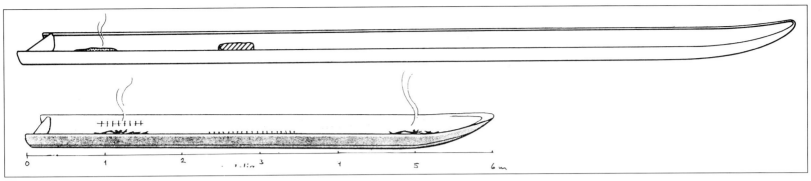

The Tybrind Vig dugout (top), dated to the later Ertebølle Culture of around 4200 BC; the boat had a fireplace or hearth aft and a large stone as ballast amidships. By contrast, the Lystrup dugout (bottom), originating from the early Ertebølle Culture of about 5200 BC, had hearths fore and aft. (Institute of Prehistoric Archaeology, Aahus University)

A carving of a moose head discovered in Finland. The holes have been interpreted as methods of attaching the carving to a boat as a form of figurehead. (National Museum of Finland)

washstrake and with inserted ribs were built in Finland well into this century, and the technique is well documented. Iron Age boats from Waaler Moor and Leck in north Germany are built in this way. The Finnish boatbuilders use aspen, while the German boats, and boat remains from the Danish island of Bornholm, are of oak. The technique used in Finland was to hollow the log through a narrow slit on the top, and then to expand the shell with the help of fire. The shape had to be stabilised with inserted ribs.

So far the Bornholm boats, used as burial coffins in a grave-field dating from the Roman Iron Age, are the only ones found in Scandinavia. Recent finds from Britain prove that the type was known in Anglo-Saxon times, probably as an idea imported from Scandinavia. However, a boat with no iron fastenings leaves few traces, and only a very careful excavation will enable correct interpretation of the faint traces in the soil.

The rock carvings of Scandinavia show many representations of boats. The older group of carvings, dating from the Stone Age, depict the world of hunters and fishermen. Reindeer, moose, geese, whales and halibut carved into hard stone probably furthered the hunters' luck. In some cases, especially in northern Norway and Karelia, boats are shown. The Norwegian ones have been interpreted as skin-boats by some scholars. The Karelian boats often have a moose head at the stem, and a wooden head found in Finland may be another such 'figurehead'. The head has large dowel holes, which are easily explained as holes for treenails securing the head to a logboat, but they are hard to explain as fastenings for a mounting on a skin boat.

The more recent carvings, found in southern Sweden and Norway, and sparingly in Denmark, depict the interests of cattle-breeders and farmers. Carvings of characteristic

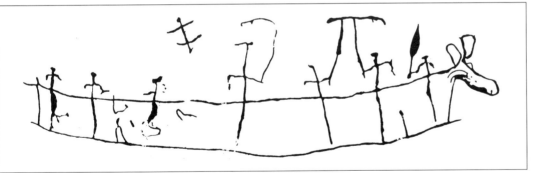

Left: The numerous carvings from Alta, Finnmark, north Norway show boats from different periods. Whether they were skin boats or logboats cannot be established. This particular vessel, dated to the period 3600–2700 BC, has a large moose head at the stem. (After Helskog 1988)

Below: The head on this fine ship from Bakkehaugen, Østfold, southeast Norway looks like a horse. Figureheads are clearly an idea of great antiquity. (Oldsaksamlingen, Oslo)

objects like bronze horns (lures) date them to the Bronze Age. The carvings show cattle, ploughing scenes, processions, etc. If we exclude plain cupmarks, the most numerous motif is ships and boats. The carvings differ, but many of them show a characteristic profile (see illustration of Bakkchaugen Skjeberg carving). They have been interpreted as skin-boats, one of the most ardent advocates being the Norwegian archaeologist Sverre Marstrander. Many of them show crew members, either as figures or plain lines. In some cases the number of lines is so large that one wonders if the carver was boasting, or whether boats carrying forty-eight paddlers really existed in Scandinavia around 1000 BC.

A number of wooden artefacts from Neolithic and Bronze Age sites show that excellent woodworking was possible with flint and bronze tools. When Captain Cook first visited Tahiti, he was met by war canoes that were longer than his three-masted bark, paddled by more than one hundred men. They were built by a Neolithic society, whose stone tools were inferior to the flint of southern Scandinavia. The canoes were logboats with added strakes, and they were stitched together. There is no technological reason to reject a similar solution for late Neolithic and Bronze Age Scandinavia, probably with an extended dugout as the bottom part of the vessel. A lucky find may one day prove this right or wrong.

The custom of carving rock pictures continued into the Iron Age, and a group of carvings have a profile which shows a striking resemblance to the oldest plank-built boat found in Scandinavia.

This is the Hjortspring boat, dated to about 350 BC. It formed part of a bog offering on the island of Als in southern Denmark. Spears, shields, and a few swords were found with the boat, and it is generally accepted that the winners sacrificed the equipment of the losers after a battle. This custom is described by classical authors as part of germanic religion in the first centuries AD, but Hjortspring is the oldest example found so far. The bog was excavated in 1921, the ship and equipment being exhibited in the National Museum in Copenhagen. A few years ago the wood underwent reconservation, and the ship was given a new, stainless steel frame to support the fragile wood.

The ship is made of lime wood (*tilia*), which is light, soft, easily worked and fairly strong for its weight. The backbone is a hollowed, and probably expanded, bottom plank. On this rest two endpieces, also hollowed. To this back-

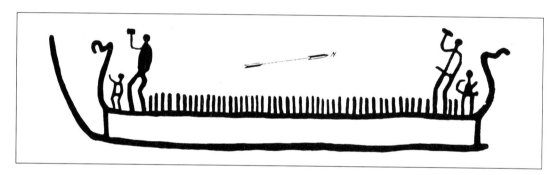

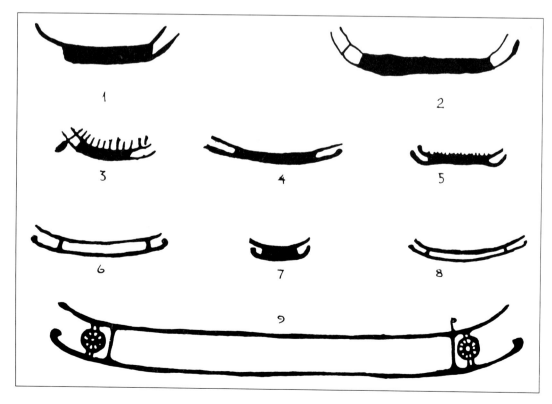

Middle: A crew of 52 men seems large for a Bronze Age vessel. It has been suggested that the big figures fore and aft are Gods, and therefore that this ship belonged to them, so may not be realistic. From Bjørnstad, Østfold. (Tracing by S Marstrander)

Left: One particular type of ship found in rock carvings bears a striking likeness to the silhouette of the Hjortspring boat. They are usually believed to be of early Iron Age date. (Tracings by S Marstrander)

*The remains of the Hjortspring boat after recent
reconservation, now displayed on a stainless steel frame
that both supports the timbers and defines the shape of
the missing sections.* (National Museum,
Copenhagen)

bone the boatbuilders sewed two side planks
and two sheerstrakes. The bottom plank and
the endpieces have long 'horns' extending the
centreline outside the hull proper. When
cutting the planks, the boatbuilders left small
cleats standing on the inside surface. Thin,
elastic hazel rods were bent to fit the transverse
curves and lashed to holes in the cleats. Vertical
and horizontal struts and thwarts at sheerstrake
level strengthened the ribs. This supporting
framework is made of ash. The plank laps and
stitching were waterproofed with a pitch-like
substance, probably based on birch tar. The
number of thwarts show that ten men on each
side paddled the boat, while larger steering
paddles were found at both ends.

The Hjortspring boat has features which can
be traced to this day in Scandinavian boatbuilding, like the light flexible hull and the lapstrake
construction. The use of cleats on the strakes
for lashing the ribs continued in use until the
Viking Age, and sewn lapstrake construction
was used by Lapp boatbuilders in the extreme
north of Scandinavia and parts of Russia until
the turn of the last century.

If we turn to Britain, we find a tradition older
than the Hjortspring boat, where a totally different approach to boatbuilding can be seen.
The vessels found at Ferriby and Brigg in
Yorkshire, a fragment from Wales and the
recently discovered boat at Dover range in date
from about 1300 BC to around 400 BC. The
boats are stitched, but the timbers are very
sturdy – one is tempted to say massive – when

*A model of the Hjortspring boat, Scandinavia's oldest
plank-built craft, the original being dated to around 350
BC. The thwarts supported ten paddlers per side.*
(National Museum, Copenhagen)

compared to Hjortspring. The wood is oak, and
the dimensions show that the boatbuilders
could handle large timbers and shape them to
perfection. In the Hjortspring boat some
carving was necessary in order to shape the
bottom plank and the endpieces, but most of
the wood was bent to shape. The boatbuilders
who built the Ferriby boats carved their timbers

to shape, the pieces being too sturdy for
bending. An elaborate system of cleats and
transverse struts probably served to hold the
various planks in position until they were firmly
stitched or lashed together with yew withies.
The framing system is not fully known, but it is
to be hoped that more information will come
from the Dover vessel when it is fully published.

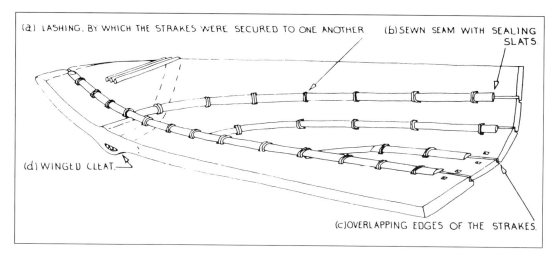

(a) LASHING, BY WHICH THE STRAKES WERE SECURED TO ONE ANOTHER (b) SEWN SEAM WITH SEALING SLATS.

(d) WINGED CLEAT.

(c) OVERLAPPING EDGES OF THE STRAKES.

The plank ends of the first Ferriby boat in an early hypothetical reconstruction by Eric McKee. The strakes, of heavy scantling, are shaped and the edges half-lapped and stitched together, with laths over the seams to seal them. (National Maritime Museum)

The 'Celtic' tradition

On the Continent, and in southern Britain, Roman influence can be seen in vessels built in the Mediterranean fashion, with flush-laid planks fastened by mortise and tenons, but there are also vessels built with flush-laid planking where the planks are not fastened together, but nailed to the frames and caulked like modern carvel ships. This tradition has been identified as Celtic. The ships are sturdy; some of them are box-like river barges, others have hulls suited for North Sea voyages, like the wrecks found near Blackfriars Bridge in London and in the port at Guernsey. Many of the vessels date from the period when Britain, France and Holland were under Roman rule.

Many of the river craft have an L-shaped plank in the transition between bottom and side. This is best explained as the remains of a logboat ancestry. A larger hull was built by

splitting the logboat, inserting planks between the two halves and building up the sides.

The river barges were a long-lived tradition, whereas later examples of the Ferriby and Celtic traditions are difficult to find. Perhaps they proved to be blind alleys in the evolution of ships and boats.

From paddles to oars

In Scandinavia, it is possible to follow the evolution from Hjortspring in a series of finds. They are widely scattered in time and space, but they seem to form an evolutionary chain, where changes and improvements can be followed over the centuries well into the late Middle Ages, when new principles were adopted for building large ships.

The Hjortspring boat was paddled, but Norwegian bog finds, dated by C14 to the first centuries AD, have given rowlocks of a type still

in use on the Norwegian west coast. They show that 350-400 years after the building of the Hjortspring boat, paddling had given way to rowing, a more efficient means of using human strength for moving a boat through the water.

In the middle of the fourth century, another victorious army sacrificed its opponents' arms and equipment to the war gods. At Nydam in southern Jutland several offerings were consigned to a sacred lake, now a bog. Large scale excavation in the early 1860s recovered two ships, one of oak, one of pine, as well as fragments of another oak vessel. The pine boat was destroyed in the Danish-Prussian war of 1864, while the magnificent oak vessel has survived several moves from museum to museum and two world wars. The 24m (79ft) long hull is now in the museum at Schloss Gottorf in Schleswig. The building of the ship has been dated by dendrochronology to about 310-320 AD and the arms and equipment found around the ship indicate that a large sacrifice took place during the second half of the fourth century.

The Norwegian scholar Eilert Sundt published several sociological studies of Norwegian rural life in the 1850s and 1860s.

The fragments of a small boat found in a bog at Halsnøy, Hordaland, west Norway, shows that by about AD 200 boats were no longer paddled, but rowed. This shape of the rowlock is still in use in western Norway. (Drawing by B Færøyvik)

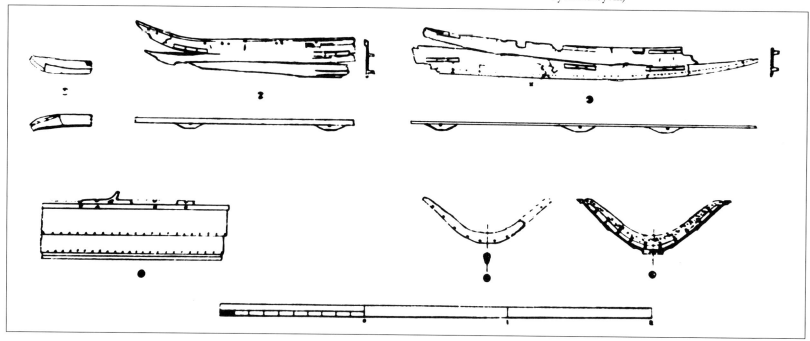

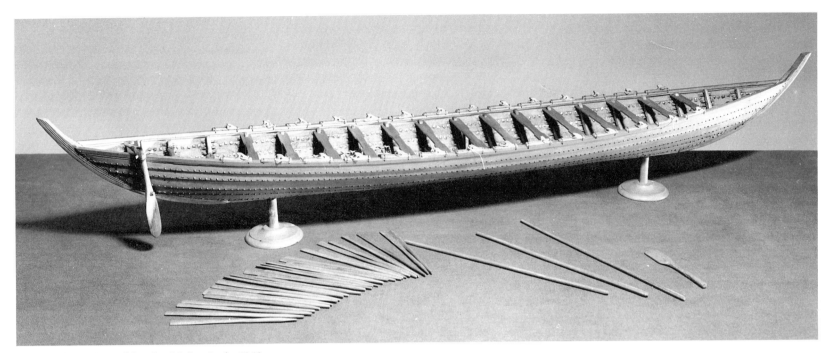

A model of the oak vessel found at Nydam in the 1860s. Dated to the early fourth century AD, it is believed to represent the kind of vessel that were used by the Angles and Saxons in their colonisation of Britain. The model shows the original interpretation of the hull form, which is very deep and narrow, but the Swedish authority Harold Åkerlund has suggested that the boat may have been wider and shallower, requiring a hogging truss to be stretched fore and aft; this later view is not universally accepted. (National Maritime Museum)

He noted the large variation among boat types of Norway, and speculated that they may have had a common background, and had developed differently due to variations in coastal geography, use and prevailing weather conditions. 'If an antiquary could find on the sea-bottom a sunken boat from Fridthiof's days, it could be an example of the ancient vessels, the great-grandmother of today's large family of boats.' Even as he was writing this, the Danish archaeologist C Engelhardt had just finished excavating the Nydam ship, the 'great-grandmother' he sought. Engelhardt knew Sundt's work, and followed up on it by comparing details from Nydam with contemporary vessels from northern Norway, demonstrating for the first time the remarkable continuity of tradition. In rural boatbuilding, the tradition still lives, and scholars studying ancient Scandinavian naval architecture are in a privileged position among archaeologists; 1500-year-old technical solutions can be explained by living craftsmen who still use them.

Engelhardt's comparison of rowlocks is the first use of living tradition in the study of ancient Scandinavian vessels. (After Engelhardt 1864)

The Nydam ship is a much stronger and larger vessel than the frail and delicate Hjortspring canoe. It is built entirely of oak, and the strakes are not sewn together, but riveted with iron nails. Five huge strakes make up the sides, while a thicker bottom strake is scarphed to the stems. The ribs are strong curved oak branches instead of the bent hazel rods of Hjortspring. Other naturally grown timbers were used as stems, and the ends of the strakes were secured in a groove on the stem, a rabbet, a method still used by many boatbuilders in Scandinavia. Rowlocks for fifteen rowers were lashed to each side of the ship, and a heavy steering oar was found near the stern. How it was fastened to the ship is not known.

The Nydam ship is a pure rowing vessel, rather narrow, low in the water for comfortable rowing, and without a proper keel. Carved stones on the island of Gotland and in mainland Sweden give vivid impressions of such ships in use. The Anglo-Saxon raids and invasion of Britain must have taken place in vessels of this type.

A large and magnificent example of a somewhat later stage in the development is the vessel used for the burial at Sutton Hoo in East Anglia in AD 630. All wood has decayed, but the hull was so well supported by sand in the trench dug below the burial mound that the iron rivets had remained in position, and it was possible to draw up a reliable reconstruction plan of the vessel, based on measurements of the rivet positions. The ship is more beamy than the older vessel from Nydam, and may have had a mast and sail, even though the keel is still more a bottom plank than a true keel. The hull shape is not well suited for tacking, so if the vessel was rigged, it would have performed best when sailing down-wind. Three close-set ribs aft, very sturdily riveted to the starboard side, tell of a more permanent fastening of the side rudder. The rowlocks stand on a thickened sheerstrake, as in Nydam, but they are no longer lashed, but more firmly fastened by vertical iron spikes. The strakes, nine on each side, are not as wide as those of Nydam, and are scarphed from several shorter pieces.

This photograph of the original excavation of the Sutton Hoo ship in 1939 reveals how well the shape and structural details of the ship were preserved, despite the decay of the timbers themselves. The vessel is thought to have been built about AD 600, since there is evidence that the ship had enjoyed a relatively long life before being interred. (By courtesy of Basil Greenhill)

ful rudder also indicates that the vessel could have carried a mast and sail. Like Sutton Hoo, the hull shape is not too well adapted to sailing; the vessels are still primarily rowing ships. The low freeboard is well suited for comfortable rowing, but would be dangerous when the ship heeled under sail. The small Kvalsund vessel found with the ship is a long, slender rowing boat, 9.5m (31ft) long and equipped with two pairs of oars. The Kvalsund vessels retain the lashings between planking and ribs below the waterline, while the upper strakes are connected to the ribs with treenails or rivets. Traces in the sand 'ghosts' of the Sutton Hoo ribs indicate that all rib fastenings in this ship were treenails.

In the centuries before the Viking Age, the societies of Scandinavia knew no towns. It has been suggested that the economy was based on a redistributive system, where the local chieftains collected fish, game and farm products as tribute or 'tax' from members of the 'tribe' they controlled, and distributed enough in return for people to live on. The surplus was used for the chief's own purposes, like feeding a band of soldiers and retainers. Long-distance trade was in luxury goods, necessary to keep up the prestige of the chiefs. There was little or no trade in goods for consumption, and no long-distance transport of cheap bulk wares.

A society of this kind would have little need for special cargo vessels, so ships built to carry the armed followers of the chief could also handle the moderate amount of valuable trade goods needed to make a trading voyage profitable.

It has been suggested, mainly by Crumlin-Pedersen in several papers, that the use of sailing cargo ships in Scandinavia goes back well before the Viking Age, while the present author has maintained that the society of Scandinavia had no need for special ships for war and trade until the Viking Age was well advanced. The ships of the pre-Viking Iron Age as we know them from the bog finds and the Sutton Hoo grave are examples of such all-purpose vessels, equally well suited for war, general travel and trade in luxury goods. At this time the difference between a boat and a ship was mainly a question of size, so a small fishing boat and the chieftain's ship would have much in common.

With a total length of about 27m (88ft) Sutton Hoo is the largest of the pre-Viking vessels of northern Europe. The shipbuilding technique, as well as many of the objects found in the grave, show that there were close connections between Anglo-Saxon England and Scandinavia.

Around 700 AD a ship and a boat were sacrificed at Kvalsund, on the Norwegian west coast north of Bergen. The find is interpreted as a war offering like the ones from southern Scandinavia, but in this case, no arms were sacrificed, only the vessels themselves. A number of pointed hazel rods were found, which have been interpreted as symbolic spears. The ship shows some changes from the Nydam/Sutton Hoo stage, the most important being that the bottom plank has a pronounced strengthening lath on the underside, which is well on its way to become a T-shaped keel. The long and power-

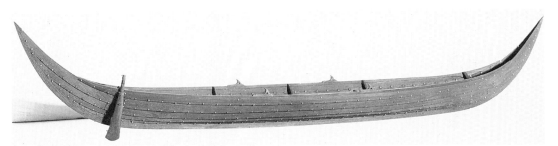

Reconstruction models of the larger Kvalsund vessel and the accompanying boat. Both ship and small boat had been sacrificed in a bog at Herøy, Sunnmøre, west Norway around AD 700. (Oldsaksamlingen, Oslo)

The adoption of mast and sail

An unsolved problem is why sailing ships were adopted so late in the north, probably not until the seventh century. At that time, the square sail had been in use for several millennia in the Mediterranean, and Scandinavians must have seen sailing ships in the southern part of the North Sea and in the English Channel. The light, flexible hulls of Norse ships were not suited to withstand the stresses of sail and rigging until the stage represented by Sutton Hoo and Kvalsund. Even these ships have a hull form better suited to rowing than sailing. They would not tack well, due to the round bottom profile and shallow keel, and the freeboard is too low to keep water out when the ship heels.

The oldest sailing ship found is the vessel used for burial at Oseberg on the west coast of the Oslo Fjord. The very substantial grave goods, and the rich wood-carving of the ship and many other objects makes this a prime source within Viking Age archaeology. Dendrochronological investigations have dated the building of the ship to AD 815-820. The wood used for the burial chamber was cut in the summer of 834, and as it was in all probability used unseasoned, this dates the burial. It has been suggested that the vessel is more of a state barge than a ship for ordinary use, and

that she was only intended for coastal trips in calm weather and sheltered waters. The Gokstad ship, on the other hand, has been seen as *the* Viking Ship, capable of sailing the

Atlantic if necessary. The Gokstad ship was built about AD 890, and used for burial some twenty years later. Until the Skuldelev vessels were excavated in 1962, little comparative

Midship cross-sections of the Kvalsund and Sutton Hoo ships to the same scale. (Sketch by author after Johannessen and Care Evans)

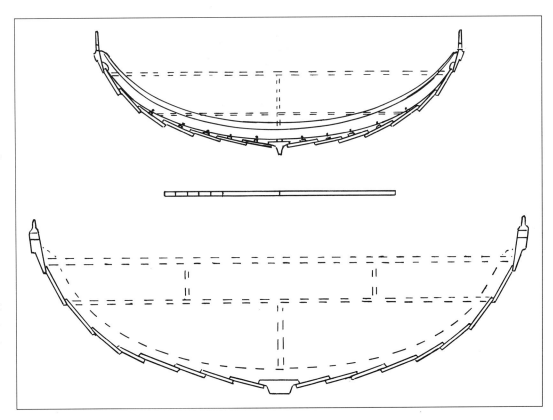

The restored Oseberg ship. Built around AD 815 – 820, this is the oldest Scandinavian vessel so far discovered which has a mast and sail. (Oldsaksamlingen, Oslo)

The Kvalsund vessel has a shallow keel, and the bottom planks amidships are nearly horizontal. This is a good shape for rowing, but gives little lateral resistance when sailing on the wind. The frames run from sheerstrake to sheerstrake, lashed to cleats on the planking in the underwater part of the hull, but with some use of treenails and iron rivets in the upper strakes. The freeboard, giving the oars a comfortable height above water, is alarmingly low when the ship heels under sail. The sheerstrake is shaped like an L turned upside-down, a shape also used in Nydam, and probably in Sutton Hoo. In addition to the surface this gives for fastening rowlocks, it strengthens the hull longitudinally. Strong bulkhead-like ribs fore and aft give added strength to the stem areas. The deep, permanently fastened steering oar is secured to the aft bulkhead. The rib system is strong enough for a rowing vessel, but there is little transverse strength, as the thwarts are not securely fastened. The stresses caused by sail and rigging may have given serious trouble to a vessel of this type. The ship is C14-dated to about 700 AD.

Oseberg, with a building date around 820 AD is 120 years, or at least four generations of shipbuilders, later than Kvalsund. We still find material existed, and all real Viking ships were thought to be of 'the Gokstad type'.

If we accept that the Norse ships did develop and improve over the centuries, and that mast and sail was adopted surprisingly late, it is necessary to take a close look at Kvalsund and Oseberg, which in this writer's opinion mark the beginning and end of the period of experiments and transition which must have followed the introduction of sail as a means of propulsion at sea. Old men must have scorned the young, 'who were too lazy to row like we did, and want to be blown across the sea'. Daring skippers with little experience in handling sail must have had very nasty experiences. Those who survived must surely have suggested improvements to the shipbuilders, and we can imagine lengthy conversations over the evening beer all winter before a new ship was built, incorporating the ideas and experience derived from sailing.

The restored Gokstad ship. Replicas that have sailed the North Atlantic prove the seaworthiness of the design. (Oldsaksamlingen, Oslo)

A replica of the Kvalsund vessel was built in 1973. It proved to be light and fast under oars. (Author)

member used his sea-chest as a rowing bench. Experiments in replicas show that the smallest of the chests found in the Oseberg burial is well suited for this purpose. Placed on the crossbeam, it is of the right height, and the rower can support his feet against the chest of the next man. In a seaway, the chests would have to be lashed in place.

Evidence from archaeology and the study of place names indicate that the first settlers from western Norway went to Shetland and the Orkneys in the eighth century, before the traditional date of the beginning of the Viking Age – 792 AD, when the monastery at Lindisfarne was sacked. This early settlement must have been undertaken in vessels of the Kvalsund type.

Excavation evidence from the Danish city of Ribe shows that Viking art was developed well before the Lindisfarne attack, and the chronology within the Viking Age may have to be revised in the light of these finds. However, the written sources in France, Ireland and England show clearly that around 800 AD the Norsemen launched a series of attacks on coasts that had been at peace for centuries. Norse settlements were established in Ireland, Scotland, England, and Normandy. The Atlantic islands were discovered – or possibly rediscovered, as there is some evidence of Irish

the high sweeping stems and the bulkhead-like ribs near the stems, the aft one doubling as rudder-rib. Most of the other constructional details have developed. The sturdy L-shaped strake is no longer the sheerstrake, but now forms the transition between the ship's bottom and topsides. Old Norse had a name for one of the strakes in a ship's side – *meginhufr*, literally translated as the Strong Strake. This is a good name for the old sheerstrake in its new place, and it is generally accepted that it is the name for this strake. The thwarts have changed function to firmly secured crossbeams, which stiffens the ship transversely. The two strakes above the *meginhufr* are supported by naturally 'grown' knees securely fastened with spikes and treenails. The rowlocks have given way to oarports in the upper of the two added strakes. The keel has a new shape, like a large T, where the old bottom board exists as the horizontal parts of the T, for rivetting the first strake, while the lath on the underside has changed into a sturdy beam, a real keel. The first strakes are fastened at a steeper angle, giving a better hull shape for sailing. The rounded hull shape of Kvalsund has given way to a V-bottom, with nearly vertical topsides above the *meginhufr*.

The mast was supported by a keelson resting on the keel, shaped on the underside to fit over two ribs. A tree with a horizontal branch was selected, the branch acting as a support for the heavy 'mast partner' placed above the crossbeams. The crossbeam in front of the mast curves upwards, and so does the mast partner, giving support to the mast about a metre above the mast step in the keelson. The problem of

giving enough support to the mast in a light and flexible hull has been solved in an elegant manner. Sailing experiments in a modern replica have shown that shrouds to the ship's side and a stay to the stem were needed as additional support. The keelson and mast partner have little support sideways, an improvement that was to come later. The added strakes and the transition from thwart to crossbeam robbed the rowers of their seats. The Oseberg ship, like the vessels from Tune and Gokstad, lack fixed seats for the rowers. No definite proof exists, but it is generally believed that each crew

The Oseberg ship looking aft. Knees standing on the crossbeams support the topsides. (Author)

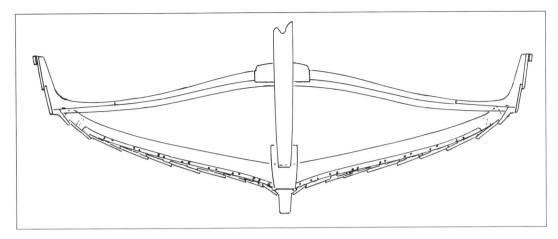

Keel, crossbeams and mast support set the Oseberg ship apart from the older rowing vessels like Sutton Hoo and Kvalsund, but the ship can still be moved by thirty oarsmen in a calm. (Drawing by Glende)

monasteries as far north as Iceland. Discovery was soon followed by settlement. Swedish Vikings traded and settled in Russia. Between 800 AD and 1000 AD, Norse seafaring had expanded from sailing the home waters to travelling, more or less regularly, on all seas from the Caspian to the North Atlantic. One man might in his lifetime have taken part in voyages ranging from Constantinople in the east to Newfoundland in the west.

The Danish society seems to have been the most developed politically, with a central government strong enough to order the building of earthworks against Frankish attacks on the southern border, and other impressive pieces of engineering like the late Viking Age ringforts. Sweden, and especially Norway, seem to have been more divided, and more sparsely populated. Even so, one of the explanations for Viking expansion is population pressure at home. Younger sons needed land outside the ancestral farm. Some cleared forested land at home, but many went abroad. Another explanation is social unrest. The old tribal society was changing into early kingdoms, a change that may have been both socially complicated and violent.

This may be relevant background to the Viking activities abroad, but the tool for all activities, plunder, trade or colonisation – the ship – is definitely the most important single clue to Viking expansion. Nearly all travel, regardless of purpose, was by water. There must definitely have been maritime trade and other contacts by sea before the Viking Age, but the scale changed radically about 800 AD. This is the time of the Oseberg ship, the time when sailing vessels had come of age in the north. For the first time ships crossed the

North Sea in considerable numbers each summer. In the Baltic, the picture is the same. The Swedes had traded across the Baltic before the Viking Age, but on a much more modest scale.

The Oseberg ship is part of a female burial, and the ship itself is richly decorated with carvings. It has been suggested that this is a royal yacht, intended for pleasure trips in sheltered waters. It may well be that this particular ship was mainly used along the coast, and probably for ceremonial voyages, but there is no reason to believe that she was less seaworthy than other contemporary ships. If a ship is built as a compromise, with some seaworthiness sacrificed, it is in order to gain something, like greater comfort on board, easier and cheaper construction or more cargo capacity. Like all other Viking ships, Oseberg is a large open boat, as uncomfortable as the others in foul weather. Cargo capacity is small, and there is nothing cheap and easy about construction and workmanship. In the author's opinion, she is typical of the ships used at the beginning of the Viking expansion, an early sailing ship, fully capable of sailing the North Sea in summer (nobody sailed in winter).

In 1992, a replica of the Oseberg ship was wrecked in the Mediterranean, in a full gale with waves up to 12m (40ft) high. The ship handled the very severe weather amazingly well, running before the wind, until a great wave broke and filled the ship. In an open

vessel there is very little one can do in such a situation, but all hands were saved due to excellent seamanship. In the Viking Age, sailors in a similar situation would have had little hope of rescue, if no other vessels close by could pick them up. Beaching the ship in shallow water could save lives, and when driven on to a lee shore, Viking skippers would head for the land under full canvas, hoping to run the ship ashore with a chance of saving the crew, and possibly some cargo.

In the ninth century ships crossed the North Sea every summer, and the assembled experience must have led to further development of hull and rigging. If the Oseberg ship of around AD 800 is compared with the Gokstad and Tune ships, built late in the ninth century, it is possible to see how ships changed as three or four generations of sailors demanded improvements from the shipbuilders. The keel is deeper, especially in the Gokstad ship, and the first two strakes are fitted at a steeper angle, to give better lateral resistance. The upper part of the Tune ship is missing, but Gokstad shows a higher freeboard than Oseberg, with two strakes added above the one with the oarports. For comfortable rowing, it was impossible to have the ports higher up, and lids have been added to close the oarports against spray when the ship was under sail. The extreme V-bottom of the Oseberg ship has given way to a smoother transition between bottom and topsides. The sheer at the stem and stern is less pronounced, so the ends of the hull do not catch as much wind. The mast is placed amidships, as against 1m further forward in the Oseberg ship, resulting in a better balance between hull and rigging.

The mast support is also much stronger. The keelson spans four ribs, against Oseberg's two, and it is secured laterally by knees mounted on the ribs. Where the Oseberg mast partner was supported sideways only by being let down into

The Oseberg and Gokstad ships lack fixed seats for the rowers, and it is believed that the crew used their sea-chests as rowing benches, as shown in this Gokstad cross-section. (Drawing by M Storm)

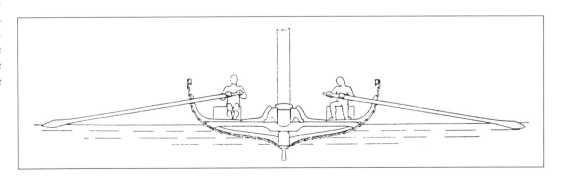

The Gokstad ship on display in Oslo. Three generations of shipbuilders separate the Oseberg and Gokstad ships. Improvements include a better underwater shape, added freeboard and lids for the oarports. (Oldsaksamlingen, Oslo)

a mortise in the crossbeam in front of the mast, the mast partner of Gokstad is mortised over six crossbeams, and supported laterally by knees securely fastened to the crossbeams. The seaworthiness of the Gokstad ship has been demonstrated by three replicas which have crossed the North Atlantic successfully, two sailing westwards, one eastwards.

From the first half of the Viking Age, we have only these three ships, Oseberg, Gokstad and Tune, and small fragments of a few others. A mast partner like the one from Oseberg has been found in the sea near Århus in Denmark; two fragmentary stems came from bogs in western Norway; a Gokstad-type mast partner has also been found in western Norway, probably remains of a wreck thrown up on the beach and overgrown by peat. These are examples of the same type of ship, and it is important to ask whether all early Viking ships were of the same

general type or not. So far, the material is not sufficient to come to a firm conclusion, but it seems reasonable to suggest that early Viking Age society did not need ships specialised for trade and war.

Post-Viking developments

At the end of the Viking Age, when the Vikings had started to adopt Christianity, and their societies were beginning to take part in European trade and politics as nations, it is known that ships for war and ships for trade had developed. They all show the common ancestry, but cargo vessels have become more beamy and high sided, more dependent on sail, while the warships are slender and low, intended only for men and arms in need of fast travel under sail or oars.

The ships used to block a sailing channel at Skuldelev in the shallow Roskilde fjord in Denmark in the eleventh century show what the situation was like in the transition from Viking Age to medieval society. Two of the ships are warships, slender, low and with oar-

ports all along the sides where the top strakes are preserved. Analysis of the timbers used in the large ship shows that it was built of Irish oak. Dublin was a Viking city, and it is reasonable to suggest that the vessel was built in Dublin for a Norse chieftain and finally ended up in Roskilde fjord after exciting service, including at least one trip across the North Sea. The small warship shows many repairs, and reused planks from another vessel were employed when it was built. It has been suggested that this is a typical levy ship, built and maintained by the local population for the use of the king. Fragments of a somewhat younger but quite similar vessel have been found in another navigation blockage, at Fotevik in Scania. Like all taxes, the duty to keep ships for the king's use is likely to have been unpopular, and the ship was built as cheaply as possible, repaired again and again, as long as she could be kept seaworthy.

This ship has many details in common with the small merchantman, Skuldelev 3, and they may have been built in the Roskilde fjord area. Both Wreck 3 and the larger merchantman (Wreck 1) had an open cargo hold amidships

Outlines, to the same scale, of the five Skuldelev ships; shaded areas indicate the preserved parts of the vessels. (The Viking Ship Museum, Roskilde)

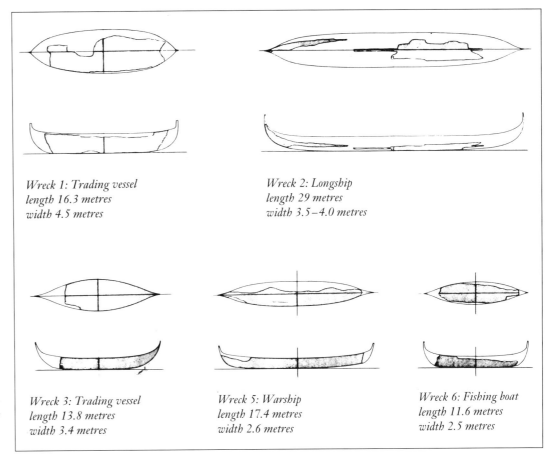

Wreck 1: Trading vessel
length 16.3 metres
width 4.5 metres

Wreck 2: Longship
length 29 metres
width 3.5–4.0 metres

Wreck 3: Trading vessel
length 13.8 metres
width 3.4 metres

Wreck 5: Warship
length 17.4 metres
width 2.6 metres

Wreck 6: Fishing boat
length 11.6 metres
width 2.5 metres

and small decks fore and aft. A few oarports show that oars could be used for getting in or out of harbour, or for turning the vessels in a tight spot, but they are primarily sailing ships. The larger of the two is mainly built of pine, which was very rare in Viking Age Denmark, but plentiful in Norway. It is possible that this is an early example of the heavy vessels built in western Norway for voyages to the Faeroes, Iceland and Greenland. The last of the Skuldelev ships is a small fishing vessel or all-purpose boat.

Probably during the tenth century, a system called *leidang* was devised for the coastal defence of the Nordic countries. It seems to have been based on an agreement between the population of the coastal districts, and a fairly strong central government, the king. In addition to defence against enemies from abroad, it could have been a means of restricting the private Viking expeditions and skirmishes of local chieftains, by firmly indicating that war was the business of the king alone. The coast was divided into districts called *skipreider*. In Norway they reached as far inland as the salmon went upriver. Each district had to build, maintain, man and provision a ship. The ship could be requisitioned by the king for defence against attack, and to a lesser degree for offensive war abroad. For the first time, an economic basis had been established for building ships that were intended only to carry men and arms into battle. At the same time, market places developed into early towns, which were dependent on the countryside for cheap everyday goods in increasing bulk. As long as trade was based on expensive luxury wares, a ship with limited cargo capacity could trade profitably. A cargo of house-timber, firewood, building stone, roofing materials or fish could not fetch the same prices, and more cargo space was needed to make a trip commercially viable. In addition, the bulky goods themselves also made it necessary to build vessels with more cargo capacity.

The types can be seen in well developed form in the Skuldelev ships, and we must suppose that the size of the cargo ships increased steadily with the trade expansion of the Middle Ages. Even after the development of special cargo-carriers and warships, the vessels did not differ very much from their common ancestry. Even

as late as the early thirteenth century, it was still possible to alter a merchant vessel to a warship by cutting oarports all along the ship's side. As warships were not built to be as seaworthy as the merchantmen, an alteration the other way is not recorded.

We have several wreck finds from Scandinavian waters which enable us to follow the gradual development of the Norse merchant vessel in the centuries following the Viking Age, but there are no finds of warships later than Skuldelev and Fotevik. The medieval

Ship carved near the old road leading to Trondheim from the south. The head indicates an early eleventh century date. (Tracing by A Stalsberg Alsvik)

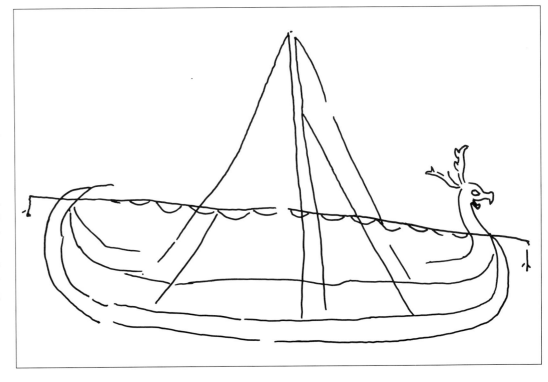

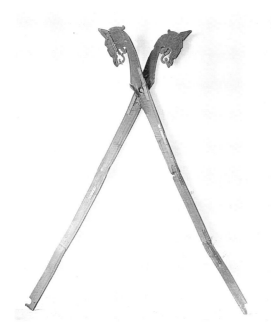

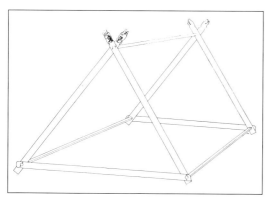

Top left: One pair of gable-boards from the tent found with the Gokstad ship – the drawing (left) shows how it was used – and (above) a replica of the large Oseberg bed. Such removable 'camping equipment' was for the use of a few selected crew members only. (Oldsaksamlingen, Oslo)

sources, especially the sagas of the Norwegian kings, contain numerous passages on ships and seafaring, but they are seldom detailed enough to give more than a brief glimpse of the vessels.

The warships were dependent on a large crew for rowing, and of course also for fighting. There were no real naval tactics, like the Mediterranean use of the ram, and the ships were more suited for the transport of warriors than for fighting at sea. It was usual to tie the ships together before battle, to make larger 'fighting platforms'. The outermost ships could still row, and as the enemy also used a similar formation, fighting was mainly over the high stems, where few men could find room. Accordingly, the best warriors were placed in the bow. A battle would start with archers, spear-throwers and stone-throwers attacking the enemy and as the ships closed, the crews would fight hand to hand with sword, spear and axe. If enough men succeeded in entering an enemy ship, it would be 'cleared' from stem to stern.

It was a total, and successful, break with the traditional tactics when King Sverre let his ships roam free at the battle of Fimreite in 1184, closing with the enemy by laying vessels alongside the outermost ones in the block of opposing ships. Furthermore, some time before the battle, he had had an extra-large ship built, and its high freeboard proved a tactical advantage, which was later adopted by other royal ships. Some of the saga passages indicate that the huge royal ships were unwieldy, and the bulk of warships confirmed to be of the 20-thwart size which was the standard levy ship.

In the late Middle Ages, the tactical advantages of high ships were again proved, when 400 pirates from the Baltic sailing seven cogs were victorious against a 'large' levy fleet during an attack on Bergen in 1429. This is the last recorded use of the levy fleet.

Even though merchant ships could be worked with small crews – less than ten men are sufficient to sail a replica of Skuldelev 1 – crews were often large for other reasons. The usual way to conduct trade, according to the few surviving written sources, was for one or more men owning a ship to make public that they intended to go on a trading voyage, usually to a

well known market. People who had surplus goods which they wanted to sell made an agreement with the owner(s) and paid for the cargo space by acting as crew members. Thus the ship might have a large crew, each with their own goods to sell. The Old Norse name for a merchant, *Farmann*, translates literally as 'travelling man'. A merchant had to travel to sell his goods.

The Norwegian laws have detailed rules for the procedure if the shipowner had invited too many people and the ship became overloaded. There are rules also for seaworthiness. The Icelandic law includes a definition of a 'plimsoll mark' – two-fifths of the ship's side amidships had to be above water. In the city law of King Magnus 'The Lawmender' from 1276 we read that:

A ship which requires bailing three times in the course of 24 hours will be declared seaworthy for all kinds of traffic; but if they so wish, the crew can entrust themselves to a more leaky ship. But if the steersman lets the ship be bailed at night, concealing this from the crew, such action is treason towards the crew, and the steersman shall be responsible for any damage or injury resulting from that, regardless of whether it affects men or cargo or both, for every man must pay for his own dishonesty.

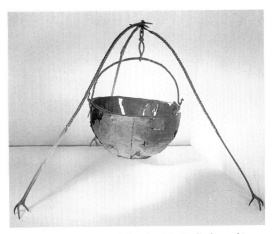

Iron cauldron and tripod found with the Oseberg ship. No fireplaces existed on board, so cooking had to be done ashore. (Oldsaksamlingen, Oslo)

As rents and taxes were paid in kind, the great landowners had a surplus to sell. Accordingly, the king, nobility, monasteries and bishops had their own ships, which were presumably sailed with more professional crews, and with less varied cargoes. Custom rolls from the early fourteenth century preserved from some of the ports of eastern England tell of ships with names such as 'the Bishop's Buza' unloading cod liver oil, dried fish and lumber.

Life on board

As the ships were mainly undecked, the seaman's life must have been wet and cold. In the Viking Age and earlier, most travel was within sight of land, and it was usual to anchor in a natural harbour at night, cook a hot meal, and probably sleep on shore. In the middle of the war between King Alfred of Wessex and the Vikings, a peaceful merchant, from northern Norway, Ottar (or Othere as his name is given in Anglo-Saxon), visited the court of Wessex. The information he gave the king was written down and included in an Anglo-Saxon version of Orosius. Othere had sailed from his home in northern Norway, and evidently spent his nights in good natural harbours along the coast. He visited the market place at Skiringsal in southern Norway, and then went on to Hedeby near the modern Danish-German border. We know nothing of his ship and its equipment, but the Oseberg and Gokstad ships

were equipped with tents and dismountable beds, and there were cauldrons of iron or copper, complete with chains or tripod for hanging the pot over the fire. A dish of stew or porridge from the great copper cauldron found in the Gokstad ship could have fed a large hungry crew: the capacity is more than 100 litres. It seems reasonable that Othere had similar equipment on his vessel.

Early medieval sources sometimes tell of special pilots, a cook and passengers. Passengers would sometimes bring their own food – there is a story of an Icelander travelling on a Norwegian ship who borrows the cooking pot and starts a quarrel by using too much time making his porridge while the hungry crew waits. The cooking on a merchant ship might be done by the crew members taking turns or by a cook hired jointly. In later times it was not uncommon for the crew of a fishing boat to have their own food, which was cooked jointly, after being marked, so that each man was sure of getting his own piece of meat or fish. Some of the small wooden 'labels' with names in runes found at Bryggen in Bergen may be such marks of ownership. The crew would all eat from the same pot, presumably, but the tents and beds were for a few selected crew members, since there is not room for all. In addition to

the shore tents, pieces of canvas or the sail was stretched over the decks fore and aft, to provide shelter for people sleeping on board. There are sources, admittedly not too precise, which speak of leather sacks used to store equipment in the day and as two-man sleeping bags at night.

How sailors of the time dressed is not known, but in more recent times fishermen used wool, and oilskins – literally, coats of tanned goatskin treated with cod liver oil to make then waterproof. On long voyages across the open sea, there would be no means of safely lighting a fire, so it must be assumed that dried, smoked or salted meat and fish was eaten, washed down with water, sour skimmed milk or possibly beer.

On board a levy ship, the steersman (appointed by the king) probably had full command, at sea as well as in battle. Merchant ships seem to have had a more democratic structure of command: the ship's council had the final word in a crisis, and could evidently overrule the shipowner. In harbour, the council, where all on board were members, met on the quay; at sea the council was convened by the mast. One Icelandic saga tells of a ship which had drifted in the fog for days, and had lost its course. When the fog lifted, the ship's

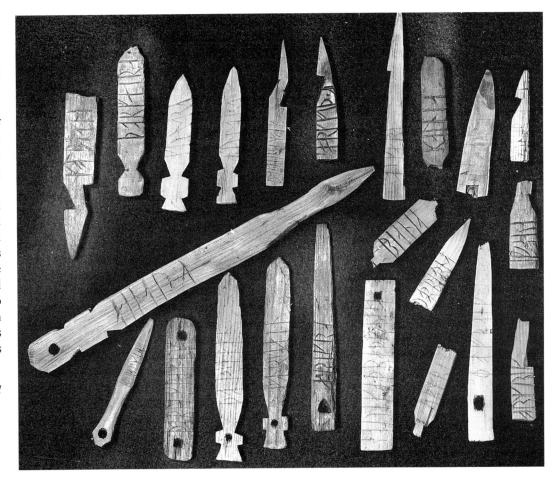

A selection of owners' marks from Bryggen, the medieval wharf of Bergen, Norway. Usually, the owner's name is written in runes, and in a few cases the goods are mentioned (woollen yarn, for example). The barbed pieces were probably stuck into a bale of goods, while the others were tied on. (Oldsaksamlingen, Oslo)

council debated which course to steer, and finally followed advice from an experienced crew member.

Navigation

Around 1220 the Icelander Snorre Sturlason wrote a text book on how to compose poetry in the Norse style. A poet had to have some knowledge of traditional myths and heathen religion, and our only description of heathen Norse cosmology is found in this work.

The earth is a round disk, where the gods live in the centre. Here the ash tree Yggdrasil stands as an immense pillar, holding up the sky. Around the land of the gods we find the homes of humans, while evil giants live close to the sea surrounding the earth. The immense sea serpent Midgardsormen lives in the sea, reaching all the way around the earth and biting its own tail. If Viking Age sailors really did believe this, the first seamen who set sail westwards into the Atlantic must have been either reckless or very daring men.

In coastal waters, navigation was by landmarks. Along the Norwegian coast, a number of mountains and islands have characteristic silhouettes which make them easy to remember. The preferred sailing channel among island and skerries was known as the *leid*, a word still current on the coast. On the long journey from northern Norway to Bergen, there were a number of landmarks with stories or fairytales connected to them. A mountain resembling a man on horseback, Hestmannen, is a supernatural being who once upon a time proposed to a fairy, Lekamøya, who declined to marry him. Furious, Hestmannen drew his bow and shot an arrow which was deflected by another supernatural being throwing his hat in its path. The result is Torghatten, an island with an open tunnel through the mountain. Even the arrow can be seen, in the form of an Iron Age standing stone. A good yarn like this would shorten long hours under oars in calm, but at the same time it would help young crew members to remember important landmarks along the *leid*. No proof exists, but it is highly probable that the stories are as old as the Viking Age or older.

People who were in a hurry, or who did not wish to be seen, would sail the *utleid*, so far out to sea that they could just see land. When travelling in unknown waters, a skipper might hire a pilot, in Old Norse called *leidsogumadr* – he who tells where the *leid* is. After a century or more of experience, the coasts around the North Sea and the Baltic held few secrets for Viking sailors. Seasoned raiders and traders might have experience in navigating the

Russian rivers, or they might even know how to find the straits of Gibraltar and enter the Mediterranean.

Artificial landmarks do not seem to have come into use until after the Viking Age, but it is highly probable that large burial cairns along the coasts were used as landmarks. Norwegian waters are too deep for successful use of the sounding lead, but it is probable that it was used when sailing the more shallow waters around Denmark, and on navigable rivers.

How Viking Age sailors navigated on the high seas has been a matter of much speculation. Most of the passages out of sight of land were fairly short: across the Baltic, from England to Norway, or from Norway to Shetland or the Orkneys. The longer voyages were across the North Atlantic to the Faeroes, Iceland and Greenland, or from Iceland to Ireland. The climate was somewhat more favourable than today, with less ice around Greenland, but nevertheless, taking an undecked vessel from western Norway across the North Atlantic to Greenland is in any terms an impressive piece of seamanship and navigation.

Some scholars – mainly Sølver, Morcken and Thirslund – have maintained that Viking Age sailors practised advanced astronomical navigation, while Schnall is more modest in his estimate of navigational methods (see Chapter 8 for more detail). The sources used by the advocates of astronomical navigation are a story in the saga of King Olav the Saint, Icelandic written sources on astronomy from the early medieval period, and a supposed bearing dial found in a Norse ruin in Greenland.

According to the saga, King Olav visited a farmer and his sons who all claimed supernatural powers. The farmer said that he could tell the directions to the corners of the world, even with no sun showing. The day was overcast and it was snowing. The king took out his 'sunstone' to check the claim of the farmer, who was pointing in the right direction. The Danish archaeologist T Ramskou has connected this source to the use of certain feldspars, cordierite and Icelandic doublespar. Both minerals polarise sunlight, and by turning them until the stone changes colour, the direction of the sun is found. It is necessary to have some clear sky, so the fully overcast day with snow is, at the very least, a misunderstanding by the saga author. Even if an early eleventh-century king did possess such a stone, there is no proof that it was a common navigational aid, and no such stones have ever been found in a Viking Age context.

The 'bearing dial' from Greenland was iden-

tified by Sølver, who was both a mariner and a maker of navigational instruments. It is the broken half of a disc of pine, about 7cm (2¾in) in diameter. Around the edge there are triangular points cut into the wood, giving an impression not unlike a modern ship's compass. The directions, however, are quite imprecise. Sølver had an idealised reconstruction made with 32 points, adding a central vertical pin and a horizontal 'course indicator'. Later Thirslund altered the interpretation, maintaining that the incised lines on the surface of the object are shadow lines. If the shadow from a centrally placed gnomon follows the line as the sun traverses the sky, your ship is correctly pointing on a course due west or east.

In the twelfth century, a gifted astronomer known as Star Oddi lived in northern Iceland. It is not known whether he was literate himself, but some of his observations have been preserved in Icelandic manuscripts. He made observations of stars and the sun, using the sun's diameter as the unit for expressing sun altitude above the horizon. He seems to have had little or no contact with the astronomers of the church. Oddi's observations, the 'sun stone' and the 'bearing dial' have together been taken as evidence for a Viking system of astronomic navigation.

This is in sharp contrast to a passage in one of the Icelandic manuscripts, which gives information on how to sail from western Norway to Greenland.

From Hernar in Norway, sail westwards. You should pass so far north of Shetland that you just see the islands in good weather, and south of the Færøy Islands, they should be halfway below the horizon [Literally 'with the sea half way up the mountains']. Sail south of Iceland, out of sight of land, but seeing whales and sea birds, and you will make landfall at the southern tip of Greenland.

Here there is no navigation by sun or stars or bearing dials, but the technique of the coastal sailor transferred to the high seas: you cross the North Atlantic using the landmarks available. Sailing was a summer occupation, and in the light northern nights stars would hardly have been visible. In spring and autumn it is reasonable to believe that the Pole Star was used as a navigational aid – its Old Norse name, *leidar stjerna*, translates as the star showing the *leid*. It is also good reason to believe that dominating wave systems, prevailing winds and other natural phenomena were known and used by Viking sailors.

Arne Emil Christensen

6

Arabia to China – the Oriental Traditions

THE STUDY of ships of the Indian Ocean and Asia is both important and complex. Firstly, the study encompasses a large and diverse geographical area which extends from Japan, through Southeast Asia, into the Indian Ocean, up to the Red Sea and the Persian Gulf and to the northern coast of East Africa. The study excludes Oceania, in the wider sense, although parts of the Philippines and Formosa have relevance to Melanesia and Micronesia. This is about one-fifth of the surface area of the world. The study covers a diverse cultural range, from simple island and coastal societies of Africa and Indonesia to complex maritime trade centres of China, Indonesia, India and Arabia. The study covers a long time span, although not as great as the range existing in Europe – the earliest boat remains are in Korea and date from the eleventh century. The evidence that survives is varied and often complex to interpret and can be obtained from ethnography, archaeology, written records, pictorial information and oral tradition. All this makes the study challenging and an interesting contrast with European/ North American maritime culture. The first part of this chapter looks at the evidence for sewn boats and their connection with the developments of shipbuilding in the region.

The *mtepe* of East Africa

The *mtepe* was a distinctive vessel which was still being built on the Swahili coast north of Lamu in Kenya at the beginning of this century. There were two types, the *mtepe* and the *dau la mtepe*. Both are now extinct, the last *mtepe* being wrecked off the Kenya coast around 1935. The only surviving evidence today is a small section of hull planking in the ceiling of a room in Fort Jesus Museum, Mombasa; a number of models; some photo-

A model of the East African mtepe, *a now disappeared type that was built using a very ancient dowelled and sewn planked hull structure.* (National Maritime Museum)

attached to the frames. Therefore there is a different technology at work. Its function in sewn boats would be to add longitudinal strength to reduce the shearing effect at the seam. It may be assumed, then, that the sewing of a seam has two functions: firstly to hold the planks together and secondly to prevent them moving longitudinally relative to each other at the seam. For that reason, lashings (bindings between holes directly opposite each other on the seam) serve to hold the planks together, but have little effect in preventing longitudinal movement. To counteract this, lashings can also run diagonally between adjacent lashing holes, thus helping to reduce longitudinal shear. However, the working of a vessel makes it inevitable that these lashings will loosen. As a result the longitudinal forces will have a much greater effect because of the mechanical advantage of this type of stress on the fibres. By introducing dowels along the seam, the shear effect will be eliminated, allowing the sewing–lashing to function more efficiently to hold the seams together.

Details of dowel and sewn fastenings on the exterior hull of an Omani kambari *(a sewn* sambuq*).* (Roger Garwood)

graphs and illustrations; and various writers' accounts of the vessels. Professor Prins, in a 1986 study of these craft, suggests that there are four classes of *mtepe*, two distinguished by form – breasthook bow versus swan-neck stem; and two by sewing technique – visible externally and invisible (*ie* cut off externally).[1]

The *mtepe* is interesting because it represents a class of Indian Ocean vessel built using dowels and sewing techniques. The *Periplous Maris Erythraei*, an anonymous account of trade and navigation in the Indian Ocean written around the first century AD, speaks of the sewn boats of the Indian Ocean. We have evidence of sewing traditions across most of the Indian Ocean, in the Arab world (Oman), in India, the Lakshadweep, Sri Lanka, the Maldives, Vietnam and southern China. The dowelling technique used in the *mtepe*, as with the Arabian dhow, is different from the technique used in Southeast Asia, where the dowels are set in holes drilled in opposite faces of the edge of the plank. With the *mtepe* the dowels are driven from the outside upwards and then planed off. This has considerable implications in the construction of the vessels and indicates that a different construction sequence is used in the two systems.

In Southeast Asia and the Maldives, the technique is as follows: the plank A, to be set on the

strake B attached to the hull, is cut roughly to shape. A series of holes to take the dowels is drilled in B separated by a fixed distance, usually about 10 to 20cm. Plank A is then brought up to B and the positions of the holes marked on A. Holes are then drilled in A. At this point a few thin dowels are usually placed in a number of holes in B, and A is then fitted in place and marked up with a spiling gauge, so that the joint can be cut and shaped to fit exactly. The holes are then set with the full size dowels and plank A is then hammered into place. In some cases a certain amount of twist and bend may be given to the plank in order to fit it accurately. However, this system cannot sustain sharp changes in curvature (twist), since the strength is only in the dowels unless the planks are burnt to induce the twist or curvature. This contrasts with the frame-first technique, where the frames have an intrinsic strength which enables the shipwright to force the strakes around the shape. Even so, frame-first construction often utilises burning or other forms of heating to give planks curvature before being applied to the framed hull.

Clearly, the oblique dowelling technique of the *mtepe* and the dhow has to operate in a different way and with a different function. For the dowels to be driven upwards, the plank that they are being driven into (the top one) has to be attached in some way to the lower one. It is assumed that the dowel 'nail' was driven after the seams had been sewn or, in the case of an unsewn vessel, after the strakes had been

1. A H J Prins, *A Handbook of Sewn Boats*, Maritime Monographs and Reports 59, National Maritime Museum (Greenwich 1986).

A Maldivian dhoni *in Malé harbour; the thwart beams are very obvious although the lashed-lug construction technique is not.* (Jeremy Green)

Maldives boats and Maldivian shipbuilding

It has been noted that Maldivian vessels have unusual features not commonly found in the Indian Ocean region. These features include thwart beams, carved lugs on the inside of the strakes to locate the thwart beams (this seems a remarkably similar construction to that used in Southeast Asia where the thwart beams are lashed to the lugs and referred to as a lashed-lug technique), strakes edge-joined with dowels, and other minor features.[2] These observations raise a number of questions: is there evidence of changes in the boat-building techniques over time? Did the boat-building techniques develop independently as a result of technological changes over time, or were they introduced from elsewhere, and if so, when? If changes were introduced, why were they adopted and what were the reasons for change and to what extent did local factors influence the adoption of these new techniques. In attempting to answer these questions it is important to consider the environment in which these vessels were built and sailed, their function, the materials used in their construction and the skills and tools available.

The vessels studied by Millar and others in 1992 included examples in use, older abandoned vessels, and vessels being constructed. The study was made in the Malé shipyard which had more than twenty *dhonis* in varying stages of disrepair; some were modern powered boats, others were older sailing vessels. One particular feature of interest seen on some of the vessels was a small lashing that penetrated the stempost, through the gunwale and around a short turned spar which was used to attach the foot of the sail. The lashing is called *kanikuredhibai* and is said to add strength, although seeming to serve a purely decorative or non-functional purpose.

An additional survey was then made on Alifushi, one of the islands of the northernmost atolls, famous for shipbuilding. In the Maldives most people return to their home island during Ramadan. The survey during this Muslim festival coincided with the return of a group of traditional boat-builders who had decided to build

a *dhoni* instead of resting. At the time of the study, the boat had been constructed up to about the sixth strake in the shell-first tradition. The first two planks were luted with coconut shavings, while cotton wool had been used for the rest of the seams. The planks had been soaked for two days in the sea and then twisted into shape under tension in the sun. A plank was held roughly in place against the hull to determine where to shape and shorten it. Blackened string was used to mark, by eye, the wood that was to be removed. This wood was adzed out and the butt joint at the hood end was carefully bevelled using soot to mark what was to be cut away. Blackened string was again used to mark where the dowel holes were to be drilled. Once this had been set, dowel holes were drilled through the full width of the plank using an electric drill.

2. G Block, 'Island craft: Gus Block looks at traditional boatbuilding in the Maldives', *Classic Boat* (22–26 February 1992); P-Y Manguin, 'Pre-Modern Southeast Asian shipping in the Indian Ocean: the Maldives connection', in New Directions in Maritime History Conference, International Commission of Maritime History (Fremantle December 1993); S McGrail, *The Gokstad Faering*, part 1: *Building the Replica*, Maritime Monographs and Reports (Greenwich 1974); K Millar, 'Preliminary report on observations made into the techniques and traditions of Maldivian shipbuilding', *Bulletin of the Australian Institute for Maritime Archaeology* 17/1 (1993), pp9–16.

Traditional shipbuilding at Alifushi in the Maldives: the section of the hull visible in the photograph has been constructed by the shell-first technique, and two additional strakes are being offered up. (Jeremy Green)

The elaborately shaped tiller of a Maldivian mas dhoni. (Jeremy Green)

The decorative lashing of the stem of a dhoni. Jeremy Green)

Block, who recorded shipbuilding on this island a few years earlier, noted then that the shipbuilders were using a hand operated rope drill. Thin dowels were then used to guide the fitting of the strake. The new plank was fitted to the hull using the pegs and a mortise gauge was used to mark how much of the plank needed to be cut away to fit. The carpenter then marked both the underneath and the top surfaces, which also gives the angle of the bevel. After the surplus wood was cut away with an axe it was adzed smooth. The plank was fitted three times using the thin pegs and the sooted surface which was then adzed back, each time making a closer fit. Next full-sized dowels were shaped to fit the holes in the new plank, and the upper surface of the plank on the hull was then painted blue and cotton wool luting applied.

The new strake, with the dowels inserted, was brought to the hull and, starting at the aft end, was knocked in using a large wooden, flat-topped mallet. The boat-builders moved forward easing the pegs into the holes with the aid of a wooden plank with a notch cut out of it to twist it to the right shape. Once the whole plank was fitted in place, the rounded tops of the dowels were sawn flat and hammered down. The shape of the upper surface of the strake was then marked using a long piece of sooted string. The aim was to leave the full width of the plank amidships and taper it off toward the stem and stern. Finally, the inside surface was adzed and planed to give a smooth finish.

Heavy lugs at every frame were only found on the older vessels which were built of coconut wood, the modern *dhonis* (made from imported timber) having no lugs or only very light lugs carved at the mast step frame. The use of lugs was dying out because it is too difficult and too expensive to cut the lugs out of the pre-dressed imported hardwood timber. It was said that shorter dowels were used twenty years

ago, but a change was made to longer dowels which penetrated through three planks rather than two. This was no doubt facilitated by the introduction of the power drill–manual drilling through the width of three planks would not have been easy.

The results of the survey revealed some significant points. Firstly, the shipbuilding traditions of the Maldives are undergoing rapid technical changes. Coconut wood is now replaced largely by tropical rainforest timber from the Indian subcontinent. The use of lugs is rapidly dying out. Although the traditional shipbuilders still build shell-first, some of the vessels built by the Fisheries Department were being built frames-first. The is no evidence of sewing, except for the small semi-decorative lashing close to the junction of the stem and the large, decorative stemhead fitting, called a *moburi*, a distinctive recurving structure which fits into a slot at the top of the stem. All the evidence indicates a very close similarity with modern-day Indonesian shell-first ship construction. The processes of construction closely parallel the methods found in many parts of the Indonesian archipelago.

This raises a number of interesting questions. Firstly, it is widely accepted that the Maldives were settled by people from southern India or Sri Lanka, certainly in Buddhist times and possibly earlier, the language having similar origins. Clearly the ships would have been of that region, but at some point in time the Maldivians adopted a Southeast Asian method of shipbuilding. It has been suggested that the Maldives may have been a 'way-station' in the Southeast Asian colonisation of Malagasi[3] and that there were extensive trading contacts between Indonesia and the Maldives. It may be through these contacts that the change in shipbuilding technology occurred.

To examine these questions it is necessary to examine also the economics of the Maldives in order to seek explanations for this technological development. The Maldives consist of about 1200 coral islands, each island being surrounded by a shallow lagoon which is enclosed by a coral reef providing protection from the sea. Hundreds of these islands, along with other coral growth, form an atoll. Coconuts and fish compose the local diet, with the majority of the population dependent on fishing for skipjack and yellow fin tuna from their *dhonis*. The Maldives must have been a wealthy society, since it was possible to build large numbers of relatively large (some 10m high) Buddhist *stupas* and other religious buildings in an environment where building materials, land area and, therefore, population were limited.

The main economic wealth of the Maldive Islands lies in their access to sea and to the coconut palm trees.

Malé, the administrative capital of the Maldive Islands, is a port of call on the direct route between Southeast Asia, Arabia and East Africa due to the monsoon winds. Shipping crossing from Southeast Asia to Southern Arabia during the winter northeast monsoon called at Malé to trade, to provision and for shore leave. Shipping was almost always westbound since shipping from Arabia travelled directly to the Indian mainland with the southwest monsoons in summer, missing the Maldives.[4] From the historical background of the islands it is clear that vessels from Arabia, India and China visited them regularly to trade in dried fish, money cowrie (*Cypraea moneta*), ambergris, tortoiseshell, fish, coconuts and coir. This trade was witnessed by Ibn Batuta on his second visit to the islands at the end of 1346, and Pyrard in 1602.[5] The islanders traded with Calcutta and Sri Lanka in their own vessels, chiefly to import rice. Bell refers to the thriving trade in money cowrie. From the ninth century money cowries had been regularly exported to India, Arabia, Africa, and other places to be utilised both as an easy medium of exchange as well as for ornament.

3. P-Y Manguin, 'Pre-Modern Southeast Asian shipping in the Indian Ocean: the Maldives connection', in New Directions in Maritime History Conference, International Commission of Maritime History (Fremantle December 1993).

4. A D W Forbes, 'Southern Arabia and the Islamicization of the central Indian Ocean archipelago', *Archipel*. 21(1941), pp55–92.

5. H C P Bell, *The Maldive Islands: monograph on the history, archaeology and epigraphy*, Ceylon Government Press (Colombo 1940); A Gray and H C P Bell, *The Voyage of François Pyrard of Laval to the East Indies, the Maldives, the Moluccas and Brasil*, Hakluyt Society (London 1887).

As late as the seventeenth and eighteenth centuries they attracted serious commercial attention even from the Dutch in Ceylon. The Maldivian success in tuna fishing depended on access to adequate quantities of the bait fish which are plentiful in the region. The Maldivians developed their vessels specifically for their fishing activities.

The historical references to Maldivian shipbuilding are diverse. The earliest dateable reference is Alberuni (AD 1030) who noted that coir was used to fasten the planks of their ships. Likewise, Ibn Batuta, who visited the Maldives in AD 1343–4 and 1346, noted that coir was used to fasten the planks of boats in the Maldives, India and Yemen and that '. . . for the Indian Sea is full of rocks, and if a ship joined with iron bolts strikes a rock, it is broken up; but when it is fastened with this cord it has elasticity and does not break.'[6] Ma Huan who visited the Maldives in 1413 and 1421 was the first to refer to wooden pegs or dowels: '. . . they never use nails; they merely bore the holes, and always use their [coir] ropes to bind [the planks] together, employing wooden pegs in addition; afterwards, they smear the seams with indigenous pitch; no water can leak in.' Similarly, Correa described Maldivian craft taken in 1503 on the Indian coast near Culicut: '. . . they were made of coconut-tree timber assembled with wooden pegs, without any [iron nails] and the sails . . .'. Barbosa elaborates on the fact that the Maldivians '. . . build many great ships of palm trunks, sewn together with thread, for they have no other timber . . .'.[7] Witsen, in his naval architectural treatise of 1671, wrote that the planks were made of coconut wood and fastened with wooden nails and sewn together with coir.

There is reference to dowels being used on Maldivian vessels in 1854. Henry Coleman Folkard notes:

> The vessels used by the Maldive islanders are of very ancient appearance, and have many peculiarities, no other vessels being built of the same material; they are constructed chiefly of cocoa-nut wood, there being no other in the islands suitable for the purposes of naval architecture. The planking is pegged together with hard wooden pegs: the large boats are particularly strong.[8]

So it seems that there was a gradual transition from sewing to dowelling, and today, the only vestige of sewing is the semi-decorative lashing

The thwart structure of a Maldivian dhoni. (Jeremy Green)

at the bow. There appears to be no recollection by any of the present-day shipbuilders of a sewing tradition, in spite of the fact that the Maldivian verb used for building a ship is to 'to bind or sew'. The transition from sewing to dowelling can be seen in an earlier stage in Oman (see below), where sewing is still used on the stem and sternpost and where the through-beams penetrate the outside of the hull; elsewhere the hull is fastened with diagonal dowels.

In addition, parallels for the lugs and thwart beams in Maldivian boats need to be sought. It could be that the lugs are a modification of those found in the lashed-lug construction of Southeast Asia (see the Butuan Boats below). Single lugs of this general type occur in the Solo region of the Philippines, and locating lugs have been noted on a Bajau *lippa* in Tawi Tawi in the Sulu Archipelago, Philippines.

The *yatra dhoni* of Sri Lanka

In Sri Lanka there exists a number of unique sewn vessels: the *madel oruwa*, *madel paruwa* and the *yatra dhoni*, or *maha oru*, meaning 'big outrigger canoe'. The first two vessels, which are still widely used for beach seine fishing, have been described extensively in recent years by Kapitän and Kentley and Gunaratne respectively.[9] No example of the *yatra* now exists, the last example having been wrecked in the Maldives in the 1930s. Hornell stated that the *yatra* ranged up to about 30m in length, but were normally about 15–18m, carried 25–75 tons of cargo, and usually averaged about 50

tons. Mookerji mentions *yatra dhonis* being about 18m in length with a beam of about 5m. They are sewn craft, planked from domba (*Callophyllum inophyllum*), at least 50mm thick. In recent times the *yatra dhoni* was used as a coastal trader and for voyages to India and the Maldives.[10]

A model of a *yatra dhoni* was recently examined and documented in the Maritime Museum in Galle, Sri Lanka by Vosmer. This model had originally been in the Kumarakanda Vihara at

6. A Gray and H C P Bell, *The Voyage of François Pyrard of Laval to the East Indies, the Maldives, the Moluccas and Brasil*, Hakluyt Society (London 1887), p444.

7. P-Y Manguin, 'Pre-Modern Southeast Asian shipping in the Indian Ocean: the Maldives connection', in New Directions in Maritime History Conference, International Commission of Maritime History (Fremantle December 1993).

8. H C Folkard, *The Sailing Boat: a description of English and foreign boats, their varieties of rig, and practical directions for sailing* (London 1854), p259.

9. G Kapitän, 'Records of native craft in Sri Lanka', *International Journal of Nautical Archaeology* 16/2 (1987), pp135-147, 17/3 (1988), pp223-235, 18/2 (1989), pp137-149, 20/1 (1991), pp23-32; E Kentley and R Gunaratne, 'The *Madel Paruwa* – a sewn boat with chine strakes', *International Journal of Nautical Archaeology* 16/1 (1987), pp35–48.

10. J Hornell, 'The origins and ethnological significance of Indian boat designs', *Memoirs of the Asiatic Society of Bengal* 7 (1920), and 'Fishing and coastal craft of Ceylon', *The Mariner's Mirror* 29/1 (1943), pp30–53; R K Mookerji, *Indian Shipping: A History of the Sea-borne Trade and Maritime Activity of the Indians from the Earliest Times.* (Bombay 1957); V Vitharana, *The oru and the yatra. Traditional out-rigger water craft of Sri Lanka* (Dehiwala 1992).

A model of the large Sri Lankan yatra dhoni *at the Maritime Museum in Galle. The constructional detail and the care with which the work was executed suggest that the modelmaker may have been a practising boat-builder.* (Patrick Baker)

Arabian Gulf and India. Planking is fastened to the frames with nails roved on the inside. The frame timbers are large but relatively few for any vessel. The total sectional area of all the frames, however, is more than adequate for strength. With the exception of the pairs of bollard timbers near bow and stern, the frames are continuous, all crossing the keel and running from sheer to sheer.

The beams are also large in section, few in number (seven) and protrude through the sides of the hull. It is presumed that the edge of the planking is slotted into them in order to lock them into place, though this cannot be discerned on the model.

A large outrigger is fitted on the port and windward side of the vessel (according to the set of the sails). The use of an outrigger is curious on a vessel which appears to possess a rather stable hull-to-rig relationship. Hydrostatic analysis of this hull form by Vosmer showed it to be a reasonably seaworthy vessel even without the outrigger.[11] It thus appears that the port side was intended to be always to windward and therefore for trading voyages it would need to utilise the monsoons. Alternatively, the sea breeze could be worked

the port of Dodanduva. It is said to be over a hundred years old and to have been constructed by a boat-builder, since it exhibited the hallmarks of his care. For example, it was noted that the four hooked scarph joints in the keel-stem and sternpost structure were made with tiny locking wedges exactly as they would have been on the real vessel. Other elements were also executed with attention to detail: the frame fastenings were roved on the inside, the sewing together of the planks was detailed, and the general finish of the components was of high quality. In view of this attention to detail, it was thought that the accuracy of the model, both in scale and detail, would make a fairly reliable source for documentation.

The hull is double-ended, with slack bilges but full mid-sections. The forward sections are only just slightly more fine than the aft sections, displaying a subtle hollow entry at the bow. The forefoot is extended forward by a gripe attached to the keel-stem and there is also a skeg aft to which the rudder is fitted. Both these devices would be aids to lateral stability,

helping to reduce leeway and balancing the helm while sailing. It should be noted that at least one drawing of a *yatra* does not show these additions.

The carvel-planked hull comprises wide planks sewn together (up to the level of the deck) along their edges. The bulk of the sewing is on the outside of the hull, a practice common to Sri Lanka but unusual in sewn craft of the

11. T Vosmer, 'The *Yatra dhoni* of Sri Lanka', *Bulletin of the Australian Institute for Maritime Archaeology* 17/2 (1993), pp37–42.

A Sri Lankan madel paruwa *on the beach at Galle. The type is a form of extended logboat, the original carved log being split longitudinally and the two halves employed as chine strakes with a number of flat strakes between. The sewn nature of the structure is readily apparent.* (Jeremy Green)

Sri Lankan oruwas *on the beach at Kalutara. They are essentially dugouts with the addition of flat washstrakes.* (Patrick Baker)

during the day to move northward along the western coast, while the southward journey could use the land breeze at night. Voyages to the Maldives could be accomplished in similar fashion, by using the monsoon winds at appropriate seasons.

The vessel is rigged as a ketch with square-headed lugsails and a jib set on a short bowsprit, a rig common to the region of the Indian subcontinent. The arrangement of the halyards was such that they prevent the mizzen yard from passing around the forward side of the mast. It must therefore be concluded that the mizzen sail on the *yatra* was never tacked, but went aback against the mast when occasionally on a starboard tack. It has been suggested that the *yatra* is a derivative of the types of vessel illustrated on the Borobudur ship carvings.

Several traditional boats are still built in Sri Lanka; these include the *oruwa* and the *madel paruwa*.[12] The *oruwa*, in its various forms, is a dugout log with two parallel sided washstrakes built up vertically along the slot of the dugout. The washstrakes are closed at each end and only allow a narrow access for the boatman to stand up. The dugout is stabilised with a single outrigger; the vessels are sewn and although effective for fishing are technologically primitive. The *madel paruwa* is also a sewn boat, but in this case the log of the dugout is split longitudinally to form two chine strakes with a number of sewn planks on the bottom to separate the chines. Again the sides are built up vertically and overall the vessel looks like an extremely primitive landing craft. It is the logical technological progression from the *oruwa* and would possibly be the precursor to the *yatra dhoni*.

In March 1992, a three-week maritime archaeology training and research programme was conducted in Galle, under the auspices of the Archaeology Department of Sri Lanka and in conjunction with the Post-Graduate Institute for Archaeology. In January 1993 a second season was carried out. The objective of the course was to provide an introduction to maritime archaeology and conservation to a range of archaeologists and conservators. The research programme involved a survey of Galle Harbour and concentrated on a number of sites. One site around a large iron wreck had for some time produced a range of material (mostly local, Chinese and European ceramics) dating from about the fourteenth century to

modern times. The objective of the survey was to determine the origins of this material and to determine if the site represented harbour jettison or a number of discrete shipwreck sites. Since Galle has a long history as a port and that ships were unloaded by lightering, there were a complex array of alternative hypotheses. Surface sampling from 1m grid squares was made at distances up to 30m from the site at selected points around the main iron wreck. At present the data is being analysed and it is too early to draw any firm conclusions. A detailed description of this work will be presented by Vosmer. In addition two wooden wrecks were examined and recorded (both early nineteenth-century European) and one cannon site. The latter site is of great interest as a large bronze bell was found with the inscription 'Amor Vincit Omnia Anno 1625'. This is almost certainly a ship's bell and is probably from an early seventeenth-century Dutch East Indiaman.[13]

Butuan Boats

The Butuan Boats represent an important part of the understanding of Southeast Asian shipbuilding technology. These vessels have a lashed-lug construction which have parallels in other parts of Southeast Asia, particularly in archaeological finds in Malaysia and Sumatra. The technique is still found in the Moluccan and Solar Archipelago and the Solomon Islands, and also has parallels in Europe.[14]

Nine boat sites have been discovered around Bancasi, Libertad, in the Butuan area of Mindanao. Three have been excavated: Butuan

1, now on display in Libertad City, Mindanao; Butuan 2, now on display in the National Museum, Manila; and Butuan 5, in the Butuan Region X Museum, Mindanao.[15]

The remains of Butuan 1 comprises a keel, a wing stem, two strakes on one side, one strake on the other and some fragments. The dowels

12. G Kapitän, 'Records of native craft in Sri Lanka'; E Kentley and R Gunaratne, 'The *Madel Paruwa* – a sewn boat with chine strakes'.

13. J N Green and S Devendra, 'Interim report on the joint Sri Lanka-Australian maritime archaeology training and research programme, 1992-3', *International Journal of Nautical Archaeology* 22/4 (1993), pp331-43; and *Maritime Archaeology in Sri Lanka: the Galle Harbour Project 1992* (Colombo, Sri Lanka 1995).

14. Sumatra: I H N Evans, 'Notes on the remains of an old boat found at Pontian', *Journal of the Federated Malay States Museum* 12 (1927), pp93-6; C A Gibson-Hill, 'Further notes on the old boat found at Pontian, in Southern Pahang', *Journal (Malay Branch) Royal Asiatic Society* 25/1 (1952), pp111-13; and P-Y Manguin, 'Late Medieval Asian shipbuilding in the Indian Ocean', *Moyen Orient & Ocean Indien* 2/2 (1985), pp1-30. Société d'Histoire de l'Orient, Paris.

The Solomon Islands: Burningham, personal communication; and G Horridge, *Lashed-lug Boats of the Eastern Archipelagoes*, National Maritime Museum Monographs 5 (Greenwich 1982); parallels in Europe, J Hornell, 'Constructional parallels in Scandinavian and Oceanic boat construction', *The Mariner's Mirror* 21 (1946), pp 411-427.

15. O V Abinion, 'The recovery of the 12th century wooden boats in the Philippines', *The Bulletin of the Australian Institute for Maritime Archaeology* 13/2 (1989), pp1-2; J T Peralta, 'Ancient mariners of the Philippines', *Archaeology* 33/5 (1980), pp41-48; W P Ronquillo, 'Highlights of Philippine prehistory: 1986', *SPAFA Digest* 8/1 (1987), pp22-6; W P Ronquillo, 'The Butuan archaeological finds: profound implications for Philippines and Southeast Asian prehistory', *Man and Culture in Oceania* 3 (1987, special issue), pp71-8.

The remains of the Butuan 1 boat-find on display at the museum in Libertad City, Mindanao, Philippines. (Jeremy Green)

are counter-pegged at every alternate dowel, except at the wing stem where they pegged at every dowel. The strakes are broad at the centre and the overall length of the remains is about 13m. The keel plank is interesting because, except at the narrow end, it has lugs in sets (transversely) of three; the outer two have been drilled to take the lashings, the middle one apparently to act as a support. All the other strakes have single lugs. There are three lashing holes on nearly all of the lugs, two of the holes being equidistant from the ends of the lug, and the third hole (possibly having been drilled later) is spaced at an equal distance to the separation of the symmetrically placed holes.

Butuan 2 is the best preserved of the three vessels.[16] The remains consist of a keel and two strakes on one side and five strakes on the other. The remains suggest there were at least fourteen sets of lugs cut into each strake and the keel and set in rows across the vessel. The lugs were rectangular (40mm x 300mm x 30mm on the keel and about 115mm x 300mm on the strakes) except for the keel lugs which were double. Each lug had two pairs of lashing holes and in many cases the original fibre could still be seen in the holes. There were some small remains of a frame or frames, but badly degraded. The dowels were set about 129mm apart without locking pins. An elaborate scarph joint system was noted at one end of the ship which ended in a complex stem or sternpost (at this time it is still uncertain which was the bow and which was the stern of these vessels). At the other end, the strakes taper to a fine point. The lugs on the strakes were aligned across the hull, although there was a lot of variation in the size of the lugs and their separation. It was noted that the dowelling pattern for all the strakes showed that the dowels were arranged in a pattern of six, possibly reflecting that a template was used to mark the holes.

16. P Clark, E Conese, J N Green, and N Nicholas, 'Philippines archaeological site survey, February 1988', *International Journal of Nautical Archaeology* 18/3 (1989), pp 255–262; P Clark, J N Green, T Vosmer, and R Santiago, 'The Butuan Two Boat known as a balangay in the National Museum, Manila, Philippines', *International Journal of Nautical Archaeology* 22/2 (1993), pp143–160; J N Green, T Vosmer, P Clark, R Santiago, M Alveres, 'Interim report on the Joint Australian–Philippines Butuan Boat Project, October 1992', *International Journal of Nautical Archaeology* 23 (1994).

An example of surviving shell-first construction employed for a boat in the Sulu Archipelago.

The remaining timbers of Butuan 5 are fairly degraded, with only a few of the planks in good condition. Those frames that remain are generally in better condition than the planking. The vessel was probably about 13m in length, though the longest remaining portion, the keel, is about only 11.5m. There are remains of eight planks on one side of the vessel and seven on the other. The planks vary in thickness from 30mm to 45mm. The maximum thickness at the lugs is 80mm, but is usually about 60–75mm. The planking is edge-joined with dowels of approximately 12mm diameter, spaced about 200mm apart. The dowels extend more than half way through the width of the plank. The relative position of dowels on opposite sides of the plank strakes are staggered slightly. The dowels on each side of the lugs are counter-pegged with hardwood locking pins, square in section and slightly tapered. In the midships part of the boat, where there is a large space between lugs, every third dowel is pegged. On plank number 8, the lugs are different from the others, being carved in a triangular cross-sectional shape. Unlike the other lugs, these triangular section lugs have no lashing holes. This was the last, or highest, strake remaining on the site, but the presence of dowels on the upper edge indicates that this was not the highest strake. Most lugs show slight compression of the timber at the frame lashing positions. In some lugs, a slightly raised ridge running across the lug about midway between the lashing holes was noted.

Remains of another unusual plank, thought to be number 7, were also noted. This strake has a continuous raised portion, similar to the keel,

Part of the Song dynasty scroll Qing ming shang he tu *painted by Zhang ze Duan about 1125; it shows river junks near Kaifeng and may provide some idea of the appearance of the Quanzhou ship.*

but off centre, and lugs pierced with lashing holes. The strake also has a series of notches cut in it between the lugs, perhaps to hold beams or uprights. The continuous raised portion certainly could have functioned as a wale, but may have been a beam shelf. The keel is a narrow plank with a raised lug running its full length. This carinate or ridged keel is different from keel planks found on the other excavated Butuan boats, numbers 1 and 2. Presumably this continuous raised lug not only serves as a frame lashing structure, but also – and primarily – increases the stiffness of the keel and decreases any tendency for the vessel to hog.

Shipwreck sites in China

A series of papers has been published in Chinese by the Museum of Overseas Communication describing the excavation and the subsequent analysis of the Quanzhou ship. These include Song Shipwreck Committee (1975), Museum of Overseas Communication (1987) and a variety of articles in *Haijiaoshi Yanjiu*. Surprisingly little has been published outside China: Salmon and Lombard (1979) published a French summary of the *Wen Wu* articles of the Song Shipwreck Committee (1975) and Green (1983) and Li Guo-Qing (1989) have produced reports on the ship.

The hull is now completely rebuilt, with some minor modern additions to the damaged bow section and bulkheads. The remains, measuring 24m long by 9m wide, consist of the keel, part of the transom, twelve bulkheads and the sides of the ship up to, and slightly beyond the turn of the bilge (fourteen strakes on the port and sixteen strakes on the starboard side). It is thought that the ship was originally 34m long, 11m wide and had a displacement of around 380 tonnes.

The keel is made of pine and is constructed in three parts. The fore and aft parts slope upwards (the fore part more than the after), and are scarphed longitudinally to the central part. In the vertical faces of both scarph joints, seven bronze coins and a bronze mirror were found. This is a *baosongkong* or longevity symbol – the coins were set in such a way as to represent the constellation of Ursa Major, and the mirror is thought to represent the moon. The *baosongkong* have Daoist significance, bringing either good luck and fair winds, or representing the Seven Star Ocean where there are many dangerous rocks; the mirror is there to reflect light and ensure a safe journey. This tradition still continues today in modern shipbuilding, the stars represented by nails and the moon by a silver coin. A square-sectioned rabbet is cut on either side of the keel to accept the garboard strake. The hull is double planked up to the beginning of the turn of the bilge, where it becomes triple planked. The planking is made of cedar, constructed in an exceedingly complex manner in a mixture of carvel and clinker design.

In order to describe this structure adequately, some liberties have to be taken with regard to conventional Western shipbuilding terms. Inner or inside refers to the surface or side facing the interior of the hull; conversely, outer or outside refers to the side facing the water. Upper refers to the part (edge or strake) away from the keel, lower refers to the part towards the keel. Carvel joint (as in the conventional definition): the edge-joint between two adjacent strakes is a flat butt-joint cut at right angles to the surface of the strakes, producing a smooth (carvel) surface on the inside and outside of the hull. Rabbeted carvel joint (unconventional definition): the edge-joint between two adjacent strakes is rabbeted along

The Song dynasty ship on display in Quanzhou museum.
(Jeremy Green)

the whole of the strake joint by a type of lap-joint. Clinker joint (as in the conventional definition): the strakes overlap one another, so that (in this case) the upper strake overlaps the lower strake on the outer surface, the jointing surface being between the outer and inner faces of the strakes. This type of joint produces a discontinuity in both the inside and outside surfaces of the hull of the ship. Rabbeted clinker joint (unconventional definition): in this case a rabbet is cut in the inside of the lower edge of the strake; the upper (uncut) edge of the lower strake in this rabbet, giving an external appearance of a clinker joint, but the thickness of the step between the strakes at the surface is reduced by the depth of the rabbet. It should be noted that a similar type of joint has been found on the Shinan ship, but in this case, the rabbet was cut out of the inside upper strake, and the upper surface of the lower strake was cut square and fitted into the rabbet.[17]

The inner planking is made of cedar and is 80mm thick; the lower edge of the garboard strake is rabbeted so that the strake lies against the horizontal surface of the keel rabbet and a short part of the vertical face of the keel. Starting from the garboard strake of the inner

planking, the first three strakes have carvel joints, the rabbets being cut in the outer edge of the lower strake and the inner edge of the upper strake. The third and fourth strakes are joined with a rabbeted clinker joint. This system of two rabbeted carvel and one rabbeted clinker joints continues for sixteen strake joints. Each rabbeted clinker joint on the inner surface of the hull has a strip or lath of wood set over the top of the joint to seal it. The outer planking is 50mm thick and is carvel joined, the planking being irregularly nailed with light nails to the inner planking. The garboard strake of the outer planking butts up against the keel, with an additional plank attached to the vertical surface of the keel forming a type of sheathing. The rabbeted clinker joint on the inner planking is cut so that the thickness of the projection of the strake on the outside is 50mm. This allows the strake edge of the outer planking to form a carvel joint. The next strake of the outer planking is then attached with a clinker joint. It could be said that the outer planking becomes the inner planking, and the whole arrangement is a type of mixed clinker-carvel construction. A third layer of planking is applied to the hull at the fourth clinker joint on the outer planking, at the turn of the bilge. This planking is 25mm thick and is carvel

joined, continuing for five strakes to the edge of the hull remains. The author's impression was that this planking was the same thickness as the second layer of planking, but it was not possible to measure this.

There are twelve bulkheads creating thirteen compartments roughly equal in size, the two aftermost compartments being slightly smaller than the rest. The bulkheads are formed by a series of cedar planks, edge joined with a similar type of rabbeted carvel joint as the inner hull planking. The lowest plank of every bulkhead, except for the aftermost and forwardmost bulkheads, has a waterway cut in it. All the bulkhead joints were sealed with luting. Some of the longer planks in the upper sections of the bulkheads are made in two parts, with a scarph joint.

On the aft sides of the bulkheads forward of the mast step, and on the forward sides of the bulkheads aft of the mast step, are heavy wooden frames. These are half-frames, not floors, and extend up to about the fourteenth strake. It is not known if there were subsequent futtocks nor is there any clear evidence for scarphs on the frames. The frames have a waterway cut in them, to match the waterways of the bulkheads. The frames are in a much poorer state of preservation than the rest of the hull, and as a result it has not been possible to identify the species of wood they are made from. The transom is flat, inclined outwards, and is constructed in two layers. The inner layer consists of horizontal planks, while the outer layer is a series of thick blocks of camphor wood. In these blocks is cut a round vertical groove which takes the (missing) axial rudder. This method of mounting the rudder allows the rudder to be raised or lowered without affecting its operation, and is a common Chinese tradition. The outer layer of the triple planking extends outwards beyond the transom, indicating that there was a type of counter projecting over the stern.

The fore and main mast steps were set on the keel, against the forward side of a bulkhead (the

Midships cross-section showing the unusual carvel-clinker planking of the Quanzhou ship.

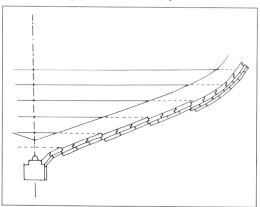

Sketch of the keel and garboard strake, with a detail of the complex plank joint, of the Quanzhou ship.

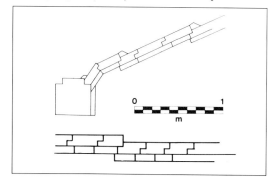

17. J N Green, 'The Song Dynasty shipwreck at Quanzhou, Fujian Province, People's Republic of China', *International Journal of Nautical Archaeology* 12/3 (1983), pp253–61; 'Two season's excavation of the Ko Kradat wrecksite, Thailand: conclusions', *Oriental Art* 29 (1983), pp59-68; 'The Shinan excavation: an interim report on the hull structure', *International Journal of Nautical Archaeology* 12/4 (1983), pp293-301; 'The Ko Si Chang excavation report, 1983', *Bulletin of the Australian Institute for Maritime Archaeology* 7/2 (1983),pp9-37; 'In search of Khubila Khan's lost fleet', *Geo Magazine* 5/4 (1983), pp58-69.

Left: Details of the bulkheads in the Song dynasty ship in Quanzhou museum. (Jeremy Green)

Lower left: The after end of the Song dynasty ship in Quanzhou museum. (Jeremy Green)

were also attached to the hull by an unusual type of iron fastening. This consisted of a flat bar which was bent at right angles at one end to form an L-shape. The bar was mounted through the inner planking and set against the opposite side of the bulkhead to the frames. The strap had four or five holes on its long side, through which it was attached with nails to the bulkhead. The short angle, flush with the outside of the inner planking, had a single hole through which it was fastened with a nail to the hull. These straps or *ju*-nails appeared to be placed so that they were centrally located on each plank of the bulkhead and are described by Li Guo-Qing and Xu Yingfan.[20]

In addition to the Quanzhou ship a further site has been excavated at Fa Shui near the city of Quanzhou. The Fa Shui ship is constructed using rather unusual wooden stiffeners. Essentially these stiffeners duplicate the func-

18. Song Shipwreck Committee, 'The Song Dynasty shipwreck excavated at Quanzhou harbour: i. The excavation; ii. History of the port of Quanzhou; iii. Naval construction during the Song Dynasty; iv. The reconstruction of the ship after recovery', *Wen Wu* 10 (1975), pp1–34.

19. J N Green and R Harper, *The Excavation of the Pattaya Wreck site and Survey of Three Other Sites, Thailand 1982*, Australian Institute for Maritime Archaeology, Special Publication No 1 (Fremantle 1983), p40.

20. Li Guo-Qing, 'Archaeological evidence for the use of 'chu-nam' on the 13th century Quanzhou ship, Fujian Province, China', *International Journal of Nautical Archaeology* 18/4 (1989), pp277–83; and Xu Yingfan, 'Origin and technique of "gua-ju" (iron cramp) connections in wooden craft construction', *Special of Ship Engineering Marine History Research Transactions of CSNAME – Marine History Research Group No 1* (Shanghai, China 1985).

Sketch of the iron fastenings attaching the bulkheads to the inner hull planking of the Song dynasty ship.

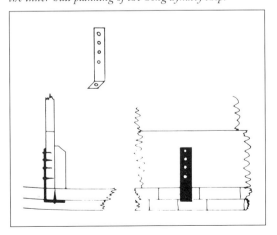

fore mast against the first bulkhead, the main mast against the sixth bulkhead). Both steps had two square sockets to take the partners of a tabernacle mast housing. The Song Shipwreck Committee report indicates that the main mast step was also braced against the forward bulkhead by two beams running parallel to and on either side of the keel.[18] This method of stepping a mast is common in the East and is discussed in Green and Harper.[19]

A square section was cut out of the upper remaining (fifth) plank of the bulkhead forward of the main mast step (bulkhead five). This, it was suggested, allowed the mast to be lowered. If this was the case, it is interesting to speculate briefly on how this was done. The first question is where did the mast pivot? It could either be from the step or from the deck. In the former case, the mast (which would lower forwards) could not be lowered completely since it would

rest on the cut-out section of the bulkhead. In the latter case, the mast would lower completely aft. From a simple inspection of the plan it is clear that the former situation is the case, simply because the height of the mast from the step to the deck is over twice the width between the bulkheads.

Iron appears to have been the main fastening material and wooden treenails have not been reported. The edge joints of the rabbeted inner planking were nailed diagonally from the outside through the joint. The outer layers of planking were nailed onto the inner planking. The rabbeted joins on the bulkheads were also nailed diagonally, but it was also reported that they were edge-joined with round iron dowels. No evidence for this was noted, and there appears to be only evidence for diagonal nailing. The strakes were fixed to the edges of the bulkheads with iron nails. The bulkheads

The 1:5 scale model of the remains of the Shinan ship in Mokpo Conservation Laboratories. (Jeremy Green)

tion of the iron *ju*-nails used in the Quanzhou ship. They also appear in the Shinan ship (below). The ship was partially excavated, the remaining unexcavated section lying under a modern-day house. The site has not been fully published but is referred to by Xu Yingfan.

Another buried ship was found at the wharf site at Ningbo. This site contains a vessel, of which the stern part is missing, that was originally about 13m long, and is thought to date from the Song Dynasty.[21] It consists of seven bulkheads, a main and fore mast step, eight strakes on the port side and four strakes on the starboard. The keel is comprised of three parts, scarphed together, with an attached stempost and with *baosongkong* or longevity holes with coins, similar to the Quanzhou ship.

Clark and Wei have reported briefly on a survey and excavation at Dinghai, Fujian where three sites were surveyed and one site (Bai Jiao) was investigated in detail.[22]

Shipwreck sites in Korea

The excavation and finds of the Shinan ship have been discussed by a number of authors – Ayres, Hahn, Keith, Keith & Buys, National Museum of Korea, Valenstein and Zaine – the discussion being centred mainly around the immense ceramic collection, which to date numbers some 16,000 items.[23] Excavation took place between 1976 and 1982, by which time the main part of the cargo had been recovered and work had commenced on the excavation of the hull. Since then the whole of the ship has been dismantled and raised, and is now undergoing conservation treatment at the Mokpo Conservation and Restoration Centre of the Cultural Property Research Institute. A number of reports have been published relating to the hull structure,[24] and a 1:5 scale model of the vessel has been constructed.[25] The site is now dated by a wooden cargo tag with the date 1323 and the last date for the coins of 1310 (there were 26.8 tonnes totalling over seven

million brass-bronze coins, the earliest date for the coins being AD 14).[26]

The remains of the ship include the keel,

21. Lin Shimin, Du Genqui and J N Green, 'Waterfront excavations at Dongmenkou, Ningbo, Zhe Jiang Province, PRC', *International Journal of Nautical Archaeology* 20/4 (1991), p299–311.

22. P Clark and Zhang Wei, 'A preliminary survey of wreck sites in the Dinghai area, Fujian Province, China', *International Journal of Nautical Archaeology* 19/3 (1990), p239–241.

23. J Ayres, 'The discovery of the Yän ship at Sinan, South West Korea', *Oriental Art* 24/1 (1978), pp79–85; D H Keith, 'A fourteenth century shipwreck at Sinan-Gun. Sunken archaeological treasure in the Yellow Sea', *Archaeology* 33/2 (1980), pp33–43; D H Keith and C J Buys, 'A new light on medieval Chinese seagoing ship construction', *International Journal of Nautical Archaeology* 10/2 (1981), pp119–132; National Museum of Korea, *Special Exhibition of Cultural Objects found off Sinan Coast* (Korea 1977); C M Valenstein, 'The Sinan shipwreck: an early Muromachi art collection', *Oriental Art* 25/1 (1979), pp103–114.

24. Cultural Property Maintenance Office, *Shinan Seabed Relics (Information Data No 2)*, Cultural Property Maintenance Office, Ministry of Culture and Publicity (Seoul, Korea 1984); Cultural Property Research Institute, *Annual Report Mokpo Conservation and Restoration Centre, 1985*, Cultural Property Maintenance Office, Ministry of Culture and Publicity (Seoul, Korea 1986); P Hoffmann, K-n Choi and Y-h Kim, 'Technical communication, the 14th-century Shinan Ship – Progress in conservation', *International Journal of Nautical Archaeology* 20/1 (1991), pp59–64.

25. J N Green, 'The Shinan excavation: an interim report on the hull structure', *International Journal of Nautical Archaeology* 12/4 (1983), pp293–301; J N Green and Z-G Kim, 'The Shinan and Wando sites, Korea. Further information', *International Journal of Nautical Archaeology* 18/1 (1989), pp33–41.

26. Conservation Science Research Department, *Component Analysis of the Shinan Coins*, Cultural Properties Research Institute, Cultural Property Maintenance Office, Ministry of Culture and Publicity (Seoul, Korea 1986).

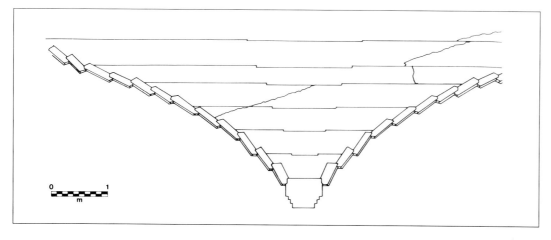

A cross-section of the Shinan ship.

A frame and bulkhead section from the Shinan ship. Note the 'clinker' construction and waterway. (Jeremy Green)

about fourteen strakes of the starboard side and six strakes of the port side of the ship, part of the pram bow and a small section of the stern transom. The vessel has seven internal bulkheads creating eight compartments. There is a fore and main mast step and structure that is possibly part of the decking of the ship. The bulkheads forward of the mast step are supported on the aft side with frames and on the forward side with stiffeners. The stiffeners are pointed wooden pegs that penetrate each strake from the outside of the hull planking, thus locating the opposite side of the bulkhead to the frames and are attached to the face of the bulkhead (these stiffeners serve the same function as the *ju*-nail described in the Quanzhou and the Fa Shui sites).

Aft of the main mast step, the reverse situation occurs. The strakes are butt-jointed. In most cases the butt-joint is a lap joint, but on the garboard strake and on at least one other place the joint is a mortise and tenon joint. On the internal face of the butt-joints there are butt plates which sit over the top of the joints and clamp them together. In some cases these butt plates are set under a frame, indicating that the frames were put in place after the completion of the planking. The strakes are rabbeted clinker construction, with the rabbet cut out of the uppermost plank, on the lower inside edge. The bulkhead floor and planks have a rebate set in the joint to locate the edge of the bulkhead. In the fore part of the ship this arrangement gradually changes to a rabbeted carvel or shiplap construction which allows a flush rabbeted joint onto the pram bow.

The research model has been built by the Mokpo Conservation and Restoration Centre at a scale of 1:5 based on measurements made of the hull timbers. This model raises a number of complex and interesting problems, although it has some limitations. Firstly, because of the poor visibility on the wreck site, it was not always possible to establish the exact orientation of the pieces, so in some cases their relationship is uncertain. Additionally, the plans of the timbers were made from individual measurements made on the timbers, but not direct 1:1 tracings. In spite of these drawbacks, the model is of great interest, and of course is just

one step in the development of a complete understanding of the structure.

One of the major curiosities that has not yet been explained is that the keel has a distinct hog, the centre being 220mm higher than the fore and aft ends. It is not certain at present if this is a feature that was incorporated into the construction of the ship, or whether it is a result of forces on the hull structure after the sinking. It is expected that further work on the research model will resolve this problem. The scarph joints in the keel have a similar arrangement to the Quanzhou ship,[27] but with coins and a mirror placed on the sloping horizontal face of the joint rather than the vertical faces, as in the Quanzhou ship.

The mast step is very interesting, showing the arrangement of the step and the three-part mast. It is possible that the orientation of the mast is wrong. The fore mast is arranged to lie against the bulkhead, while the bulkhead, it seems, has been specially angled so that it is aligned with the rake of the mast. The use of a pin to fix the base of the masts is also interesting. The way that the pram bow is attached to the keel is also not absolutely certain. However, it is double planked. A single cant frame was recovered. It is unusual because it has a series of semi-circular holes cut from the upper through to the side face of the frame. The purpose of these holes is unclear. The arrangement of the upper part of the side of the ship is also uncertain. It is thought that the structure that projects into the body of the ship is a deck of sorts. However, it has also been suggested that this may have been a coaming. Thus it is not certain if the timbers that are associated with this were separated from the main part of the hull or not. The bulwark associated with this has 150mm circular holes cut in them. It is not clear what these holes were for. They may have been scuppers or possibly holes for oars. Until the

position of the bulwark on the section of the hull is known more precisely, the function of the holes is uncertain.

The Wando ship was discovered in 1984 in southwestern Korea. The cargo of 30,000 pieces of celadon originated from a kiln in Haenam Province and are thought to date from around the second half of the eleventh century. The construction and timber species of the vessel indicates that it was built in Korea. The construction is distinctive and unusual and the original length of the vessel would have been about 9m. There is no keel, the construction employing instead five heavy longitudinal timbers (180 to 200mm thick and 300 to 350mm wide) which are pinned together with a complex series of mortise and tenon joints. The centre three planks have six mortise and tenons that run through the three planks. The two

Details of hull construction on the Shinan ship.

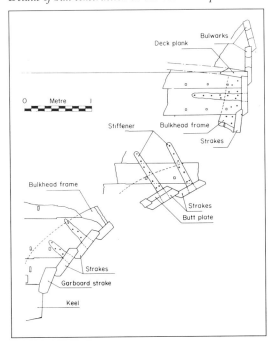

27. J N Green, 'The Song Dynasty shipwreck at Quanzhou, Fujian Province, People's Republic of China', *International Journal of Nautical Archaeology* 12/3 (1983), pp253–61.

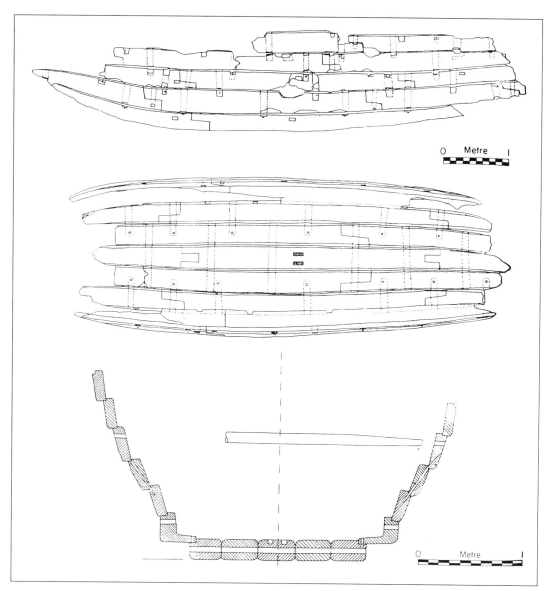

Details of the construction of the Wando ship. Top: port side planking. Middle: plan of bottom planking. Bottom: midship section.

the Mokpo Conservation Institute of Maritime Archaeological Finds.[29] The boat was a dugout vessel originally about 19m long and 2.3m broad, built in three parts, and is described as a three-piece logboat. The vessel had six bulk-heads, with a mast step in front of the third bulkhead. The vessel is thought to be Chinese because it has the *baosongkong* with coins in the holes and the timber is camphor wood, indige-nous to South China. The coins date from AD 1111–1117 and a carbon date of AD 1260–1380 is given for the timber and putty. The bow and stern sections were attached to the main body of the hull in rabbeted joints with a brace in the form of a longitudinal beam set over the joints.

Shipwrecks of the Gulf of Thailand

In 1975, a wreck site was discovered near the island of Ko Khram in the southeast of the Gulf of Thailand. The excavation of this site was the beginning of an underwater archaeology pro-gramme in Thailand. Since then a number of

28. Z G Kim, *Study of Korean Ship History* (in Korean), Korean Cultural Studies Research Institute Research Series No 24 (Seoul National University 1985); J N Green, 'The Shinan excavation: an interim report on the hull structure', *International Journal of Nautical Archaeology* 12/4 (1983), pp293–301.

29. Mokpo Conservation Institute, *Report on the excavation of the Jindo Logboat*, Mokpo Conservation Institute for Maritime Archaeological Finds (Mokpo, Korea 1993).

outer planks also have six mortise and tenons, but in this case they penetrate through the outer plank, but only partially into the outer edge of the second strakes. The side planking is attached to the bottom with chine planks. These are L-shaped planks which are rebated into the upper edge of the outer bottom plank and fastened with mortise and tenons. There are five strakes of the sides of the ship arranged in a rabbeted clinker construction. The upper edge of each strake has a rebate cut in the outer edge. The strakes are attached with mortise and tenons, the tenon being driven through the upper strake and partially in the lower. There is evidence that the third strake was penetrated with a thwart beam. All these features are asso-ciated with Korean ship construction.[28]

The Jindo logboat was excavated in 1992 by

The mast step of the Pattaya wreck showing tabernacle sockets for mast partners and waterway on either side of the keel.

The Pattaya wreck site. Top: side elevation. Bottom: plan.

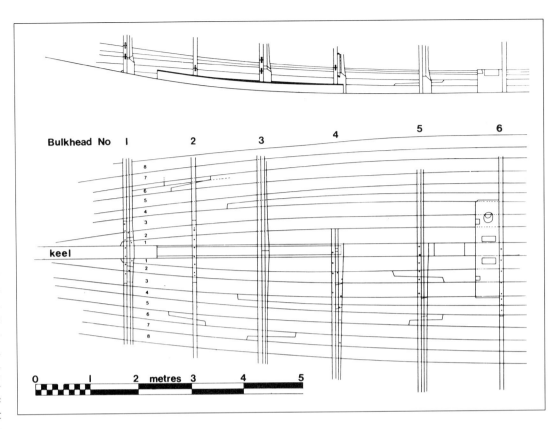

Bulkhead No 1   2   3   4   5   6

keel

0   1   2 metres 3   4   5

sites have been examined in the Gulf of Thailand; some have been completely excavated, some have only been surveyed.[30]

The Ko Khram site was excavated by a Joint Thai-Danish team from 1975 to 1977.[31] A very large quantity of Thai ceramics was recovered from the site (in excess of 5000 pieces). It has been stated that the Sukhothai and Sawankhalok ceramics account for between 60 and 75 per cent of the total ceramic cargo, the remainder probably being Vietnamese and some of an unclear origin. Sisatchanalai celadons include plates and bowls with tubular support marks on the base, jarlets, eared bottles, potiche and small bowls. Earthenware rice pots and unglazed stoneware storage jars and basins are thought to have been produced at kilns north-northwest of Lopburi. The underpainted fish and floral designed plates and bowls were produced in the Sukhothai kilns. Green glazed bowls with an unglazed ring in the inside centre are thought to be Cham. A blue and white jarlet and a saucer are thought to be Vietnamese. In 1987, the site was visited to obtain timber and ceramic samples. It was noted that the site is still remarkably intact, with no evidence of recent looting; in fact the site is one of the largest and best preserved that has been noted in the region, and certainly warrants further investigation at some future date. In a number of places the ceramic material was still stacked in rows.

The Ko Kradat wreck in Trat Province can be definitely dated by a blue and white porcelain base sherd bearing the inscription *Da Ming Jiajing Nian Zhi* ('made in the Jiajing reign of the Great Ming Dynasty' [1522-1566]). Other porcelain sherds suggest a date from the Wanli period, 1573-1619. The presence of these Chinese ceramics clearly dates the Sawankhalok products which were encapsulated together with the porcelain at the time of the wreck, indicating that the Sawankhalok kilns must have been producing in the mid sixteenth century, with strong evidence for the latter half of the century. Ceramics which can be definitely attributed to Sawankhalok include small cover boxes with a thin glaze fusing the base to the lid, indicating that the article had never been used and had probably come straight from the kiln.[32]

The Pattaya site consists of a 9m length of the hull with a maximum width of 4.5m with six bulkheads together with eight strakes on either side of the keel. The hull profile had a marked V-shape next to the keel. This flattened out,

finishing in an upward curve at the turn of the bilge. Here, obviously, the continuing sides of the ship had broken away and disintegrated. The keel consisted of a large, apparently single timber, 300mm wide, with 45-degree bevels on the upper edges, giving an upper keel surface of 200mm. The planking consisted of three layers – the inner was 70mm thick, whilst the second and third layers were 40mm thick. The garboard strake of the inner layer of planking was attached to the bevel on the upper part of the keel by a series of dowels, 20mm in diameter, spaced 160mm apart. It was noted that the strake scarph joints all occur under bulkheads and do not have any logical system to them.

Traces of six bulkheads were found on the site. The bulkheads consist of two components: the bulkheads themselves and a lightly constructed, bevelled frame, locating and securing the bulkhead to the hull. In all cases, the bulkhead frames were on the side of the bulkhead nearest midships. The bulkhead consisted of a number of parallel planks 70mm thick, dowelled together with round pegs in the same manner as the strakes of the hull planking. The ends of the planks were shaped so that they fitted flush with the hull planking, and appeared to be lightly nailed to the planking at the narrow ends. There was no evidence of dowels being used to join the bulkheads to the hull. The lowest bulkhead plan is regular in section, lying symmetrically over the keel. The extreme ends of the planks were also trimmed

in the same way as the scarph-joint of the planks.

The waterways consisted of two circular

30. J N Green and R Harper, *The Maritime Archaeology of Shipwrecks and Ceramics in Southeast Asia*, Australian Institute for Maritime Archaeology Special Publication No 4 (1987).

31. R Brown, 'Preliminary report on the Ko Khram sunken ship', *Oriental Art*, 24/1 (1975), pp356-70; R Brown, *The Ceramics of Southeast Asia, their Dating and Identification*, Oxford University Press (Kuala Lumpur 1977); J N Green, 'Further light on the Koh Khram wrecksite', *Transactions of the S.E. Asian Ceramic Society* 8 (1981), pp18-26; P C Howitz, 'Two ancient shipwrecks from the Gulf of Siam. A report on archaeological excavations', *Journal of the Siam Society* 65 (1977), pp1–22; P C Howitz, *The Research into the Old Sailing Ships Wrecks which are found in the Gulf of Thailand* (in Thai), Special publication (Bangkok 1978); J N Green and R Harper, 'Maritime archaeology in Thailand – seven shipwrecks', in W Jeffery and J Amess (eds), *Proceedings of the 2nd Southern Hemisphere Conference on Maritime Archaeology*, South Australian Dept Environment and Planning and Commonwealth Dept of Home Affairs and Environment (Adelaide 1983), pp153-174; K Atkinson, J N Green, R Harper and V Intakosai, 'Joint Thai-Australian underwater archaeological project 1987-88. Part 1: Archaeological survey of wreck sites in the Gulf of Thailand, 1987-1988', *International Journal of Nautical Archaeology* 18/4 (1989), pp299–315.

32. J N Green, R Harper and S Prishanchittara, *The Excavation of the Ko Kradat Wreck Site: Thailand 1979–80*, Report - Department of Maritime Archaeology, Western Australian Maritime Museum: No17 (Fremantle 1980); J N Green and R Harper, 'The excavation of the Ko Kradat wreck site, Thailand', *International Journal of Nautical Archaeology* 11/2 (1982), pp164-71; P C Howitz, 'Two ancient shipwrecks from the Gulf of Siam. A report on archaeological excavations', *Journal of the Siam Society* 65 (1977), pp1–22.

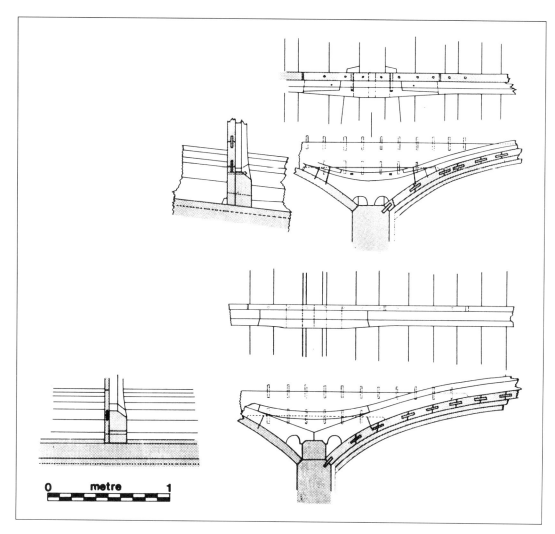

Bulkheads from the Pattaya wreck site showing dowel construction. Top: bulkhead 1. Bottom: bulkhead 3.

with lime remains and a stirrer), wooden bungs, sappanwood (also recovered from the *Risdam* site), musket stock and a grindstone.[34]

The Ko Si Chang 2 site is interesting because the ceramics from the site are complex and include material thought to originate from Thailand, southern China and a small group of uncertain origin. Also recovered was a portion of an oriental style oven. Metal objects include a square lead ingot and a Chinese cash coin. The survey of the hull of the Ko Si Chang 2 site showed some unusual features not previously encountered on vessels in the Gulf of Thailand. Firstly, the ship's planking is joined with iron nails driven diagonally from about the middle of the inside of the hull planking, downwards through the abutting surfaces into the next strake. This method of fastening is unknown in the region; Southeast Asian fastenings of adjacent strakes are usually edge-joined dowels and Chinese and Korean are diagonal iron nails from the outside. On this site there is no doubt that in the remaining strakes, the nails are driven from the inside. This seems to be unusual, since as hull cross-sections are invariably concave, the angle at which the nail is driven will make the task more difficult from

33. J N Green and R Harper, *The Excavation of the Pattaya Wreck Site and Survey of Three Other Sites, Thailand 1982*, Australian Institute for Maritime Archaeology, Special Publication No 1 (Fremantle 1983). J N Green and V Intakosai, 'The Pattaya wreck site excavation, Thailand. An interim report', *International Journal of Nautical Archaeology* 12/1 (1983), pp3-14.

34. J N Green, 'The Ko Si Chang excavation report, 1983', *Bulletin of the Australian Institute for Maritime Archaeology* 7/2 (1983), pp9-37. J N Green, R Harper and V Intakosi, 'The Ko Si Chang One shipwreck excavation 1983-1985. A progress report', *International Journal of Nautical Archaeology* 15/2 (1986), pp105-122.

holes, 110mm in diameter, lying on either side of the keel. The frames lodge against the side of the bulkhead nearest the midships. The central frame was a floor in all cases except for bulkhead 3, where it was a half-frame. In this case the two half-frames were clamped with chocks. In all other frames, the first futtocks were scarphed to the floors. A mast step was located on the southern side of bulkhead 6. Two large rectangular holes, 110mm by 260mm, were cut 90mm deep, equidistant from the middle line, which formed the recess for the tabernacle of the mast. On the west side is a round hole 110mm in diameter which is inclined at about 50 degrees towards the centre –possibly a pump hole. A further two small notches, 90mm by 80mm, are located on the southern edge of the top surface, which were possibly for longitudinal braces. The mast step has two waterway holes similar to the other waterway holes in the other bulkheads.[33]

The Ko Si Chang 1 wreck, Chonburi

Province can be dated by a Chinese blue and white porcelain bowl bearing the inscription *Da Ming Wanli Nian Zhi* ('Made in the Great Ming Year Wanli'): Wanli reigned from 1573 to 1620. Non-ceramic items from this site include lacquer ware with a dragon motif, pyramidal-shaped lead ingots as found on the Ko Si Chang 3, Pattaya and *Risdam* sites, a copper bowl, lidded copper lime container (complete

Traditional Thai vessels called rua chalom *being used as lighters in the Chao Phraya river. Note the survival of the quarter rudders.* (Jeremy Green)

Excavation of the Ko Si Chang 3 wreck site, showing the compartments in the wreck.

the inside than the outside. There has to be an advantage to fastening in this manner, but it is not immediately obvious.

It is unfortunate that the site has suffered badly, both from the effects of trawler activity and from looters. It was reported, during a brief inspection of the site in 1985, that timbers were projecting from the seabed at an angle of about 20 degrees; this was almost certainly the result of a trawler net snagging the end timbers on the site and ripping them up. It is thus not possible to determine what happened on the strakes further up the hull. One possibility is that the vessel was flat bottomed and this method of fastening was used in this area, but changed at the chine. The two outer strakes that remain of the inner planking are narrower than the other planks and consequently the nails are driven into the plank at the outer edge.[35]

The Ko Si Chang 3 wreck, Chonburi Province was excavated in 1986 by a joint Thai-Australian-SPAFA team. Unlike many other sites, it has not suffered at the hands of looters, although trawling activities disturbed the surface to an extent. Despite this, a very accurate estimation of the quantity of the cargo and its placement could be assessed. The hull structure consisted of the keel, the planking (at the maximum, six strakes on the starboard side and five strakes on the port), the remains of nine bulkheads and the mast step. It is evident that the site, and in particular the hull structure, has been damaged by bottom-trawlers. There is also evidence that the stern part of the structure has collapsed. The keel appears to have separated at the scarph joint, causing the stern part of the keel to drop, which has resulted in the garboard strakes separating from the keel.

At the stern on the port side, the remains of six planks were discovered, lying below the main planking. These planks ran at an angle to the keel, but it is thought that they are part of the outer planking which has become detached from the inner planking. Additionally, three unusual blocks, sitting on the keel were noted. These are thought to be associated with the complex scarphing arrangement on the keel. The ship would have been slightly more than 20m long, with a beam of about 6m. Compartments were about 1.2m wide, suggesting about sixteen over the length of the ship. It seems that the ship may have been quite old at the time of the loss because of the evidence of repairs. In particular, the scarph on strake three (starboard) between bulkheads 51 and 52 shows

evidence of a repair. Also, strake two, on the port side, has two scarph joints very close together (between bulkheads 45–46 and 46–47), less than a metre apart.[36]

The Rang Kwien site was excavated by the Fine Arts Department between 1978 and 1981.[37] It had been extensively looted by sports divers, but the Fine Arts Department excavation recovered 200kg of copper coins, copper ingots, ceramics, gongs, bells, elephant tusks, and a number of other interesting items. Additionally, a large section of the hull of the ship survived, including the keel which had an unusual waterway cut out of the centre. In 1987, the survey group visited the site to recover timber samples for dating and analysis. During the visit, the keel was found to be exposed and so a series of cross-sectional measurements were made to record the keel waterway.[38]

In February 1992 the Royal Thai Navy arrested a salvage vessel operating in the country's Exclusive Economic Zone. A large quantity of ceramic material was confiscated and the vessel was ordered out of the Thai waters. This is the first time that a country in the region has arrested a vessel involved in large-scale looting.

Vietnam

A number of sites have been salvaged by treasure hunting groups with permits issued by the Vietnamese government. Flecker (1992) has reported on the recovery of a late seventeenth-century vessel off Con Dao and he concludes that from the design of the vessel it was proba-

bly a *lorcha*.[39] In addition there has been a report of a shipwreck off Phu Quock. In all cases the findings in Vietnam support the work in Thailand. The vessels seem to be traditional to this particular region. Subsequently Blake and Flecker reported another site at Phu Quock.[40] This site is extremely interesting since it has features found both in Southeast

35. J N Green and R Harper, *The Excavation of the Pattaya Wreck Site and Survey of Three Other Sites, Thailand 1982*, Australian Institute for Maritime Archaeology, Special Publication No 1 (Fremantle 1983); and 'Maritime archaeology in Thailand – seven shipwrecks,' in W Jeffery and J Amess (eds), *Proceedings of the 2nd Southern Hemisphere Conference on Maritime Archaeology*: South Australian Dept of Environment and Planning and Commonwealth Dept of Home Affairs and Environment (Adelaide 1983), pp153-174; K Atkinson, J N Green, R Harper and V Intakosai, 'Joint Thai-Australian underwater archaeological project 1987-88. Part 1: Archaeological survey of wreck sites in the Gulf of Thailand, 1987-1988', *International Journal of Nautical Archaeology* 18/4 (1989), pp299–315.

36. J N Green, R Harper and V and Intakosai, *The Ko Si Chang Three Shipwreck Excavation, 1986*, Australian Institute for Maritime Archaeology Special Publication No 4 (1987).

37. V Intakosi, 'Rang Kwien and Samed Ngam shipwrecks', *SPAFA Digest* 4/11 (1983).

38. K Atkinson, J N Green, R Harper and V Intakosai, 'Joint Thai-Australian underwater archaeological project 1987-88. Part 1: Archaeological survey of wreck sites in the Gulf of Thailand, 1987-1988', *International Journal of Nautical Archaeology* 18/4 (1989), pp299–315.

39. M Flecker, 'Excavation of an Oriental vessel of c. 1690 off Con Dao, Vietnam', *International Journal of Nautical Archaeology* 21/3 (1992), pp221-244.

40. W Blake and M Flecker, 'A preliminary survey of a South-East Asian wreck, Phu Quock Island, Vietnam', *International Journal of Nautical Archaeology* 23/2 (1994), pp79-91.

Two of the traditional ship types that survive on the Omani coast, a ghanjah *and a* shu'i. *(Tom Vosmer)*

traditions of basket boats, sewn boats and bamboo raft boats.[41]

Oman

In 1987 a small maritime archaeological reconnaissance of the coast of Oman was carried out by Green and Vincent. As part of this project, a number of traditional vessels were recorded, either in use or abandoned on the beaches. In continuation of this work, and with an Earthwatch grant, Vosmer returned to Oman and between 1992 and 1995 recorded a large number of these craft. What is interesting about the vessels of the Omani coast is that they reflect many of the features that are common to the Indian Ocean region. The sewn *sambuq*s of the Dhofar coast show the criss-cross pattern

Asia (see Thailand above) and China. The hull consisted of three layers of planking and was edge joined with dowels. The vessel had sixteen compartments, with double waterways next to the keel/keelson and the bulkheads carefully sealed with luting. These features are similar to the wrecks found in the Gulf of Thailand. In addition there was an extra waterway on the

second plank of the bulkhead. The vessel also had stiffeners supporting the bulkhead on the other side to the frame. This is the first time this feature has been reported on a Southeast Asian vessel, although it was found on the Shinan ship in Korea and the Fa Shui ship in China.

The present-day boats of Vietnam are also of great interest, since the country is relatively underdeveloped, and one can see the remaining

The internal framing of an Omani sewn boum *at Sohar. (Tom Vosmer)*

41. N Burningham, 'Notes on the watercraft of Thanh Hoa province, northern Vietnam', *International Journal of Nautical Archaeology* 23/3 (1994), pp229-238; anon, *Blue Book of Coastal Vessels: South Vietnam*, Remote Area Conflict Information Centre (Columbus, Ohio 1967).

An Omani battil qarib *at Sharyah, Musandam. Note the sewing around the thwart beams.* (Jeremy Green)

century. They exhibit the unusual stem and stern extension and a balanced axial rudder, often turned by lanyards.[42] There are also the larger vessels which are more traditionally thought of as dhows. These include two classes: those with transoms and those that are double ended. The former class include the *baghlah*, the *jalibut*, the *ghanjah* and the *sambuq*. In the latter class is the *boum*.[43]

---

42. R K Vincent and J N Green, 'A reconnaissance along the coast of Oman', *INA Newsletter* 17/1 (1990), pp8–11; T Vosmer, 'Traditional Boats of Oman, links past and present', *Proceedings of the Conference on Techno-Archaeological Perspectives on Shipbuilding in the Indian Ocean* (Delhi 1994); T Vosmer, *Traditional Boats of Oman*, Ministry of National Heritage and Culture, Muscat (1994); T Vosmer, R Margariti, A Tilley and I Godfrey, *The Omani Dhow Research Project, Final Report, Fieldwork 1992*, WA Maritime Museum Report No 69 (1993).

43. H A Jewel, *Dhows at Mombasa* (Nairobi 1969); Sultanate of Oman Ministry of Information and Culture, *Oman, A Seafaring Nation* (Oman 1978).

A sambuq *from Aden, one of the many variations on the Arab ship type known to the West as a dhow, in the harbour of Mombasa.* (Jeremy Green)

stitching and the diagonal dowelling. The *huri* is a dugout canoe, usually with a small built-up washstrake. There is the *shashah* which is a reed boat. There is a group of vessels including the *baggarah* which incorporates some sewn construction and the badan. Both vessels have undergone recent change and it is thought that both were sewn vessels in the nineteenth

Indonesian traditional craft at Madura. In the foreground is a jangollan *being built shell-first; the bow and transom will not be fitted until the shell has been finished.* (Nick Burningham)

It has been suggested that the double-enders are an older type of Arab design and that the transom stern is a European innovation. Like many of these Eurocentric statements, it does not hold up under close examination. Certainly, the two illustrations from the Iranian *Maqamat* of al-Hariri (1225–35) show classic double-enders with axial rudders and a sewn construction. However, examination of early atlases of the Indian Ocean show local craft with transom sterns (Lopo Homen-Reinéis Atlas of 1519 in the Bibliothèque Nationale in Paris). This situation is similar to the claim often made that the Portuguese brought the technique of fastening planks with nails to the Indian Ocean. Moreland suggests that all Arab vessels were stitched before the arrival of the Europeans in 1498.[44] However, in 1509 Moreland cites the example of a fleet of vessels being built in Goa to attack the Portuguese. Following their capture by the Portuguese, the storehouses supplying the shipyards were found to contain, among other things, nails. The author continues: 'The mention of nails might suggest that their use was familiar to the shipwrights of Goa, but in fact these ships were not of the local build, but were imitations of the Portuguese; and the true reading . . . I think, to take it as showing that Indian builders were quick to appreciate and imitate, Portuguese practice.' It is unlikely that eleven years after Vasco da Gama arrived in Calicut the Indian shipbuilders changed from a sewing technique to building ships with nails. The modern method of shipbuilding is still shell first, and the hull planking is built up using external clamps, rather like the seventeenth-century Dutch shell-first technique.

Pakistan, India and Bangladesh

The development of the dhow in the north-western part of the Indian Ocean is connected with the Arab seafarers. The dhows of this region utilised the monsoonal wind pattern. Dhows traded up the Persian Gulf to Basra, along the Pakistan and along the Malabar coasts, then to Malagasy. The voyages could continue to Dar es Salaam, Zanzibar and up the east coast of Africa. Other dhows came south along this coast and returned with the Southwest Monsoon. It was, at one time, not unusual to see Adeni, Omani, dhows from the Gulf, and Pakistani and Gujarati dhows in Mombasa Harbour.

However, the coasts of Pakistan, India and Bangladesh have their own characteristics in terms of weather, climate and coastal topography and thus their own individual boat types.

44. W H Moreland, 'The ships of the Arabian Sea about AD 1500', *Journal of the Royal Asiatic Society of Great Britain and Ireland* (January and April 1939), pp63-74 and 12-192.

The region has been studied by many authors, but little work has been done systematically. A number of authors have written about specific areas; Hornell wrote on the boat types of India, Greenhill on the boats of Pakistan and of Bangladesh, and in general the west coast has been studied more than the east.[45] The north-western coastline has traditions that are similar to Arab boatbuilding in origins, whereas the southern and eastern coastline have a more traditional Indian origin. In particular, the dugout and outrigger are found in the central west coast. On the east coast the catamaran is the characteristic fishing vessel, except for the sewn boats such as the *masula*, the dugout and the *toni*.[46]

Indonesia

The Indonesian archipelago covers an area of almost 750,000 square miles and an enormous cultural diversity. Within this region, understandably there is an enormous variety of ship-building traditions. The most distinctive aspect is the technique of edge-joining with dowels that is common to most traditional vessels of the region. Much has been written about these vessels and the reader is referred to these texts for further details.[47]

Moko shurai ekotoba, a scroll showing an attack on a large Chinese vessel, useful iconographical evidence for the appearance of the ships of the period

Japan

In 1982 a project under the leadership of Professor Mozai, Merchant Marine Department, Tokai University, Tokyo was conducted to search for the remains of Kubila Khan's fleet that was destroyed in 1282 by a typhoon in and around the Bay of Imari, Kuyushu. A wide variety of ceramic material was recovered from the seabed, together with examples of projectiles of some sort, thought to be associated with *P'ao* – a type of fire-ball or projectile fired from either a trebuchet or early cannon.[48] There is an illustration, by an unknown artist, in *Moko shurai ekotoba* [*Illustrated Narrative of the Mongol Invasion*], a work which was written in about 1292 by the Japanese warrior Takezaki who took part in the campaign of 1282. The scroll describes his battle experiences, and at one point shows him being dismounted by an exploding device of some sort.[49] The scroll shows a number of Japanese and Chinese ships and is one of the oldest contemporary illustrations of Japanese and Chinese ships.

Jeremy Green

45. Hornell, 'The origins and ethnological significance of Indian boat design'; B Greenhill, *Boats and Boatmen of Pakistan* (Newton Abbott 1971), and 'The boats of East Pakistan: a preliminary study', *The Mariner's Mirror* 43 (1957), pp106-134 and 203-215.

46. E Kentley, 'The *masula* of India's East Coast'; G A Thivakaran and G V Rajamanickam, 'Indigenous sailing traditions of Tamil Nadu', both in *International Seminar on Techno-Archaeological Perspectives of Seafaring in the Indian Ocean, New Delhi 28 February–4 March 1994* (New Delhi 1994).

47. C W Hawkins, *Praus of Indonesia* (Lymington 1982); G A Horridge, *The Design of Planked Boats of the Moluccas*, Maritime Monographs and Reports No 38 (Greenwich 1978), *The Konjo Boatbuilders and the Bugis Prahus of South Sulawesi*, Maritime Monographs and Reports No 40 (Greenwich 1979), *The Lambo or Prahu Bot: A Western Ship in an Eastern Setting*, Maritime Monographs and Reports No 39 (Greenwich 1979), *The Prahu. Traditional Sailing Boat of Indonesia* (Kuala Lumpur 1981), *The Lashed-lug Boat of the Eastern Archipelagoes*, Maritime Monographs and Reports No 54 (Greenwich 1982); N Burningham,

'Reconstruction of a nineteenth century Makassan perahu', *The Beagle* 4/1 (1987), pp103-128, 'Description of Hati Marege, a replica 19th century Makassan perahu', *The Beagle* 5/1 (1988), pp155-161, 'Four double-ended perahu lambo', *The Beagle* 6/1 (1989), pp179-193, 'The structure of Javanese Perahus', *The Beagle* 6/1 (1989), pp195–219, 'Stemless boats from Ende Bay', *The Beagle* 7/1 (1990), pp105–119, 'Bajau lepa and sope: a seven-part canoe building tradition in Indonesia', *The Beagle* 10/1 (1994), pp193–222, 'Notes on the watercraft of Thanh Hoa province, northern Vietnam', *International Journal of Nautical Archaeology* 23/3 (1994), 229–238.

48. T Mozai, 'The lost fleet of Kubila Kahn', *National Geographic* 162/5 (1982), pp635-649; J N Green, 'In search of Kubila Khan's lost fleet', *Geo Magazine* 5/4, pp58-69.

49. Kubota Beisan, *Moko shurai ektoba* [*Illustrated Narrative of the Mongol Invasion*], facsimile edition (Japan 1916); F P Purvis, 'Ship construction in Japan', *Transactions of the Asiatic Society of Japan* 23 (1919), p51; Ikeuchi Hiroshi, *Genko no Shin Kenkyu* [*New Studies of the Yuan Invasion*] (Tokyo 1931).

7

Problems of Reconstruction and the Estimation of Performance

THE NATURE and performance of various ship types of the ancient past is a field of study that is of interest not only to archaeologists, historians and philologists but also to people with a practical approach to the sea, such as naval architects, officers and sailors, as well as the growing number of yachtsmen and -women around the world. In addition, much interest has been aroused in general by Thor Heyerdahl's experiments in crossing the tropical oceans on rafts and reed-boats, Tim Severin's voyage across the cold North Atlantic in a skin-boat intended to represent a sixth-century AD Celtic vessel, and the Anglo-Greek project of building a hypothetical Athenian trireme warship of the third century BC and testing this under oars and sail. All these projects have their merits in drawing attention to the basic conditions that met sailors of the past in fragile vessels constructed in ways that are unfamiliar today.

At best such projects – besides providing exciting armchair reading – may be eye-openers that enable modern man to understand pictorial or literary evidence of past maritime cultures. In fact, several theories launched from writing desks have had to be scuttled following

The traditional way of building reed boats on Lake Titicaca in the Andes was demonstrated in 1990 at the Viking Ship Museum in Roskilde by Paulino Esteban from Bolivia. In 1970 he took part in the construction of Thor Heyerdahl's large Ra II which crossed the Atlantic in 57 days. (Viking Ship Museum)

Viking, *a Gokstad ship replica, leaving Bergen bound for New York in 1893.* (Universitetets Oldsaksamling, Oslo)

a successful voyage in one of these 'floating hypotheses'. So even though these vessels are not true replicas, since none of them is based on actual finds of boats that could be replicated, these experiments have been crucial for our understanding of the potentials of unfamiliar materials or building techniques for the construction of seaworthy watercraft in early times.

Living tradition versus 'floating hypotheses'

The technical problems encountered in the process of constructing these vessels have served to draw the attention of ship archaeologists to the few remaining places in the world where these materials have remained in use in local boatbuilding to within living memory. Thus the surviving reed boat tradition on Lake Titicaca in South America, or among the Marsh Arabs in Iran, enables us to study old methods, skills and beliefs, etc related to the building of these boats, even though they were never meant to cross the oceans. Such studies serve as a guide in tracing some of the roots of the various basic boatbuilding traditions around the globe. But at the same time they demonstrate the complexity of the issue, as the boats are not manifestations of technology

alone but fully integrated elements of life in society at several levels.

In general the shiphandling skills that were needed to carry the early vessels safely across the sea cannot be traced in the archaeological sources or in the written or pictorial evidence of the past. However, some ancient elements of seamanship and navigation may still be recorded among sailors and fishermen working under similar conditions at a pre-industrial stage in odd corners of the world. But again such rudimentary memories of past techniques will probably relate to inland or coastal navigation rather than to ocean crossings.

So even if there are anthropological sources to draw from, there must be reservations about the value of the 'floating hypotheses' as true reflections of the actual conditions of deep-sea navigation in the past. Contemporary Europeans and Americans are based in a modern world where their minds and hands are not trained from childhood in the intricate art and craft of building and handling 'simple boats' in direct interplay with the elements of nature. Thus the experience gained from such attempts at scholarly experiments may turn out to be misleading – we may have taken a wrong starting position, or we may not be capable of building or handling the vessels properly because of lack of experience, or because our

experience is guiding us the wrong way.

The vessels mentioned above have been built on the basis of textual and iconographic evidence, supplemented by assumptions and qualified guesses, but without a base in well-preserved remains of such a craft found within the region and from the period in question. Thus they are in contrast to the true ship replicas based on the analysis and reconstruction of vessels that have actually survived until this day in such a condition that practically all the basic features of the ship or boat can be studied in detail. Such replicas may still be hypothetical in parts of the reconstruction – often the rigging, for example – but they enable us to establish a much closer and certainly much more well-founded contact with the sailors of the past. Examples of ships that have served as a basis for proper replicas range from the Kyrenia ship of the fourth century BC,[1] through the Scandinavian Viking ships of the ninth to the eleventh centuries AD,[2] to the thirteenth-century Gedesby ship[3] and the Bremen cog of 1380.[4]

A pioneering project of 1893

The tradition of building and sailing replicas of Viking ships dates back over a hundred years to when, after the Gokstad ship had been excavated, a replica of this ship from the tenth century was launched in Norway in 1893. The ship was named *Viking* and was sailed across the North Atlantic on its own keel by a Norwegian crew under captain Magnus Andersen.[5] Unfortunately the archaeologists of the time either took little interest in the project or directly opposed it, and the published report of the voyage is very brief with respect to matters that characterise the performance, as well as the extraordinary

1. J Richard Steffy, *Wooden Ship Building and the Interpretation of Shipwrecks* (College Station 1994), pp42ff.

2. See below, notes 5 and 7-13.

3. Jan Bill, 'Gedesbyskibet. Middelalderlig skude- og færgefart fra Falster', in *Nationalmuseets Arbejdsmark 1991* (Copenhagen 1991), pp188-198; O Crumlin-Pedersen, 'Original and replica', *Maritime Archaeology Newsletter from Roskilde* 3 (1994), pp4-7.

4. Uwe Baykowski, *Die Kieler Hansekogge. Der Nachbau eines historischen Segelschiffes von 1380* (Kiel 1991).

5. Arne Emil Christensen, '*Viking*, a Gokstad Ship Replica from 1893', in O Crumlin-Pedersen and M Vinner (eds), *Sailing into the Past. Proceedings of the International Seminar on Replicas of Ancient and Medieval Vessels, Roskilde, 1984* (Roskilde 1986), pp68-77.

The Bayeux Tapestry illustrates the various shipbuilding techniques in use in the eleventh-century Nordic/Norman tradition. (By courtesy of Basil Greenhill)

features of the ship, such as the flexibility of the hull, the efficiency of the side rudder and the good tacking ability of the single square sail rig.

At that time vessels of an appearance and rig very similar to that of the Gokstad ship were still being built and sailed in western and northern Norway, craft like the cargo-carrying *jægt* and the various sizes of *Nordlandsboat* for fishing. Thus there was relevant expertise at hand amongst boatbuilders and fishermen in that part of the country in dealing with a vessel similar to the Gokstad ship. Nevertheless it was not these men, but south Norwegian ship-builders and deep-sea sailors with a back-ground in the large square-riggers of the time who built and sailed the *Viking*. For this reason they did not hesitate to rig a headsail and even topsails and studding sails in favourable winds – in direct conflict with the evidence of Viking-period depictions of ships, which show only one mast and a single sail on each of these boats. In spite of these drawbacks, the *Viking* experience was of great value in effectively demonstrating the seaworthiness of the Gokstad ship, even if this type of ship was hardly used by the Vikings themselves on the

Radial splitting of an oak trunk into halves, quarters, eighths etc, for planking for the Skeldelev 3 replica Roar Ege. (Viking Ship Museum)

Building the Roar Ege. *The sides of the planks were dressed with copies of the Viking shipbuilder's broadaxe.* (Viking Ship Museum)

transatlantic route, but was more commonly employed along the Norwegian coast and across the North Sea.

Three Skuldelev ship replicas

With the excavation in 1962 of the five Skuldelev ships of the eleventh century,[6] a basis was created in Denmark for experimental ship archaeology. The ships had been sunk as part of a navigational barrier in Roskilde Fjord, and subsequently conserved and restored in the Viking Ship Museum in Roskilde. Here the five ship types represented in the Skuldelev ships offered an opportunity for studying the construction and performance of ships of widely differing character. Between the years 1982 and 1991 replicas of three of these ships, numbers 1, 3 and 5, were constructed in close collaboration between the archaeologist responsible for the analysis and publication of the original ships and the building team. Thus the construction and trials of these replicas served two purposes: as an integrated part of the archaeological analysis of the original ships, and as a splendid way of illustrating for the visitors to the museum these ship types, as they would originally have appeared during construction and under sail.

In order to build and test a proper ship replica that will be of use in the scholarly study of the original ship, many issues have to be dealt with. The true shape and the structural layout, as well as the tools and materials to be used for making the hull and rig, the manning and handling of the ship at sea, steering, and ballasting are some of the aspects that need to be dealt with in a competent way. This presents a great challenge to the archaeologist in charge of the find because many of the answers to these questions can be found in the shipwreck itself, if it is studied properly, while other answers may be found in relevant sources elsewhere, leaving a minimum of issues open to pure guesswork. In the end a fully functional vessel, fit for its purpose and the conditions it is built to meet, should result from the efforts.

Boatbuilding practice in replica-building

Apart from Noah, all ship- and boatbuilders over the centuries were taught their skills by means of a transmission of expertise from one generation to the next. The learning process is crucial in establishing the basis for every building tradition, even at a time when new impuls-

es tend to change the trade rapidly. Therefore it may be problematic for the construction of replicas to employ boat- and shipbuilders who are professionally trained in the present-day techniques of wooden boats. They may not be sufficiently open-minded to appreciate the technical solutions used by their predecessors, and they may tend to use the tricks of the trade known to them, rather than to follow an ancient practice they may find impractical or insecure. On the other hand the boatbuilder's learning process also includes a training of the eye to judge the lines of a ship or boat and to appreciate lines that are functional for the vessel, and this qualification is also needed for the work. Thus either a replica should be built at a boatyard working within the same line of tradition as the original vessel, or a special group of builders should be assembled, combining the necessary high-quality skills with an open-minded approach to the job.

The three Skuldelev replicas to be illustrated here are good examples of this policy. One of these, the *Saga Siglar*, a replica of the deep-sea trader Skuldelev 1, was built at a local boatyard in an area of western Norway where the original ship may also have been built more than nine hundred years ago. In this part of Scandinavia the boat traditions are directly related to those of the Viking era and this is reflected in the lines and layout of the boats as well as in the terminology. Thus it presented no problem for Sigurd Bjørkedal and his sons to build this ship for Ragnar Thorseth on the

basis of plans and instructions from the staff of the Viking Ship Museum in Roskilde. The two other replicas were built in Roskilde by a group of young people especially selected for the job and combining a wide variety of backgrounds, from woodworking to philosophy.

Building materials

But the builders alone do not make the ship. They need building materials of the right kind to suit the standard of the original ship, and this may be very problematic. Thus it would be virtually impossible today to replicate several of the ships of the past, like the sun-ship found beside the pyramids in Egypt, the Viking warship from the harbour of Hedeby/Haithabu in north Germany or the medieval Utrecht ship from the Netherlands, because of the immense size of the largest wooden elements in these ships. At the time these ships were built, such timbers could be cut from trees in the primaeval forests, but now these have all been cut down in Europe and around the Mediterranean. At best they have been replaced by forests with monocultures of trees to be felled as soon as they have reached a reasonable size, leaving no room for tree trunks of extraordinary dimensions. Even for the relatively small size vessels replicated in Roskilde, the

6. Olaf Olsen and Ole Crumlin-Pedersen, 'The Skuldelev Ships II. A Report of the Final Underwater Excavation in 1959 and the Salvaging Operation in 1962', in *Acta Archaeologica* 38 (1968), pp95-170.

Left: Building the Roar Ege *in 1983. The frames have been cut to a close fit to the planking and are being fastened with treenails. (Viking Ship Museum)*

Below: The stages in the construction of the Skuldelev 3 ship could be indentified at an early stage in the analysis of the ship. (After Crumlin-Pedersen 1970)

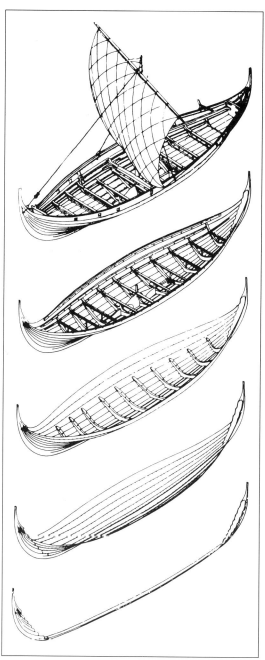

13.8m (45ft) long Skuldelev 3 replica *Roar Ege* and the 17.5m (57ft) long Skuldelev 5 replica *Helge Ask*, it was very difficult to find trees large enough and of sufficiently high quality for the radially split planks.

Another problem is the processing of the wooden parts. In vessels that were built without the use of saws, like the Viking ships, it is crucial to follow the ancient wood-technology instead of using sawn planks, whenever this has

an effect on the result. Planks which are split out of the tree-trunk are extraordinarily strong, as none of their fibres have been cut across. If a tree has spiral growth or many knots, its trunk is useless for split planks, but it may still provide sawn planks, though of a much inferior quality. At the same time, the radial orientation of most ancient oak planks improves their strength in comparison with any of the orientations in the cross-section produced with the

saw, because the structure of the fibres with pith-rays between the pith and the bark reinforces the radially cut plank, and thus it will hardly ever split along the middle. For the pine planks found in, for example, Skuldelev 1, the conditions are different, however. Here the tangential splitting of the straight-grown trees produced planks of a quality very similar to that of sawn planks. Therefore the *Saga Siglar* could be constructed with normally sawn planks, as

The hull of Roar Ege *at Roskilde, ready for launching.*
(Viking Ship Museum)

long as the quality of the wood matched that of the original planks.

Constructing the hull

There are important differences between modern practice and the Viking tradition, even in the way the hull was built. In wooden boat-building today, in practically all cases, the hull planking is shaped against a pre-erected skeleton of frames or moulds. But this technique is relatively young, based as it is on the technique of drawing plans of the ship's lines in plan and sections as the basis for the design, and this was certainly not a procedure in use by the Vikings. They built up their ships in stages, with the three-dimensional lines of the hull subjected to constant visual checking. The first step was the mounting of the keel and stem pieces on the building blocks. Then the bottom planking was built up strake by strake, with each plank cut to such a curvature that it created the desired lines. The edge fastenings between the planks served to keep these in the right shape, occasionally aided by studs from the outside or small loads of stones from the inside. Frames or floor-timbers were then inserted to strengthen the shell before the upper part of the planking was

added, again without internal support during the formative stage. At the final stage cross-beams and side-frames etc were inserted, as were the side-rudder, floorboards, mast and rig.

With the Skuldelev ship replicas the original hull shape had been established by a working process in which 1:10 scale moulds of each pre-served length of planking had been assembled into a three-dimensional model of the vessel as preserved. Then the model's hull was complet-ed by adding the missing sections. In the ships referred to here this could be done in such a way that the main dimensions of the original hull could be estimated very accurately, with an uncertainty of only ± 0.1-0.2m. A wooden model at 1:10 scale was then built of the hull, and measurements at fixed points were taken off this to be used as control-measurements in the replica. In this way it was possible to build up the replica to the exact shape of the original hull without resorting to the use of moulds. The three ships had very different proportions, as well as lines. *Saga Siglar* (Skuldelev 1) was broad and sturdy with a bluff bow that may have been characteristic of the seagoing *knarr*-type,[7] whereas *Roar Ege* (Skuldelev 3) was built as a small coaster with sharp lines and elegantly pointed stem- and sternposts.[8] The Skuldelev 5 replica *Helge Ask* was a long and slender vessel,

well fit for service as a patrol craft in Danish waters.[9]

Rig and sail

In the Skuldelev ships no parts of the rigging or steering gear were found during the excava-tions. In many pictures of Viking ships of the eighth-ninth centuries, on coins and on the Gotland stones, the sails are shown as being very broad, with a width that is two to three times that of the height of the sail. Whether

7. Olaf Olsen and Ole Crumlin-Pedersen, 'The Skuldelev Ships II. A Report of the Final Underwater Excavation in 1959 and the Salvaging Operation in 1962', in *Acta Archaeologica* 38 (1968), pp96ff; Ragnar Thorseth, *Saga Siglar. Århundrets seilas Jorda rundt* (Ålesund 1988).

8. Ole Crumlin-Pedersen, 'Aspects of Viking Age Shipbuilding in the light of the Construction and Trials of the Skuldelev Ship-Replicas *Saga Siglar* and *Roar Ege*', in *Journal of Danish Archaeology* 5 (Odense 1987), pp209-228. O Crumlin-Pedersen and M Vinner, 'Le projet *Roar Ege*. Reconstitution et expérimentation d'un caboteur viking', in *Le Chasse-Marée* 30 (1987), pp16-45; O Crumlin-Pedersen and M Vinner, 'Roar og Helge af Roskilde - om at bygge og sejle med vikingeskibe', in *Nationalmuseets Arbejdsmark 1993* (Copenhagen 1993), pp11-29.

9. Ole Crumlin-Pedersen, 'Gensyn med Skuldelev 5 – et ledingsskib?' in *Festskrift til Olaf Olsen* (Copenhagen 1988), pp137-156; O Crumlin-Pedersen and M Vinner, 'Roar og Helge af Roskilde – om at bygge og sejle med vikingeskibe', in *Nationalmuseets Arbejdsmark 1993* (Copenhagen 1993).

The launching of Roar Ege *in Roskilde, August 1984.*
(Viking Ship Museum)

the proportions between the hull and rig of more recent square-rigged boats, and this gave a sail that had almost the same height as the width.[10] Similarly the rigging of the other replicas was designed with blocks and toggles copied from originals found in the Hedeby/Haithabu harbour.

In the replicas the first rigs and sails were made of natural fibres, but not of the same materials as were used in the original ships. Finds of ropes in Viking and medieval ships indicate that lime bast was used extensively for cordage, but of a higher quality than normally seen in areas where the technique has been in use until recently. Therefore hemp ropes were used for the prototype rig, and attempts were made to produce lime bast ropes of the required quality. Such materials as horse hair and walrus hide may also have been relevant for the rigging of Viking ships, for example in the bolt-ropes of the sail and the halyards respectively, as a consequence of the special demands made on these ropes.

The sails of the prototype rigs were made of hemp or cotton, whereas in all likelihood the original sails of most Viking ships were made of wool. A few fragments of original Viking ship sails are preserved, from the Oseberg and Gokstad ships as well as a few other early ships of the north. From these pieces, and from later traditional sails in Norway, it is evident that wool was the primary material for sail-cloth.[11] The Viking sheep, however, had a different blend of bottom-wool and cover-hair from that of present-day breeds, which have been developed to produce a maximum of bottom-wool. Thus, when the production of a woollen sail for *Roar Ege* was decided upon, a search had to be made for sheep of the old type of breed. A small flock of the old breed was located on an island in a Norwegian fjord, and the wool from these was then spun and woven – rather loosely – into sail-cloth. With a bolt-rope of horse-hair the sail was then sewn to match the shape of the prototype sail, and interestingly enough the wool sail was lighter, even after having been treated with a coating of horse tallow and ochre. The wool sail proved to be more flexible and thus to adjust better to wind-pressure than the hemp sail, but the latter was tighter woven and

this reflects reality or was a product of iconographic conventions is not known, but such a sail would have been useful only in down-wind sailing. In the best preserved Skuldelev ship, number 3, some holes in the top-strakes indi-

cated where the ropes of the rigging had been fastened when sailing close-hauled. This gave a maximum width for the lower part of the sail in this ship. The approximate length of the mast was determined on the basis of a close study of

10. Bent Andersen and Erik Andersen, *Råsejlet – Dragens Vinge* (Roskilde 1989).

11. Erik Andersen, 'Square sails of wool', in *Shipshape. Essays for Ole Crumlin-Pedersen* (eds O Olsen *et al*) (Roskilde 1995), pp249-270.

Roar Ege *under sail on Roskilde Fjord.* (Viking Ship Museum)

held a better wind. With a wool cloth of tight weave as in the original sails the wool sail would probably have matched the hemp in efficiency.

Trials under sail

On trials the sails proved to be a fit size for the hulls and, with side rudders copied from other contemporary finds and with appropriate ballast, all three ships sailed in perfect balance. In fact, the balance was so good that under most conditions the ships were steady on the course without any action at the helm. On one occasion the tiller of *Roar Ege* broke, just as the ship was about to enter Hundested harbour in a strong wind. With no control over the side rudder the skipper managed to turn the ship away from the breakwater into the open sea again by trimming the ship with the crew as mobile weights, and to keep the ship steady while a new tiller was made. This is a good illustration of the need for good seamanship as a basic element in this aspect of experimental archaeology.

The *Saga Siglar* project was initiated by Ragnar Thorseth in order to enable him to sail the ship across the North Atlantic to Iceland and Greenland. The original Skuldelev 1 ship may have done the same, though with its cargo capacity of only 20-25 tons it may have been one of the smaller ships on this newly-opened trade. In fact Thorseth not only crossed this ocean but went on through the Panama Canal to the Pacific and the Indian Ocean, passed through the Suez Canal and the Mediterranean before returning to Norway. For the first time ever an open boat without a permanent weather-deck had circumnavigated the world, a striking demonstration that the reconstruction of this ship had produced a vessel fit for its purpose.[12]

The *Saga Siglar* closely followed the original Skuldelev 1 in construction, but with a small diesel engine installed, as well as satellite navigation equipment. The engine ensured manoeuvrability in harbours etc, but on the long runs under sail alone the propeller reduced the speed slightly. Nevertheless the ship maintained a daily average of 150 nautical miles under sail over a period of 20 days and

12. Ragnar Thorseth, *Saga Siglar. Århundrets seilas Jorda rundt* (Ålesund 1988).

Roar Ege *and* Saga Siglar *cruising together on the Roskilde Fjord in 1986.* (Viking Ship Museum)

nights in fair winds of 7-12m/sec (15-25mph) in the Pacific. Before this the ship had logged a top speed of 13kts in a storm in the North Sea, in the lee of the Shetland Islands. A sudden storm, rising to a wind-speed of 35m/sec (78mph), was encountered between Greenland and Newfoundland, and here the *Saga Siglar* logged a speed through the water of up to 8.5kts, scudding bare-poled for ten hours. In 1992, however, the then rather old and worn out *Saga Siglar* was lost in terrible conditions in the Mediterranean after sailing for hours in a storm with wind speeds reported up to 45m/sec (100mph), fortunately without the loss of lives.[13] Few, if any, other archaeological experimental projects have been tested so exhaustively by Nature.

Roar versus Helge

The two other Skuldelev replicas represent coastal vessels, fit for navigation in Danish home waters and the Baltic, but not constructed for crossing the oceans. They have been tested accordingly on trial runs in Roskilde Fjord and Isefjord, where there is hardly any tide or currents and a limited build-up of waves. Electronic equipment was used for the recording of the wind, as well as of the speed and direction of the ship in the water and over the ground.

The results from the trials and from other trips with these ships show how the differences in ship types are reflected in the speed potentials and manoeuvrability of the ships. The *Roar Ege*, the local 'farm boat' with a capacity of 4-5 tons of cargo, required a crew of four or five men. The top speed recorded was 8.5-10kts, and an average of 6.5kts was maintained under favourable conditions. Against the wind the ship could maintain a VMG ('velocity made good' directly against the wind) of 1.5-2.0kts, tacking at an angle of about 65° to the direction of the wind. With six oars *Roar Ege* could be rowed at 2.0kts at best, but as soon as the wind increased, speed was reduced drastically.

The course of Roar Ege *tacking against the wind to reach the harbour of Nykøbing in October 1984, recorded on the electronic navigator giving the exact position at any time during the trial run.* (Viking Ship Museum)

For *Helge Ask*, the 17.5m long warship built to carry twenty-six warriors and a skipper, the sprint-speed recorded under oars was 5.4kts, with 4.5kts as an average over longer periods with twenty-four rowers, and 3.6-4.0kts with only twelve rowers. Thus the ship could be rowed by half the crew with the other half resting with only a slight reduction in speed and with the potential for rowing over long distances. Under sail a VMG of 0.8-1.4kts indicates that this ship did not tack as well as *Roar Ege*, but a working speed of 7.8kts was recorded in favourable winds, and under extreme conditions speeds up to 14kts have been recorded. Against a wind blowing 5-7m/sec (11-15mph) the speed under oars was recorded as 4.7kts, and 2.9kts at 12-17m/sec (26-38mph). The lowering of the mast was essential for reduction of wind resistance, and this procedure was practised to perfection. Thus it could be established that the Skuldelev 5 replica would have been able to catch up with any trading ship under all weather conditions except in a storm.

Even in the sheltered waters of Denmark, however, sudden squalls may cause tense moments for sailors. In 1993 *Helge Ask* capsized in Holbæk Fjord in the process of turning through the wind, and in 1995 a sudden storm sank the ship at its mooring outside the Viking Ship Museum in Roskilde and smashed the planking of the upperworks. On neither of these occasions were there any casualties, and each of these unfortunate events, in their own way, serve as lessons in the struggle to learn how to handle the Viking ships properly. One does not know the performance potentials of these ships until certain limits have been crossed. And to be true to the reality of the past: even in the Viking Age ships were lost, as recorded on some of the rune stones, as, for example, on an eleventh-century stone from Ny Larsker, Bornholm:

> Sasser had the stone set in memory of Alvard,
> his father.
> He drowned at sea with all the crew.
> Christ help his soul eternally.
> May this stone stand in memory.

Ole Crumlin-Pedersen

13. Max Vinner, 'A Viking-ship off Cape Farewell 1984', in *Shipshape. Essays for Ole Crumlin-Pedersen* (eds O Olsen *et al*) (Roskilde 1995), pp289-304.

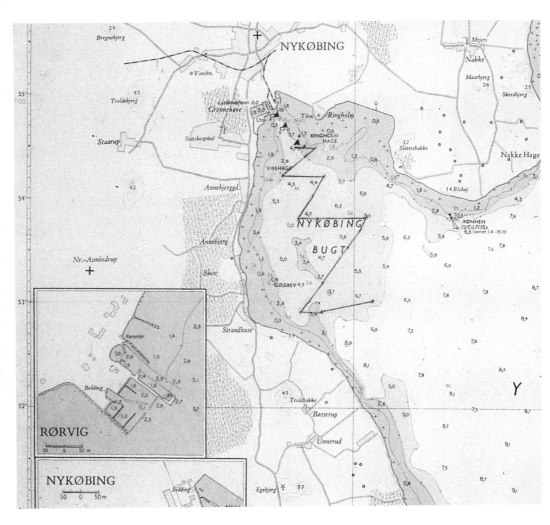

8

Early Shiphandling and Navigation in Northern Europe

THERE is no significant body of evidence on shiphandling and navigation in European history before the so-called Viking Age, so this chapter concentrates on this period.

At the height of the Viking Age, the countries of northern Europe formed the hub of a shipping network which extended from Novgorod and the Black Sea in the east to Greenland and Newfoundland (Vinland) in the

The vessels of the Viking era were optimised as warships (which were essentially oared vessels with auxiliary sail), or as cargo carriers (which were seaworthy sailing craft that were occasionally rowed). This specialisation was reflected in the proportions of the hull, the warship being longer and lower. This is perfectly demonstrated by the Viking Ship Museum's Helga Ask (right) – a replica of Skuldelev 5, a small warship – compared with Roar Ege (centre) – a replica of Skuldelev 3, a small cargo carrier. The third craft is the Faroe boat Ask. (Photo by Werner Karrasch; The Viking Ship Museum)

west, and from the Mediterranean in the south to the Polar Sea in the north. It is therefore only natural that the techniques of seafaring and navigation which were developed by the Norsemen should influence at the very least the shipping of adjacent regions – from around the Baltic to the southern coasts of the North Sea and the British Isles. It was only from the beginning of the thirteenth century, with the rise of the economically successful Hanseatic League, that there was any challenge to the influence of the Scandinavians in the field of navigation. The best 'tools' the Vikings possessed were their ships, which in terms of design were unequalled by any other vessels in Europe at that time.

From the very beginning of the Viking Age it is possible to discern two clearly different types: warships and cargo vessels. The former belong to the family of traditional northern

rowing craft, with a sail only for use as an auxiliary means of propulsion, so were manned by a numerous crew of warriors, whereas cargo vessels had only a limited number of sailors. Their main propulsion was the sail, although for short distances – while manoeuvring, for example – some oars could be employed forward and aft of the middle section which formed the ship's hold. It is self-evident that long-distance voyages were undertaken under sail; nobody could have contemplated rowing, for example, from Norway to Byzantium and Jerusalem, or to Iceland, Greenland and America.

Sailing directions

Though these long-distance passages to the Mediterranean or across the North Atlantic are the most renowned voyages of the Viking Age,

Even the predominantly sail-powered cargo vessel could be moved under oars in light or sheltered conditions, and would be used, for example, when manoeuvring in harbour or other confined waters. This is here demonstrated by Roskilde's Roar Ege, *a replica of* Skuldelev 3, *a small cargo carrier.* (Photo by Werner Karrasch; The Viking Ship Museum)

where he lived (in Helgeland, in the latitude of the Lofoten Islands), south to Skríringssal, then an important market place on the Oslofjord; from Skríringssal to the famous Haithabu (near Schleswig); and from northern Norway to the White Sea. This last voyage, undertaken between AD 870 and 880, is the first known circumnavigation of the North Cape by a Norseman, and though it looks no more than a traveller's tale, it actually contains all the details necessary for anyone wishing to repeat the expedition. Othere wanted to find out how far to the north this land (Norway) extended and if people inhabited the northern desert. He sailed along the coast in a northerly direction for three days, having the waste land on the starboard beam and the open sea to port. This was the northernmost point to which the whale-hunters regularly sailed. He then continued his voyage north for another three days, where the land turned in an easterly direction - or the sea indented the land in that direction (he did not know which, but he knew that he had to wait for wind from the west or a little north of west). He next sailed along the coast for four days, after which he had to wait for a northerly wind, because the land turned to the south. These geographical and navigational hints are always accompanied by remarks concerning the economy and ethnology of the region.

The details themselves are not always very clear. The number of days, for example, that Othere needed to reach the North Cape (where the land turned to the east) does not equate with the number of days necessary to sail along the northern coast of the Kola peninsula - but he gives no indication of the force of the wind. But the most important point, the North Cape, is clearly mentioned, and nobody sailing this route could overlook this landmark, for he had to keep the coastline within sight to starboard all the time. For this reason it was neither necessary to indicate the true direction – strictly speaking, northeast for the Norwegian coast instead of 'in northerly direction' – because it was simply a matter of following the coastline. This rather rough method of indicating directions is to be found in Norway throughout the Middle Ages, the directions between the four cardinal points of the compass being defined by

it must not be forgotten that seafaring in the Middle Ages was mainly confined to coastal shipping. Over centuries northern mariners had developed an effective system of coastal navigation, and when they began to sail across to the British Isles, to Ireland and the North Atlantic islands in the eighth and ninth centuries, they transferred their principles of coastal pilotage to oceanic navigation. Therefore it is necessary to look in a little more detail at the means of coastal navigation, to be found in some written sources, in order to understand the deep-sea navigation of the Middle Ages in northern Europe.

The most important aid to coastal navigation during the Middle Ages in northern Europe were sailing directions, and fortunately a few examples from the ninth century up to the end of the fourteenth century survive, though the source material in respect of navigation for that period is rather scarce. The accounts of two travellers, the Norseman Othere and the Englishman (?) Wulfstan, written down by King Alfred the Great in the geographical introduction of his *Orosius*, give a good idea of how such sailing directions were generated and what they looked like. Othere described three different voyages: from northern Norway,

their relationship to the mainland: northeast was *landnorðr*, northwest *útnorðr*, that is, 'land-north' and 'outnorth'. Giving Othere credit for knowing a lot about his routes, it must be concluded nevertheless that he does not speak as a

geographer or a learned man, but as a practical seaman, and for a practitioner the information he gave was quite sufficient.

Wulfstan describes the voyage from Haithabu to Truso, a market near modern-day

Elbing on the river Vistula. The main features of his account are comparable to Othere's: he gives directions and duration (while sailing with a favourable wind), and the location of the different countries in respect to the ship's course. It is pure chance that these early sailing directions have been handed down, because the northern countries themselves only began their written tradition two or three hundred years later. Thereafter, however, there are so many references to coastal shipping in northern and northwestern Europe that it is possible to reconstruct a good deal of the system of shipping routes in this region. There were two main routes along the Norwegian coast: the *pjóðleið* (common or people's route), running between the mainland and the numerous islands and skerries, where navigation was hazardous but sheltered against waves and storms from the Atlantic; and the *útleið*, the outer route, on the open sea, where only the tops of the mountains of Norway were visible – this was dangerous because of the possibility of bad weather, but faster and safer if sailing unseen and undiscovered was a priority. Centuries later, a similar situation pertained on the southern coast of the North Sea: the *binnen duinen* route between the mainland and the islands, and the *buten duinen* route on the open sea.

Sea marks

There were few aids to this kind of navigation beyond the sailing directions themselves. Othere had mentioned the North Cape as a prominent landmark, characterised by the fact that the coastline distinctly changes direction, and similar natural landmarks – mountains, hills, rivers, islands, forests, etc – are to be found in nearly all known medieval sailing directions. The obvious next step was to include artificial marks, which were not originally meant as sea marks, but acquired this secondary function because of their utility. Grave-mounds seem to have had such a function as early as the Bronze Age: in the Old English epic of *Beowulf*, it is written that his mound was erected right on the coast so that it could be seen from far away by seafarers. In the Middle Ages, tall secular and religious buildings like windmills, towers, castles, and churches helped

Despite the widely known long-distance voyages of the Viking Age, most seafaring of the time was distinctly coastal. The replica warship Helga Ask *– seen here in Roskilde Fjord – demonstrates why the low freeboard of such ships made sheltered waters preferable for voyaging, particularly under sail.* (Photo by Werner Karrasch; The Viking Ship Museum)

It is now widely believed that the famous voyages of Viking discovery were carried out by the knarr, *a sturdy and seaworthy cargo-carrying type rather than the long, low warship. The size of the former type is well shown by the Skuldelev 1 replica* Saga Siglar, *built at Sigurd Bjørkedal's boatyard in Norway. The hull is seen here during launching in 1983. (Ragnar Thorseth Adventures)*

the seaman to take bearings, and some people are of the opinion that the extraordinary height of some of the churches in Hanseatic towns – which are often situated miles upstream from coastlines without distinctive landmarks – was designed as an aid to visual bearings for seamen approaching the coast. An example taken from the Low German *Seebuch*, written down in the fourteenth century, mainly from Flemish sources, shows clearly how this worked: '. . . and hold the church of Elsinore and the *backhus* [beacon-house?] in such a manner that you can see between them, then you will not steer a false course with 7 fathoms at the Lappesand, and you will not sail too near to this

1. *Seebuch*, A, XII, 12.

shoal . . .'[1]. The *Seebuch* itself is the most important source for coastal navigation in the late Middle Ages, for it is a collection of numerous sailing directions from Cadiz in Spain up to the Baltic, including the English Channel and southern Norway.

A major innovation was the introduction of special signs for seafarers, sea marks proper. The earliest examples on the north European coasts marked entrances to harbours, reflected in their old Norwegian names *hafnarkross* ('harbour-cross') or *hafnarmerki* ('harbour-sign'), but there were comparable terms used on other coasts (*signum portus* for Travemünde/Lübeck, for example). A second form of such sea marks was the so-called *varða* ('look-out'), mostly in the form of a stone cairn, erected at dangerous points along the coast. In the Old Icelandic *Landnámabók* ('Book of the settlement of Iceland') there is a story which mentions that Flóki Vilgerðarson, one of the Norse discoverers of Iceland, piled up such a look-out, before he set off on his voyage around AD 875. Even at the end of the Middle Ages, in the year 1431 the Italian Piero Querini

records that his ship navigated by such signs along the whole Norwegian coast from the Lofotens to Oslo.

Although it is known that even in the Viking Age fires were lit in certain cases to help ships through dangerous waters, it was only around 1200 that special lighthouses were constructed (Hook Point, Ireland; mention of a 'phararius' for Dover in 1201). Similar structures had been common in southern Europe in ancient times, and Charlemagne had later tried to reactivate this system of sea marks, but without success. However, in the thirteenth and fourteenth centuries, the number of lighthouses increased considerably.

Navigational instruments

The only instruments which were used in coastal navigation during the Middle Ages were the sounding-lead and the sounding-rod. Neither is known from written Scandinavian sources, but they are both well documented in Old and Middle English and Middle Low German texts. That the Norsemen also used these instruments is clearly shown on the famous Bayeux tapestry (dating from shortly after 1066). The sounding-rod (*sund-gyrd* in Old English) was a thin stick that could only be used in very shallow waters and so was not very important, but the role of the lead can hardly be overestimated. This instrument is the oldest known technical aid to navigation; it was mentioned by Herodotus, and played an important part in the story of St Paul's shipwreck. The medieval form, which was termed *sund-ráp* or *sundlíne* in Old English and *lot* in Low German and related languages, still looked like the classical model: a cone of lead, hollowed out at the bottom to take a wax or similarly sticky filler which allowed soil samples to be brought up to the surface. The art of finding the right course 'by lead and line' was so perfected that, for example, an Anglo-German fleet in 1147 found its position off the western point of Britanny by means of the sounding-lead and the darker colour of the water alone, the land itself being obscured by fog. Furthermore, many of the sailing directions in the *Seebuch* mentioned earlier depend chiefly on soundings. It is not surprising, therefore, that in the eyes of southern Europeans the use of the lead plainly characterised navigation in the Baltic and the coastal waters of the North Sea: the illustrations on Fra Mauro's famous world map of 1458 may be quoted as an example.

Far less is known about the last aid to navigation to be mentioned here, the 'pilot'. In the Middle Ages the word did not imply a 'member of a guild, especially trained for certain routes', but only a person who happened to know a particular waterway or the routes of a region better than others. He might have been a sailor, a fisherman, a farmer, hired – or sometimes forced – to serve as *ladman* (High German) or *leiðsogumaðr* (Old Norse), the man who tells the way. Normally, a member of the crew was chosen for this job.

This simple system of coastal navigation obviously functioned satisfactorily for centuries. New technical equipment was introduced only reluctantly, as can be seen in case of the compass (detailed below) – although invented around 1200, the first mention of its use in Hanseatic sources are in 1433 for the North Sea and in 1460 for the Baltic. When in 1578 the Spanish envoy Francisco de Eraso had to cross the Baltic from Stralsund to Kalmar in Sweden, he was terrified by the local 'art of

The Helga Ask *on Roskilde Fjord, with the city's cathedral in the background. Tall structures, like the cathedral's spire, were very important in Viking pilotage. (Photo by Werner Karrasch; The Viking Ship Museum)*

navigation': none of the modern aids like a compass and charts were on board – only a tiny booklet, obviously full of sailing directions - and there was no knowledge of newly developed instruments such as the quadrant, astrolabe, or cross-staff.

Oceanic navigation and the compass

When the Norsemen started their direct crossings, first of the North Sea at the end of the eighth century, then, step by step, of the North Atlantic to the Faeroe Islands and around AD 875 to Iceland, they tried to transfer as much as possible of the functioning system of navigation to deep-water sailing. Though most details of Viking Age oceanic navigation are still unknown – because of the lack of archaeological and written evidence – there can be no doubt, that sailing directions were the most important tools of the new navigation, as they had been in coastal waters. A closer investigation of the best known of these guides, the sailing direction from Norway to Greenland, handed down in the *Landnámabók* mentioned earlier, it becomes clear that the structure is comparable to traditional forms: 'From Hernar in Norway you have to sail north of Shetland so that you can just sight it in clear weather, and south of the

Faeroe Islands, so that the sea is half-way up the mountains, and then south of Iceland, that you will have birds and whales therefrom'.[2] This is clearly a form of sailing by direction and land-/sea marks. Shetland and the Faeroe Islands serve as landmarks – considering the height of these islands, the course must have been around 37 nautical miles (nm) north of Shetland and 37nm south of the Faeroe Islands. Even the region where birds from Iceland and whales could be observed can be clearly defined and in this way regarded as a fixed point in the open sea: it must have been the zone where cold polar currents meet the warm Irminger current and thus offer ideal feeding conditions for whales as well as for sea-birds. That area is about 60-70nm south of Iceland.

A very interesting detail is that the direction 'due west' is given, which is much more precise than would be found in comparable sailing directions for coastal navigation (though it must be admitted that it does not fit with the course described, which required two changes of heading, off Shetland and off the Faeroe Islands). The reason might well be that in the Atlantic there was no coastline to follow, so that a more definite direction was needed.

2. *Landnámabók, Hauksbók,* Ch 2.

The oceanic capabilities of the Viking merchant ship has been proved many times over in recent years by the exploits of various replicas. One of the most adventurous was the voyaging of the Saga Siglar, seen here among the ice floes of Godthåb Fjord in Greenland in 1984. The ship sailed round the world, and was eventually lost in very bad weather in the Mediterranean. (Ragnar Thorseth Adventures)

tised needle, pushed through a blade of straw. This straw was put in a bowl, filled with water, where the pin turned in a north-south direction. It is evident that this instrument was very unreliable, so that it was used only in situations where all other methods had failed, because of fog or absolute darkness, for example.

During the thirteenth century, the magnetic needle was considerably improved and combined with a wind- or compass-rose, so that when it finally reached northern Europe it was able to render good services in ocean navigation, not only for the Norsemen, who called this instrument *leiðarsteinn* ('way-stone'), but also from the middle of the fourteenth century on board English ships. In regions where coastal shipping predominated, the compass was not introduced until a century later. It is important to remember that the problem of magnetic declination must have bewildered the first users of the compass.

Other navigational instruments

All the other alleged Viking instruments of navigation either have no written or archaeological evidence whatever, or at best a very weak basis in reality. Many of the proposals seem to result from the same preconception dominating the discussion of whether the Vikings possessed a compass or not (in fact they did not): for a historian of the nineteenth and twentieth centuries it was inconceivable that the Norsemen could have crossed the North Atlantic regularly without a compass or other technical means of navigation.

In recent decades the most prominent items in the argument about possible Viking instruments have been the 'sun-stone' and a sort of bearing-dial. The theory concerning the *sólarsteinn* is that the Vikings used a certain mineral – for example, feldspar or cordierite – as a sort of twilight compass, for these crystals can work as a polarizer. This means that the colour of the stone changes when held at a certain angle to the direction of the sun, provided that the zenith is cloudless. This method certainly works, but the question is whether the Vikings used it. Sun-stones are mentioned ten times in Old Icelandic manuscripts, eight times

It must be added that some of these sailing directions also quote distances. For the open sea this was not a linear measure – it was impossible to log distance in the Atlantic – but of time, the unit being the *dœgr*, a half-day of twelve hours. They always gave the shortest crossings with a fair wind: for instance the 'distance' between Hernar in Norway and Iceland was eight *dœgra* or four days. However, from this measure of time a form of linear distance could be derived, because the speeds of Viking ships were comparable, so that it would take nearly all ships, say, twelve hours to sail from a certain point to another, which might be 75nm in this case.

One of the greatest mysteries of seafaring in the Middle Ages is the question of how the Norsemen were able to navigate across the ocean regularly and safely, for they really were relatively certain to make their intended landfall, and the crossings were indeed regular, with hundreds of voyages between Europe and Iceland, Greenland and sometimes to America. There is not a single hint of a suitable navigational device in the written sources, nor any unambiguous archaeological evidence. For the Viking Age itself, the *Landnánmabók* contains a brilliant story in connection with Flóki Vilgerðarson: he is said to have taken three ravens on board his ship, when he began his search for Iceland. When he released the first

one, the raven flew up and then returned to the ship; so did the second, but the third flew away in the direction that Flóki finally found Iceland. Though ravens as a navigational resource are possible, it nevertheless seems to have been the exception – if there is any truth whatever in the story. However, much is known about the use of birds in navigation, from ancient Ceylon to Noah's Ark.

The only statement about a real instrument of navigation occurs nearly 450 years later. Haukr Erlendsson comments in his version of the *Landnámabók* on the story of Flóki's ravens, that he took the birds on board because 'in those times [the ninth century] there was no compass in the northern countries'. From this it is possible to conclude that Haukr himself, who wrote between 1306 and 1308, knew the magnetic compass very well and that it was introduced in northern navigation by at least the thirteenth century. The history of this instrument, which became one of the most important aids to navigation, is relatively well known, though its origins are not undisputed. It may have been invented in the region of the Channel, for the first mentions are to be found in the works of Alexander Neckam, first in *De utensilibus* (1187), and then by Guiot de Provins, a poet from northern France, who describes this rather primitive instrument in his poem *La Bible* (1206) as a simple iron magnein church inventories, and once in a story about a bishop and his doctor.

The only description of the use of a sun-stone is in a legendary story about the saintly Norwegian king Olaf. Only the king himself, who has a divine relation to the sun, uses the stone to find its position, on land, during a snow-storm, *ie* under circumstances, where a polarized compass would not function at all. In the author's opinion, it is extremely questionable whether such a stone was used for navigation.

The same is true in case of the so-called bearing-dial. Excavations at the Unartoq Fjord in Greenland in 1948 unearthed a fragment of

Understanding of the characteristics of Viking era vessels has advanced at a great pace in recent decades, thanks to the large number of well-researched replicas built by museums and other interested parties. Central to this effort has been the Viking Ship Museum at Roskilde, which regularly hosts meetings of such craft; comparative sailing trials, as shown here, have been very enlightening. (Photo by Grethe Schantz; The Viking Ship Museum)

an oak disk of approximately 7cm in diameter, ornamented with jags. This fragment was interpreted as part of a bearing-dial, though the jags are carved very roughly and the small size makes the use – at least of this example – nearly impossible. Though leading historians of navigation immediately rejected the interpretation, this 'old Norse instrument' can be found in many publications and even in museums. Once again it is necessary to consider that there is not a single hint of such an instrument in written sources, and no similar archaeological find has been discovered, except for part of a circular shaped sandstone, found in Lolland (Denmark), which is interpreted as a Viking Age sun-dial, because of the symbols scratched on it. But the function of this piece is as doubtful as that of the wooden disk, and there is no other source material which could help to support the bearing-dial interpretation. On the other hand, there is a valid argument against such theories. It is clear that the introduction of an instrument made ocean navigation safer. Before the compass came to the North during

the thirteenth century, the Old Norse sagas often remark that after a period of misty weather seamen lost their orientation: they got what was called *hafvilla*. After the Norse seamen could rely on the help of the magnetic needle, no further comments on the state of *hafvilla* occur. No such hints to any significant improvement that might suggest the use of other instruments can be found in the source material.

Other theories about more or less intricate aids to navigation, such as a knife on the thumb or the mysterious 'sun table', can be ignored because they seem to be entirely the products of imaginative historians of navigation.

Navigational techniques

All these alleged instruments are thought to have enabled the Norsemen to use celestial bodies for their navigation – and it is relatively certain that a part of their method was astronomical, though there is no precise information on how important this element was or

Above: The 7cm wooden fragment discovered in Unartoq Fjord, Greenland in 1948; it has been interpreted as a 'bearing-dial'. (Nationalmuseet, Copenhagen)

Below: A reconstruction of a Viking 'bearing-dial' based on the Unartoq Fjord fragment; there is still intense debate about this interpretation. (Photo by Henrik Jørgensen; The Viking Ship Museum)

which particular techniques were used. In darker nights, when the stars were visible, they steered by the Pole Star, which they called 'way-star' (*leiðarstjarna*). They were able to determine the cardinal points with the help of the sun (*deila ættir*), and it is most likely that they did it using their thumb, their hands or arms. In this context, it is worth remembering that the Icelandic abbot Nikulás was able to determine the geographical latitude of the river Jordan in 1150 with an error of only 1° by the simplest methods: lying on his back, he bent his right knee, put his fist upon it and stretched out his thumb! Finally, it is not impossible, that they even used stars which were not so high above the horizon, for it is difficult to use the Pole Star for steering in higher latitudes, the angle being too large.

Furthermore, it seems as if the sun, or better its shadow, helped to determine the latitude. There is a text, unfortunately corrupt, about an expedition by ship to the coasts of Greenland, in which the northernmost point reached is defined in the following way: 'We have been so far north that the shadow of the gunwale at noon on St James' Day hit the face of a man, lying athwart the deck of the ship.' That is, of course, a very rough and inexact measure, but methods like this seem to have been sufficient for the mixture of latitude sailing and dead reckoning which the Norsemen preferred in the pre-instrument period of navigation. It is at least questionable how much of the learned astronomy, which also existed in northern and northwestern Europe in those times, was known to a skilfull seaman.

But there were other means by which northern mariners could obtain valuable data for shaping their course: natural phenomena. Seamen of the Middle Ages were trained to observe not only weather conditions, like a steady wind or the characeristics of low-pressure areas, but also the slightest change in their surrounding, to a degree which is unthinkable in the present technology-dependent world. Land birds, as already mentioned, particular species of fish or whales, the colour of the water, direction, height and form of waves, characteristic driftwood, clouds indicating land – everything could be useful in determing position and shaping the course. Such features were noted, collected and set down in sailing directions and had to be learnt by heart.

Seamen with a lot of this knowledge were considered to be 'wise men' and were well qualified as pilots, for even the pilot system was transferred from coastal shipping to deep-water sailing. It was laid down by law that each ship should have one master (*styrimaðr*); only ships which were sailing to Iceland might have two. However, the master was not necessarily the one with the greatest experience of particular courses or waters, and many stories are told in the sagas of how skilled some seamen were. Some of them still had a good idea where they had been driven after numerous misty days with variable winds. One of these stories, which had important consequences, runs as follows. One summer, Bjarni Herjulfsson, who was born in Iceland, returned from Norway to the island and discovered that his father Herjulf had sailed away to settle in Greenland. Bjarni and his crew decided to sail to Greenland, too, and he comments on this decision: 'Our voyage will look unwise, because none of us has previously sailed in the Greenland Sea . . .'. The result of this voyage is well known: they missed Greenland and discovered America.

In the Old Norwegian *Konungs skuggsjá* ('Kings's Mirror'), a didactic work written in the middle of the thirteenth century in the form of a dialogue between a wise father and a son full of intellectual curiosity, there is an enumeration of what is worth knowing in respect of navigation: the light in the different seasons, the movement of the celestial bodies, the succession of the hours of the day, the division of the horizon, and the tides. 'That is valuable knowledge and must be understood by those who want to be seafarers.'

Ship husbandry

In this book there are also snippets of advice concerning the ship herself and the necessary equipment. A good seafarer and merchant should always have good ships, or shares in good ships, for good ships attract good crews. The ship has to be tarred regularly. The equipment should be of good quality and should include good material for the sail, many needles, thread and twine, many well-fitting nails and rivets, boathooks, hatchets and axes, chisels, drills, augers and all the other tools necessary for work on board the ship. The young man, the son, is training to become a merchant, and if a merchant has to know as much about ships and seafaring, how skilled will a more or less professional sailor have been. One of the reasons for this good training and thorough knowledge may have been the fact that most of the people on board a cargo vessel were free men who might have shares in the ship. Nevertheless, they were required to take part in all the work of the seaman, from sail-handling to baling. The crews on cargo ships were not very numerous, so that even passengers, who had paid for their passage, had to participate in the daily work. The handling of the sail, the main means of propulsion, seems to have been the most labour-intensive business on board. Judging by some of the Swedish picture-stones of the eighth century, many sails had no sheets, but a large number of ropes suspended from the sail, each of which had to be handled by one person. On warships this was no problem at all, the crew being very numerous and embracing so many members that often there were two persons for every oar. Therefore these ships were independent of the wind and weather, so that their attacks could be carried out very rapidly. However, in peaceful times even warships sailed – and as has been shown by practical experiments with replicas, they sailed fast and were easy to handle. The rudder worked well, and when close-hauled, angles of less than 50° to the wind could be attained, with a leeway of up to 10°, and with a fair wind a speed of about 15 knots was possible.

All these advantages were jettisoned, however, when increasing trade required more transport capacity. At the end of the Middle Ages, bulkier types ousted the rapid and manoeuvrable north European ships. At the same time, new methods of navigation came into use – though reluctantly – and new forms of the social system within the crew were developed.

Uwe Schnall

Saga Siglar *in Greenland: Viking ships penetrated to the ends of the known world.* (Ragnar Thorseth Adventures)

Bibliography

Edited by Robert Gardiner from material supplied by the contributors.

GENERAL AND INTRODUCTION

The most up to date information on archaeological work is to be found in the specialist journals. For maritime subjects the most important is the *International Journal of Nautical Archaeology* (since 1971), although the older *Mariner's Mirror* (since 1911) has much of value, particularly in its earlier years. Another form of publication that is crucially important in the field is the series of monographs known as British Archaeological Reports—almost universally abbreviated to BAR—published in Oxford from about 1974; there are two numbered series, British and International, the latter numbered with the prefix S for Supplementary. Museums and research institutes also publish regular or occasional reports, like the bi-annual *Maritime Archaeology Newsletter* from Roskilde, detailing their activities.

As introductions or general surveys of the discipline of maritime archaeology, the following can be recommended.

BASIL GREENHILL and SAM MANNING, *The Evolution of the Wooden Ship* (London 1988).
Comprehensively illustrated and discussed evolution of wooden boats into ships as understood by the authors, who combine the skills of a maritime historian and a practical shipwright. Only part is relevant to this bibliography, but it is thought-provoking throughout.

BASIL GREENHILL and JOHN MORRISON, *The Archaeology of Boats and Ships: An Introduction* (London 1995).
A new and entirely revised edition of the standard primer on the archaeology of seacraft. Very full bibliographical listing.

PAUL JOHNSTONE, *The Seacraft of Prehistory* (London 1980).
A very good general survey of the subject, although lacking the latest evidence.

SEAN MCGRAIL, *Rafts, Boats and Ships: From Pre-historic Times to the Medieval Era* (London 1981).
A concise, well illustrated summary of the evidence relating to the pre-modern ship. In the National Maritime Museum's 'The Ship' series.

ERIC MCKEE, *Working Boats of Britain* (London 1983).

The best study of working boats, their building, their use, their men, their evolution, and their handling ever published anywhere. Despite being apparently outside the scope of this volume, *Working Boats* is a unique work of outstanding importance for anyone interested in the boat as a basic tool of mankind.

KEITH MUCKLEROY (ed), *Archaeology under Water* (London and New York 1980).
Subtitled 'An Atlas of the World's Submerged Sites', this volume explores both archaeological techniques and the ship-finds themselves, in chapters contributed by some of the world's leading authorities.

J R STEFFY, *Wooden Shipbuilding and the Interpretation of Shipwrecks* (College Station, Texas 1994).
An outstanding book by the recently retired Professor of Nautical Archaeology at Texas A&M University. The second part of the book contains technical descriptions and drawings of selected wrecks from the ancient world.

PETER THROCKMORTON (ed), *History from the Sea: Shipwrecks and Archaeology* (London 1987).
Simultaneously published in New York as *The Sea Remembers*, this volume is a series of essays by real authorities on the major underwater discoveries to date, in many ways replacing the similar but older *A History of Seafaring based on Underwater Archaeology* edited by G F Bass (London 1972). For the themes of this volume, Chapters 2 and 3 (on the ancient Mediterranean) and Chapter 5 ('Dark Age Seafarers') are the most relevant.

THE BEGINNINGS OF BOATBUILDING IN CENTRAL EUROPE

G BOSINSKI, 'Gönnersdorf. Eiszeitjäger am Mittelrhein', *Ausstellung des Landesmuseums Koblenz* (Koblenz 1981).
Short and instructive information on the hunters' camp. Description of the different materials in the camp and where they came from; but their transport in boats is not worked out here.

D ELLMERS, 'The earliest evidence for skin boats in late-Palaeolithic Europe', SEAN MCGRAIL (ed), *Aspects of Maritime Archaeology and Ethnology* (London 1984), pp41-55.
Reconstruction of a skinboat after the antler frame from Husum; Germany and Norwegian rock carvings.

—, 'Kogge, Kahn und Kunststoffboot. 1000 Jahre Boote in Deutschland', *Führer des Deutschen Schiffahrtsmuseums*, Vol 7 (Bremerhaven 1976).

General survey of boats in Germany from late Palaeolithic to present day.

— and D EVERS, 'Schiffe der Jäger und Bauern. Vorgeschichtliche Felsbilder aus Skandinavien', *Bildmappe des Deutschen Schiffahrtsmuseums*, Vol 7 (Bremerhaven 1981).
Very detailed copies of Scandinavian rock-carvings, done by D Evers with archaeological comments by D Ellmers.

—, 'Frühe Schiffahrt in West- und Mitteleuropa', H MÜLLER-KARPE (ed), *Zur geschichtlichen Bedeutung der frühen Seefahrt* (Munich 1982), pp163-190.
Survey on the use of boats in western and central Europe in prehistory.

—, 'Frühe Schiffahrt auf Ober- und Mittelweser und ihren Nebenflüssen', *Schiffahrt, Handel, Hafen. Beiträge zur Geschichte der Schiffahrt auf Weser und Mittellandkanal* (Minden 1987), pp17-50.
Traces of the use of boats in the Weser valley from late Palaeolithic to the end of the Middle Ages.

—, 'Archäologischer Kommentar zu dem Gedicht von Venantius Fortunatus über seine Moselreise', *Andernach im Frühmittelalter*, Andernacher Beiträge 3 (Andernach 1988), pp25-68.
The first pages deal with late Palaeolithic transports by boats on the Mosel and Rhine in the light of finds from Gönnersdorf, Germany (near Andernach).

—, 'Zwei neolithische Bootsmodelle donauländischer Kulturen', *Kulturen zwischen Ost und West* (Berlin 1993), pp9-17.
Comments on the clay model boats from Einbeck, Germany, and Telis, Bulgaria, and the trade connections from the Danube to northern Germany.

O-H FREY, 'Varna—ein Umschlagplatz für den Seehandel in der Kufperzeit?', J LICHARDUS (ed), *Die Kupferzeit als historische Epoche*, Symposium Saarbrücken und Otzenhausen 6-13 November 1988 (=Saarbrücker Beiträge zur Altertumskunde 55) (Bonn 1992), pp195-210.
In his discussion of Varna as a transit port for the trade across the sea the author publishes three clay models of 'Copper Age' boats found in Bulgaria.

F LAUX, 'Die mesolithischen und frühneolithischen Fundplätze auf den Boberger Dünen bei Hamburg', *Hammaburg* NF 7 (Neumünster 1986), pp9-38.
Short and instructive information on the finds in three small islands in the river Elbe upstream from Hamburg. However, the author did not realise that these islands were a riverbank market, where the farmers came by boats from the south to trade with the hunters.

F RIECK and O CRUMLIN-PEDERSEN, *Både fra Danmarks Oldtid* (Roskilde 1988).
Detailed survey of all prehistoric boats excavated in Denmark.

G SCHWARZ-MACKENSEN and W SCHNEIDER, 'Wo liegen die Hauptliefergebiete für das Rohmaterial donauländischer Steinbeile und -äxte in Mitteleuropa?', *Archäologisches Korrespondenzblatt* 13 (Mainz 1983), pp305-314.

— and —, 'Fernbeziehungen im Frühneolithikum. Rohstoffversorgung am Beispiel des Aktinolith-Hornblendeschiefers', *Frühe Bauernkulturen in Niedersachsen* (Oldenburg1983), pp166-176.
Research on the origin of early Neolithic stone axes and adzes. The transport by boat is not worked out but obviously shown in the distribution map.

W VAN ZEIST, 'De mesolithische boot van pesse', *Nieuwe Drentse Volksalmanak* (Assen 1957), pp4-11.
Report on the oldest dugout found in Europe.

THE BRONZE AGE IN NORTHWEST EUROPE

S MCGRAIL, *Ancient Boats in NW Europe* (London 1987).
Subtitled 'The archaeology of water transport to AD 1500', this contains a wealth of information in a most compact form. Essential reading for the serious student.

—, *Logboats of England & Wales*, BAR 51 (Oxford 1978).
Discussion of the construction and use of 179 finds of logboats dated from c1500 BC to c1500 AD. Catalogue entry for each find. Reconstruction drawings and performance assessments for selected boats, with comparative material from European and other countries. The basic text on logboats.

—, *Brigg 'Raft' and her Prehistoric Environment*, BAR 89 (Oxford 1981).
Report of the excavation of a stitched plank boat of c800 BC, with reconstruction of original boat and assessments of performance. Also comparative material from other early boat finds and from ethnographic stitched boats.

— and E KENTLEY (eds), *Sewn Plank Boats*, BAR S276 (Oxford 1985).
Proceedings of a Greenwich conference on archaeological and ethnographic examples of boats with stitched planking from around the world. Nine papers are on northern Europe.

G ROSENBERG, *Hjortspringfundet* (Copenhagen 1937).
Detailed, illustrated account, in Danish of the 1921-2 excavations. With a 9-page summary in English, and captions to illustrations also in English.

E V WRIGHT, *Ferriby Boats* (London 1990).
Definitive account of the excavation of the Bronze Age boats from the north foreshore of the Humber and of 50 years' research on them. Includes reconstructions and assessments of performance.

SAILING SHIPS OF THE ANCIENT MEDITERRANEAN

G F BASS, 'Cape Gelydonia, A Bronze Age shipwreck', *Transactions of the American Philosophical Society* 57/8 (1967).
Report on a wreck found off southwest Turkey dated to thirteenth century BC. Later material in *A History of Seafaring based on Underwater Archaeology* (London 1974) edited by Bass.

LIONEL CASSON, *Ships and Seamanship in the Ancient World* (Princeton 1971; new edition 1986).
The best general work on the subject, with full coverage of Mediterranean sailing vessels, including small craft. Well illustrated.

C J EISEMAN and B S RIDGWAY, *The Porticello Shipwreck: A Mediterranean Merchant Vessel of 415-385 BC* (College Station, Texas 1987).

PAUL F JOHNSTON, *Ship and Boat Models in Ancient Greece* (Annapolis, Maryland 1985).
A catalogue of 137 models, usefully listing some of the physical evidence for the characteristics of ancient craft, although many are galleys rather than sailing ships.

BJORN LANDSTRÖM, *Ships of the Pharoahs* (Stockholm 1970).
A very approachable study, although some experts find the author's well-known artist's reconstructions less than entirely satisfactory.

PAUL LIPKE, *Royal Ship of Cheops*, BAR S225 (Oxford 1984).

F MEIJER, *A History of Seafaring in the Classical World* (London 1986).
Covers both military and mercantile shipping.

JOHN MORRISON, *Long Ships and Round Ships: Warfare and Trade in the Mediterranean 3000 BC-500 AD* (London 1980).
A concise, well illustrated summary of the evidence relating to both galleys and sailing ships in the ancient Mediterranean. In the National Maritime Museum's 'The Ship' series.

A J PARKER, *Ancient Shipwrecks of the Mediterranean* (Oxford 1987).
A BAR report comprehensively surveying every known wreck site dating from classical times.

JEAN ROUGE, *Ships and Fleets of the Ancient Mediterranean* (Middletown, Connecticut 1981).
Somewhat overshadowed by Casson's work, but some alternative interpretations make it a useful survey.

J R STEFFY, 'The Kyrenia ship: an interim report on its hull construction', *American Journal of Archaeology* 89 (1985), pp71-101.
Report on the important discovery of a fourth-century BC merchant vessel.

CELTIC PLANK BOAT AND SHIPS, 500 BC – AD 1000

B ARNOLD, 'Architecture navale en Helvétic à l'époque romaine: les barques de Bevaix et 'Yverdon', *Helvetia Archaeologica* 77 (Zürich 1989) pp2-28
Short survey of Romano-Celtic dugouts and boats found in Lake Geneva and Lake Neuchâtel.

—, 'Batellerie gallo-romaine sur le lac de Neuchâtel', *Archéologie Neuchâteloix* 12 and 13 (Saint Blaise/Neuchâtel 1992).
Profound analysis of the Romano-Celtic dugouts and boats found in Swiss lakes.

J BIEL, 'Frühkeltische Fürsten', *Das keltische Jahrtausend* (Mainz 1993), pp40-46.
This paper shows how attractive the courts of the Celtic princes were for Greek and Italian merchants, and among other things publishes the beam of a pair of fine Greek scales found at Hochdorf.

G DE BOE and F HUBERT, 'Une installation portu-aire d'époque romaine à Pommeroeul', *Archaeologica Belgica* 192 (Brussels 1977).
Report on the excavation of the Romano-Celtic dugouts and boats and a lot of small finds in a small river harbour at Pommeroeul, Belgium.

M D DE WEERD, *Schepen voor Zwammerdam* (Amsterdam 1988).
Final publication of the Romano-Celtic dugouts and boats and one raft found in the Rhine in front of the Roman camp of Zwammerdam/Netherlands.

M EGG, 'Das Grab eines unterkrainischen Kriegers in Hallstatt', *Archäologisches Korrespondenzblatt* 8 (Mainz 1978), pp191-201.
This paper gives an example of sovereign trade in the Hallstatt period: a member of the warrior aristocracy of Lower Kraina had travelled to Hallstatt together with several of his retainers, who following his death buried him there in his full finery.

D ELLMERS, 'Keltischer Schiffbau', *Jahrbuch des Römisch-Germanischen Zentralmuseums* 16 (Mainz 1969), pp73-122 and tables 16-18.
First survey of Celtic boatbuilding traditions: most of the Romano-Celtic inland vessels have been discovered since this was written, but fit well into the pattern established here.

—, 'Antriebstechniken germanischer Schiffe im 1. Jahrtausend n. Chr.', *Deutsches Schiffahrtsarchiv* 1 (Hamburg 1975), pp79-90.
Different means of propulsion of Celtic and of Germanic ships are compared.

—, *Kogge, Kahn und Kunststoffboot. 10,000 Jahre Boote in Deutschland*, (Bremerhaven 1976).
Celtic boats and ships are shown as part of a long development of water craft in central Europe.

—, 'Der Nachtsprung an eine hinter dem Horizont liegende Gegenküste. Die älteste astronomische Navigationsmethode', *Deutsches Schiffahrtsarchiv* 4 (Hamburg 1981), pp153-167.
Navigation by the pole star was only possible at night. This article discusses the written sources and maps are worked out which show routes where this method of navigation was possible for rowing boats and for sailing vessels.

—, 'Frühe Schiffahrt in West- und Nordeuropa', *Zur geschichtlichen Bedeutung der frühen Seefahrt. Kolloquien zur Allgemeinen und Vergleichenden Archäologie*, Vol 2 (Munich 1982), pp163-190.
Celtic seafaring is discussed and compared with that of Germanic tribes in Scandinavia.

—, 'Punt, barge or pram – is there one tradition or several?' in SEAN MCGRAIL (ed), *Aspects of Maritime Archaeology and Ethnology* (London 1984), pp153-172.
The question in the title is answered in favour of several traditions which differ very much in detail.

—, 'Vor- und frühgeschichtlicher Boots- und Schiffbau in Europa nördlich der Alpen', *Das Handwerk in vor- und frühgeschichtlicher Zeit*, Vol 2 (Göttingen 1983), pp471-534.
The development of the art of boatbuilding is described through the ages. Celtic boatbuilding is seen as a development from dugouts to boats larger than a single tree trunk but still having elements of dugouts in their construction.

—, 'Die Archäologie der Binnenschiffahrt in Europa nördlich der Alpen', *Untersuchungen zu Handel und Verkehr der vor- und frühgeschichtlichen Zeit in Mittel- und Nordeuropa*, Vol 5 (Göttingen 1989), pp291-350.
All aspects of building and using inland vessels including the waterways and the harbours are discussed from an archaeological point of view.

O HÖCKMANN, 'Spätrömische Schiffsfunde in Mainz', *Archäologisches Korrespondenzblatt* 12 (Mainz 1982), pp234-250.
First report on not less than ten fragments of boats and one raft, excavated in the city of Mainz in 1981-82.

—, 'Keltisch oder römisch? Bemerkungen zur Typengenese der spätrömischen Ruderschiffe von Mainz', *Jahrbuch des Römisch-Germanischen Zentralmuseums* 30 (Mainz 1983), pp403-434 and tables 86-92.
The Mainz boats of the late fourth century are military types, designed after Mediterranean patterns but using the Celtic method of joining strakes and frames with iron nails secured by rebending their points into the timber again.

G KOSSACK, 'Die Donau als Handelsweg in vorgeschichtlicher Zeit', *Osbairische Grenzmarken. Passauer Jahrbuch* 31 (Passsau 1989), pp168-186.
This paper shows how the Danube and all its tributaries have been used as a natural line of communication in different ages.

PETER MARSDEN, *A Ship of the Roman Period, from Blackfriars in the City of London* (London 1967).
For the first time in the world this author here identified an excavated ship as a work of Celtic handicraft by comparing it with the report of Julius Caesar on the ships of the Celtic Veneti.

SEAN MCGRAIL, 'Assessing the Performance of an Ancient Boat – the Hasholme Logboat', *Oxford Journal of Archaeology* 7/1 (Oxford 1988), pp35-46.
Hydrostatic curves and speed-related coefficients are used to assess the dugout from Hasholme.

— (ed), *Maritime Celts, Frisians and Saxons*, CBA Research Report No 71 (London 1990).
Papers of a conference held at Oxford in 1988 dealing with different questions of Celtic boats and harbours.

—, N NAYLING and D MAYNARD, 'Barland's Farm, Magor, Gwent; a Romano-Celtic boat', *Antiquity* 68 (1994), pp596-603.
Report on a 16m long wreck of a Romano-Celtic boat found in the estuary of the river Severn, south Wales.

—, 'Romano-Celtic boats and ships: characteristic features', *International Journal of Nautical Archaeology* 24 (1995), pp139-145.
The author gives a short history of research into Celtic boats and ships and tries to define their boatbuilding tradition and to establish subgroups within this tradition.

—, 'Celtic Seafaring and Transport', in M J GREEN (ed), *The Celtic World* (London and New York 1995), pp254-291.
Survey of all aspects of Celtic boats and ships: propulsion, steering, different craft and their boatbuilding traditions, overseas routes, inland travels and harbours.

S NEU, 'Ein Schiffsrelief vom Kölner Rheinufer', *Boreas, Münstersche Beiträge zur Archäologie* 5 (Münster 1982), pp133-138 and table 9.
Report on the fragmentary relief found near the Roman harbour of Köln (c90 AD).

J DU PLAT TAYLOR and HENRY CLEERE (eds), *Roman Shipping and Trade: Britain and the Rhine provinces*, CBA Research Report No 24 (London 1978).
Papers of a symposium held at Cambridge in 1977; many of the papers deal with finds or pictures of Romano-Celtic boats.

H R REINDERS, 'Drie middeleeuwse rivierschepen gevonden bij Meinerswijk, Arnhem', *Flevobericht* Nr 221 (Lelystad 1983), pp21-37 and drawing p62.
Report on the *Oberländer*.

PROTO-VIKING, VIKING AND NORSE CRAFT

R L S BRUCE-MITFORD and A CARE EVANS, *The Sutton Hoo Ship Burial*, Vol I: The Ship (London 1975).
The definitive report on the excavation, although some more recent work has been done.

A W BRØGGER and H SHELTIG, *The Viking Ships: their ancestry and evolution* (Oslo 1971).
Although somewhat outdated, this book remains the most widely available source on Nordic craft; covers a wider period than the Viking Age proper, and many aspects of seafaring.

A E CHRISTENSEN, *Boats of the North* (Oslo 1968).
A standard work by one of the foremost authorities.

— , *Boat Finds from the Bryggen*, Bryggen Papers main series Vol 1 (Bergen 1985).
Report on excavations on the medieval Bergen waterfront.

— , 'Boat finds from Mangersnes', in O OLSEN et al (eds), *Shipshape. Essays for Ole Crumlin-Pedersen* (Roskilde 1995).

OLE CRUMLIN-PEDERSEN, 'Skin or wood? A study of the origin of the Scandinavian plank-boat', in *Ships and Shipyards, Sailors and Fishermen* (Copenhagen 1972).
An important article arguing for the expanded dugout as the ancestor of northern planked craft.

— , 'Cargo ships of northern Europe, AD 800-1300', in A E HERTEIG (ed), *Conference on Waterfront Archaeology in Northern European Towns*, No 2 (Bergen 1985).

C ENGELHARDT, *Nydam Mosefund* (Copenhagen 1865).

— , 'Nydambåden og nordlandsbåden', *Aarbøger for nordisk oldkyndighed og Historie* (Copenhagen 1866).
With the above title, the original publication of the Nydam boat find.

K HELSKOG, *Helleristtningene i Alta* (Alta 1988).

P MARSDEN, *Ships of the Port of London, first to eleventh centuries AD* (London 1994).
A good survey of Thames shipping based on excavations on various waterfront sites.

S MARSTRANDER, *Østfolds jordbruksristninger, Skjeberg* (Oslo 1963).

O OLSEN et al (eds), *Shipshape. Essays for Ole Crumlin-Pedersen* (Roskilde 1995).
A *Festschrift* for one of the great scholars of Viking maritime history containing a number of highly significant essays on related subjects. Includes a particularly full bibliography of Crumlin-Pedersen's writings.

OLSEN and O CRUMLIN-PEDERSEN, *Five Viking Ships* (Copenhagen 1978).
A comparative study of the best preserved vessels.

R REINDERS, *Cog Finds from the Ijsselmeerpolders* (Lelystad 1985).
Some of the craft discovered while draining these Dutch polders are relevant to the Viking Age.

G ROSENBERG, *Hjortspringfundet* (Copenhagen 1929).
See comments in the section 'The Bronze Age in Northwest Europe'.

H SHETELIG and P JOHANNESSEN, *Kvalsundfundet* (Bergen 1929).
The original report on the Kvalsund boat find.

C L VEBÆK and S THIRSLUND, *The Viking Compass* (Helsingør 1992).
Proposes the concept of the 'bearing dial', which has still to be universally accepted.

E V WRIGHT, *The Ferriby Boats* (London 1990).
See comments in the section 'The Bronze Age in Northwest Europe'.

ARABIA TO CHINA – THE ORIENTAL TRADITIONS

Much of the recently discovered information about oriental ship types is only to be found in academic articles in the learned journals. Specific references are given in the footnotes to the relevant sections of this chapter, so repetition is unnecessary. Therefore, this list concentrates on more general background works.

BASIL GREENHILL, *Boats and Boatmen of Pakistan* (Newton Abbot 1971).
A pioneering study by a man who was to become one of the foremost names in maritime history.

A C HADDON and J HORNELL, *Canoes of Oceania*, 3 vols (Honolulu 1936-8; reprinted as 1 vol Honolulu 1975).
Slightly outside the geographical scope of this chapter but relevant in terms of parallel techniques of construction; a very detailed work.

J HORNELL, *Water Transport* (Newton Abbot 1970).
A pioneering study, with much reference to eastern waters, but some conclusions have been superseded by more detailed fieldwork.

ADRIAN HORRIDGE, *Sailing Craft of Indonesia* (Oxford 1986).
A small but authoritative booklet by one of the foremost specialists in the field. This author also published an excellent series of National Maritime Museum Monographs on various Asian boat types: *The Design of Planked Boats of the Moluccas* (1978); *The Lambo or Prahu Bot: A Western Ship in an Eastern Setting* (1979); and *The Lashed-lug Boat of the Eastern Archipelagoes* (1982).

G F HOURANI, *Arab Seafaring in the Indian Ocean in Ancient and Early Medieval Times* (Princeton 1951; new edition 1995).
Standard academic history of the Arab peoples at sea; not primarily about their vessels, but tends to cover what early references there are.

PAUL JOHNSTONE, *The Seacraft of Prehistory* (London 1980).
See Introduction section for general comment, but includes survey of eastern craft.

J NEEDHAM, *Science and Civilisation in China*, Vol 4, Part 3 (Cambridge 1971).
The water transportation volume of this monumental study of the history of Chinese science and technology. A summary of existing knowledge, but in depth.

A H J PRINS, *Sailing from Lamu* (Assen, Netherlands 1965).
Subtitled 'A study of maritime culture in Islamic East Africa', this is an ethnographic and technical work by a prominent Dutch anthropologist.

G R G WORCESTER, *Junks and Sampans of the Yangtse*, 2 vols (Shanghai 1947-8; reprinted with revisions Annapolis 1971).
A classic study by a man who spent his whole working life on the rivers of China as an official of the maritime customs service; well illustrated.

— , *Sail and Sweep in China* (London 1966).
A broader study of the river craft of China.

PROBLEMS OF RECONSTRUCTION AND THE ESTIMATION OF PERFORMANCE

BENT ANDERSEN and ERIK ANDERSEN, *Råsejlet-Dragens Vinge* (Roskilde 1990).
Extensive documentation (in Danish) of the principles of reconstructing the hulls, rigs and handling characteristics of Viking ships.

ERIK ANDERSEN, 'Square sails of wool', in O OLSEN *et al* (eds), *Shipshape. Essays for Ole Crumlin-Pedersen* (Roskilde 1995), pp249-270.

The article presents and discusses the archaeological and ethnological evidence for woollen sails in Scandinavia.

UWE BAYKOWSKI, *Die Kieler Hansekogge. Der Nachbau eines historischen Segelschiffes von 1380* (Kiel 1991).
Popular book with many technical details on the building of the replica of the Bremen cog in Kiel in 1987-89, and on the first sea trials.

JAN BILL, 'Gedesbyskibet. Middelalderlig skude- og færgefart fra Falster', in *Nationalmuseets Arbejdsmark 1991* (Copenhagen 1991), pp188-198.
Publication of the excavation of a small Baltic cargo ship of the late thirteenth century.

ARNE EMIL CHRISTENSEN, '*Viking*, a Gokstad Ship Replica from 1893', in OLE CRUMLIN-PEDERSEN and MAX VINNER (eds), *Sailing into the Past. Proceedings of the International Seminar on Replicas of Ancient and Medieval Vessels, Roskilde, 1984* (Roskilde 1986), pp68-77.
Brief description of the first Viking ship replica.

OLE CRUMLIN-PEDERSEN, 'The Viking Ships of Roskilde', in *Aspects of the History of Wooden Shipbuilding*, Maritime Monographs and Reports No 1, pp7-23 (London 1970).
Early presentation of the Skuldelev find.

— , 'Aspects of Viking Age Shipbuilding in the Light of the Construction and Trials of the Skuldelev Ship-Replicas *Saga Siglar* and *Roar Ege*', in *Journal of Danish Archaeology* 5 (Odense 1987), pp209-228.
Discussion of experimental ship archaeology and its contributions to our knowledge of Viking Age technology, etc.

— , 'Gensyn med Skuldelev 5 – et ledingsskib?' in *Festskrift til Olaf Olsen* (Copenhagen 1988), pp137-156.
Discussion of the origin and characteristics of the Skuldelev 5 warship and related finds.

— and MAX VINNER (eds), *Sailing into the Past. Proceedings of the International Seminar on Replicas of Ancient and Medieval Vessels, Roskilde, 1984* (Roskilde 1986).
Twenty-three papers devoted to many aspects of replicas and their performance, etc.

— and — , 'Le projet *Roar Ege*. Reconstitution et expérimentation d'un caboteur viking', *Le Chasse-Marée* 30 (1987), pp16-45.
Well illustrated presentation of the Skuldelev 3 replica *Roar Ege*'s construction and sea trials.

— and —, '*Roar* og *Helge* af Roskilde – om at bygge og sejle med vikingeskibe', in *Nationalmuseets Arbejdsmark 1993* (Copenhagen 1993), pp11-29.
Presentation of the results of the *Roar Ege* and *Helge Ask* projects.

OLAF OLSEN and OLE CRUMLIN-PEDERSEN, 'The Skuldelev Ships II. A Report of the Final Underwater Excavation in 1959 and the Salvaging Operation in 1962', *Acta Archaeologica* 38 (Copenhagen 1968), pp95-170.
Detailed preliminary publication of the Skuldelev ships.

RAGNAR THORSETH, *Saga Siglar. Århundrets seilas Jorda rundt* (Ålesund 1988).

Popular Norwegian book on the construction of the Skuldelev 1 replica *Saga Siglar* and her trip around the world.

MAX VINNER, 'A Viking-ship off Cape Farewell 1984', in *Shipshape. Essays for Ole Crumlin-Pedersen* (eds O Olsen *et al*) (Roskilde 1995), pp289-404.
Report on the North Atlantic sea trials with the Skuldelev 1 replica *Saga Siglar* in 1984.

EARLY SHIPHANDLING AND NAVIGATION IN NORTHERN EUROPE

ALAN BINNS, *Viking Voyagers. Then and Now* (London 1980).
Discussion of the whole system of Viking navigation by a learned seaman, together with a report of experiences on *Odin's Raven*, a replica of a longship.

DETLEV ELLMERS, *Frühmittelalterliche Handelsschiffahrt in Mittel- und Nordeuropa*, Deutsches Schiffahrtsmuseum's Publication, Vol 3 (Neumünster 1972).
Important work about medieval shipping, including routes and crews and speed etc.

SIBYLLA HAASUM, *Vikingatidens segling och navigation*, Theses and Papers in North-European Archaeology, Vol 4 (Stockholm 1974).
General view of Viking navigation; focusses on the sailing quality of Viking ships.

GWYN JONES, *The Norse Atlantic Saga* (London 1964).
History of the conquest of the North Atlantic, with the Norsemen's discovery of America.

GEOFFREY J MARCUS, *The Conquest of the North Atlantic* (Woodbridge 1980).
Description of the gradual conquest of the North Atlantic from the beginnings to Hanseatic and English traders. With exhaustive discussion of the means of navigation.

ALBRECHT SAUER, 'Die Bedeutung der Küste in der Navigation des Spätmittelalters', in *Deutsches Schiffahrtsarchiv* 15 (1992), pp249-278.
Thorough investigation of the role of coastal navigation in the late Middle Ages.

—, 'Zur Praxis der Gezeitenrechnung in der frühen Neuzeit', in *Deutsches Schiffahrtsarchiv* 17 (1994), pp93-150.
Outstanding description and discussion of the attempts to calculate the tides in early modern times (English resume).

UWE SCHNALL, *Navigation der Wikinger*, Deutsches Schiffahrtsmuseum's Publication, Vol 6 (Oldenburg 1975).
Description of the Viking navigation and discussion of the source material.

—, 'Bemerkungen zur Navigation auf Koggen', in *Jahrbuch der Wittheit zu Bremen* 21 (1977), pp137-148.
Discussion of the navigation on board Hanseatic ships.

—, 'Practical navigation in the late Middle Ages. Some remarks on the transfer of knowledge from the Mediterranean to the Northern Seas', in C VILLAIN-

GANDOSSI *et al* (eds), *Medieval Ships and the Birth of Technological Societies*, Vol 2 (Malta 1991), pp271-279.

EVA G R TAYLOR, *The Haven-Finding Art* (Third edition London 1971).
Standard work on the history of navigation from the beginning to the eighteenth century.

Vikingernes sejlads til Nordamerika, catalogue published by the Vikingeskibshallen (Roskilde 1992).
Essays on all aspects of the North Atlantic crossings of the Vikings.

THORSTEINN VILHJÁLMSSON, 'Af Surti og Sól. Um tímatal o.fl. á fyrstu öldum Íslands byggoar', in *Tímarit Háskóla Íslands*, Vol 4 (1989), pp87-97.

Precise description of the astronomical and mathematical possibilities in navigation in medieval Iceland (English resume).

Glossary of Terms and Abbreviations

Complied by Robert Gardiner with the assistance of the contributors. This list assumes some knowledge of ships and does not include the most basic terminology. It also avoids those words which are defined on the only occasions in which they occur in this book.

Ahrensburg Culture. Named after the village near Hamburg where there are two late Paleolithic sites, the main one at Stellmoor being dated to *c*8500 BC. The site has produced the first conclusive evidence of the use of the bow and arrow, in a collection of some fifty pine arrow shafts with notches for bowstrings. The Ahrensberg people were hunters, primarily of reindeer.

amphora (plural amphorae). A storage jar of the ancient Mediterranean, usually large, of tapering shape, with a narrow mouth and a pair of handles. They were cheap, and large deposits of broken amphorae on many sites suggest that they were regarded as 'disposable' in much the same way as modern packaging.

aphlaston. The fan-like ornament at the stern of ancient Mediterranean vessels in which the up-curving timbers of the hull terminated. Later known as the *aplustria*.

artemon. The small, square fore sail of ancient Mediterranean vessels.

Baalberge Culture. A post Neolithic central European society dating from around 4500-3600 BC named after the excavation site near Bernburg, northwest of Halle. This culture continued to make considerable use of flint and bone implements, but some copper has been found. Its pottery shows some similarities with Rössen Ware (*qv*), and the Baalbergers introduced tumulus and stone cist burials, unlike the earlier flat graves without monumental additions.

bast. The flexible inner bark of the lime or linden tree.

Battle Axe Culture. Also known as the Corded Ware Culture from the twisted cord motifs that characteristically decorated their pottery, these peoples were found over large parts of the north European plain in the third millenium BC. They used stone battle axes, although some groups also had metal artefacts, and they practised single burial under round barrows. Thay may have domesticated the horse, and employed wheeled vehicles.

bevel. To cut at an angle, or the edge so formed; commonly applied to reducing a square edge to an angle. Bevel joints, where two timber ends were cut to complementary angles and lapped, could be used to join timber end to end.

black-figure pottery. An ancient Mediterranean style with figures painted in black on a an unglazed or slightly glazed red background.

Blockkahn. A logboat-derived small boat found on some north German lakes; the bow and stern were formed of solid blocks which gave the vessel its name. It is thought to be the distant ancestor of the cog (*qv*).

boom. In rigging a relatively light spar, most commonly used to stretch the foot of a sail.

braces. Rigging that pivots the yards; to brace up was to swing them to as sharp (*ie* smallest) an angle with the keel as feasible; bracing in was the reverse.

brails. Rigging lines used to reduce and control the area of sail catching the wind.

Bremen cog. The name generally applied to the Hanseatic cog discovered in the river Weser near Bremen in October 1962. The ship, which was washed away during a storm before completion, is now in the Deutsches Schiffarhtsmuseum, Bremerhaven where it has been conserved and re-assembled.

buntlines. Rigging from the foot of a square sail passing over the forward surface to the yard; used to spill the wind from the sail when necessary.

carbon 14 (abbreviation C14). *See* radiocarbon dating.

carvel. A method of construction in which the strakes of planking butt at the edges, creating a flush hull surface – as opposed to clinker (*qv*) in which the strakes overlap and are clenched through this overlap. Carvel as a method of construction implies the initial setting up of a frame to which the strakes are fastened, which in turn means that some form of preconceived design is necessary in order for a properly faired shape to result. The technique was probably imported into northern Europe from the Mediterranean, where in late Antiquity frame-first carvel had replaced the earlier shell-first structure where mortise and tenon joints formed the connections between strakes.

caulk. To ram fibrous material (caulking) hard into a seam to make it watertight and to prevent the planks of the hull from sliding upon each other when the hull is subjected to longitudinal bending stresses.

chine. The meeting of the hull side and bottom. If there is a sharp change of angle, forming a sort of fold or knuckle, the craft is said to be hard-chined; but if it is more rounded then the vessel is soft-chined.

clench. To bend the protruding part of a spike or nail over to prevent it pulling out of timber; also, specifically, to rivet the end of a nail over a washer, or rove.

clinker. Method of construction in which overlapping strakes are fastened along the edges (usually with nails 'clenched' over roves, from which the term derives). It is a shell-first technique, without the benefit of a pre-erected frame, although strengthening timbers are sometimes added later.

cog. The classic sailing ship of northern Europe in the high Middle Ages, the cog was developed on the Frisian coast from whence its usage spread to down the North sea coasts and into the Baltic before reaching the Mediterranean. Its capacious flat-bottomed form, with straight raked stem- and stern-posts, is believed to derive from the technology of expanded logboats, but by the thirteenth century the type had evolved into a seagoing vessel of several hundred tons in its largest form. It acquired a stern rudder on the centreline to replace the steering oars and was powered by a single square sail.

coracle. Small boat usually associated with the Celtic areas of Britain (Wales and Ireland predominantly), constructed of wickerwork and originally covered with hides but more recently pitch or tarred canvas has been used. The Welsh version is usually small and round (or a rounded rectangle) in shape, man-portable and designed to carry one or at most two people, usually for fishing on rivers and lakes. The Irish *curach* is larger, more boat-like, and very seaworthy.

cotter. A locking wedge, key or bolt fitting through the body of an item to keep it firmly in its position.

cowrie. Shell of the shallow-water mollusc *Cypraea moneta*, abundant in the Indian Ocean region and traditionally used as money in parts of Africa and southern Asia.

crank. Of ships, lacking in stability.

cuculus. Latin term for an item of Celtic foul-weather gear, a hooded cloak popular with boatmen; survived into the Middle Ages with its name corrupted to 'gugel'.

Culture. As specifically used in archaeology, the term refers to a recognisable collection of artefacts or characteristic aspects of living that define a prehistoric people. Since thay are not known through written sources, each Culture tends to be named after a major archaeological site, like the Hallstatt Culture (*qv*), or some readily identifiable aspect of its lifestyle (*eg* Linear pottery Culture).

curach. *See* coracle.

cutwater. The leading edge of the bow, sometimes a separate structural member, that cleaves the water when the craft is under way.

dead reckoning. The estimation of a ships's progress across the surface of the sea, arriving at the estimated present position by taking into account course steered and calculated distance run, after due allowance has been made for tides, currents and leeway, since the last known position.

dendrochronology. An archaeological technique for dating timber artifacts based on an analysis of the annular growth rings in trees. The width and structure of such rings depends on the weather during the relevant growth period, measurements which can be plotted in the form of graphs. Starting from known dates it is possible to build up a 'map' of climate changes in particular areas and for specific periods and tree species against which the tree-ring graphs of undated timber can be compared. This can often produce quite accurate felling dates, which help to pinpoint the date at which the artifact was made.

dhoni. Small sailing craft of the Maldive Islands, built by a shell-first technique.

dhow. A generic term for the lateen rigged sailing coasters native to the Red Sea, Persian Gulf and Indian Ocean (there are many sub-variants); originally built by dowelled shell-first techniques, later examples have become frame-first, or partially so.

displacement. The mass of the volume of water occupied by the ship when afloat.

dovetail joint. A timber joint in which a tongue is cut to be wider at its extremity, forming the flat-ended fan-shape of the dove's tail. The tongue is fitted into a correspondingly shaped aperture; because it is wider at the end it cannot work free.

dowel. Round rod of wood, usually driven into holes drilled into timber as a fastening or filling.

dragon boats. Very long canoes paddled by large crews from southeast Asia, surviving today for ceremonial and racing purposes but originally used for war and piracy.

dugout. Synonymous with logboat (*qv*).

Ertbølle-Ellerbek Culture. A late Mesolithic society named after a coastal site in Denmark. Pottery, in a rather coarse form, seems to have been introduced by this culture.

expanded/extended dugout (or logboat). A craft in which the single-trunk logboat (*qv*) construction has been extended by the addition of a strake or strakes to the hull. Some historians prefer the term 'extended' for this form of construction, confining 'expanded' to a process of softening the dugout's sides with fire and water in order to get them to take on a more curved and boat-like shape.

fay. To fit together closely.

firrer. Type of steering oar used on *kahns* (*qv*) and sail-powered logboats. The rig was balanced in such a way that immersing the *firrer* to a greater or lesser extent altered the fore and aft centre of gravity, causing the boat to turn into or off the wind. The *firrer* differed from normal steering oars in that its blade did not need to be turned itself in order to manouevre the boat.

floor. In shipbuilding, transverse timbers across the keel and bottom planking.

fluit, fluyt, flute, etc. Characteristically Dutch merchantman, ship rigged and of large carrying capacity, extreme tumblehome and a narrow 'flute' stern. They were usually austere in decoration, with a plain stemhead, few if any guns, and a small crew relative to tonnage; there were, however, more conventional versions, with more powerful armament, for trading in dangerous waters. They were essentially a product of the late sixteenth century, but dominated the Dutch carrying trade in the seventeenth. Known as 'flyboats' to the English.

forefoot. The forward extremity of the keel; extended beyond the line of the stem in a ram bow.

frame-first. A term used by modern historians for ship- and boatbuilding in which the hull strakes are fastened to a pre-erected framework, as opposed to shell-first construction like clinker. In many contexts it is synonymous with carvel (*qv*), but is preferred as being a more precise definition than the old dichotomy between carvel and clinker, since there are methods of building hulls shell-first other than clinker.

freeboard. The height of the top edge of the hull amidships, or the bottom edge of an opening in the ship's side, above the surface of the water when the ship is afloat.

Funnel Beaker Culture. The earliest identified Neolithic (*qv*) culture of northern Europe (covering southern Scandinavia, northern Germany and Poland, and the Low Countries) in the later fourth and early third millenium BC. It is believed to have been developed by contact between the earlier Mesolithic peoples and the Linear Pottery Culture (*qv*) further south. It is also known as TRB Culture from the German *Trichterbecher* or Danish *Tragterbecher*.

garboard. Strake of planking next to the keel, and by extension that general area of the hull.

Geometric. The term applied to Greek painted pottery with geometrical decoration of the period 900-700 BC.

Gokstad ship. A Viking vessel found in a burial mound at Gokstad in southern Norway in 1880. Dating from about AD 890, the craft was large (79ft, 24m long) and relatively high-sided with shuttered tholes for the oars; that the craft was seaworthy was proved by the sailing of a replica across the Atlantic in 1893. The original was carefully reassembled and is now in Oslo's Viking Ship Museum.

graffito. A rough drawing scratched on a wall or other suitable surface.

gugel. See *cuculus*.

half-lap joint. A connection of timber formed by cutting away half the thickness on alternate sides of each piece to be joined and overlapping the resulting parts.

Hallstatt Culture. Early Iron Age culture named after the village in Austria which produced some of the richest finds, especially of metalwork. The main site is a hillside cemetery, but there are also extensive salt mines in the area. Based in the Danube region, the culture spread to southern Germany, and parts of eastern and central France. Evidence from the early phase (900-700 BC) suggests a relatively poor warrior aristocracy, but later grave deposits show a greater differentiation between rich Celtic chieftains and their peoples, their wealth being based on intense trading links with Mediterranean civilisations. It was succeeded by the La Tène Culture (*qv*).

Hasholme dugout. A large cargo-carrying dugout, over 12m long, with fitted transom and composite bow, found at Hasholme, North Humberside, United Kingdom. It is dated to about 300 BC.

heel. Of a ship, angle of inclination from the upright.

Hellenistic. A term used by historians to denote the post-Classical Greek world, in the period roughly between the death of Alexander the Great in 323 BC and the hegemony of the Romans some three centuries later.

hogging. Bending or shearing of a ship's hull so that its ends drop relative to the middle; caused by wave action in a seaway.

hogging truss. A device stretching fore and aft on relatively long or weak vessels to prevent hogging (*qv*). In early craft it usually took the form of tensioned cables run over crutches amidships and fastened at the extremities of the hull.

holc. *See* hulk.

hulc or hulk. Rather mysterious ship type of North Sea origins whose working career paralleled, and eventually outlasted, that of the cog. What small iconographical evidence there is suggests a banana-shaped hull of very rounded form. A Dorestad coin of AD 800 may show one, and documents of the period indicate that the hulk was a very important carrier in trade between Britain and continental Europe. As a regular type-name the word declined in the fifteenth century, and eventually changed its meaning to indicate a dismasted vessel or one laid up and unfit for sea; if there is any connection between the two usages scholars have been unable to make a convincing case for it.

jekta. Norwegian coastal vessels with a single square sail that represent a survival of Viking boat design and construction down to the early twentieth century when the last of the type were still in use.

Kahn. German inland barge of the Oder region.

kayak. Inuit (Eskimo) skin canoe used for hunting or fishing, it has an enclosed hull except for the small aperture through which the paddler's torso emerges; it is paddled from a sitting position. The term is also applied to a modern derivative of generally similar design, though often of higher-tech construction, widely used for sport and recreation.

keel. Lowermost structural member of a ship's hull; in a frame-built vessel effectively the backbone, the frames forming the ribs.

keelson or kelson. Longitudinal member laid over and secured to floors inside a ship above the keel.

knaar. The sea-going cargo carrier of the Viking era, famous from many references in the sagas and other Scandinavian literature. Compared with longships, the *knaar* was shorter, deeper and more capacious, and probably not intended for regular beaching; relatively seaworthy, the *knaar* was the most probable vehicle of the Viking exploration of the North Atlantic.

knee. In shipbuilding a bracket joining the ship's side to a cross beam.

knot. Nautical measure of speed, 1 knot being one sea, or nautical, mile per hour. This equals 1 minute of latitude per hour or 1852 metres.

krater. A big, deep bowl for mixing wine; ancient Greek.

Ladby boat. A tenth-century craft found in a chieftain's burial mound on the Danish island of Funen in 1935. Only the impression remained of a vessel some 67ft long.

lap-strake. Another term for clinker (*qv*).

lateen. Sail or rig characterised by triangular canvas set from long yard attached to the mast at an angle of about 45 degrees from the horizontal, the forward end being the lower. It was a fore-and-rig rig dating from at least late Antiquity and was the usual form of sail for most types of medieval Mediterranean craft. In the late Middle Ages it was also added to square rigged vessels, usually as a small after sail to help balance the rig and aid going about, and retained this role with the development of the three-masted ship rig.

La Tène Culture. A later Iron Age Celtic society named after the site on Lake Neuchâtel in Switzerland where its remains were first excavated. Its history is usually divided into three periods (La Tène I from 500 to 300 BC; II 300-100 BC; and III 100 to the era of Christ), it originated in the area of the middle Rhine, but expanded to cover the traditional territories of the earlier Hallstatt (*qv*) peoples, as well as the rest of Gaul, northern Italy, northern Germany, Britain and central Scandinavia. A sophisticated, if warlike, tribal culture, it was capable of exquisite and the construction of massive hillforts and *oppida* (*qv*), but also enjoyed firmly established trading contacts with the Mediterranean world. It eventually clashed with the Romans and under equal pressure from German and Nordic tribes it was eventually absorbed into the Roman sphere of influence.

lath. A thin and narrow strip of wood.

lee. The side or direction away from the wind or downwind (leeward); hence 'lee shore' is one onto which the wind is blowing.

leech. The side of a square sail; the after edge of a fore-and-aft sail.

lift. In rigging a rope from the masthead to the outer extremity (yardarm) of a yard (*qv*), used to square it (ie to keep it perpendicular to the mast).

Linear Pottery Culture. The first farming society of central Europe, dating from around 4500-4000 BC at its cultural centre, but lasting as late as 3200 BC on its periphery. It was characterised by the construction of timber long houses and decorated pottery with painted linear designs. Its areas stretched from the Netherlands to eastern Hungary and eventually to Poland. It is known as *Linienbandkeramik* in German, or LBK for short.

logboat. A dugout craft essentially constructed from a single piece of timber. *See also* expanded dugout.

loose-footed. Of sails, a pattern without a boom to stretch its lower edge.

lorcha. A hybrid oriental vessel combining a European sailing ship's hull form with the Chinese junk rig; thought to originate from Macao, the early Portuguese settlement in China.

madel oruwa/madel paruwa. Two types of Sri Lankan outrigger (*qv*) canoe, used for beach seine net fishing.

Magdalene. A late Paleolithic (*qv*) culture (about 16,000-10,000 BC) named after the archaelogical site of La Madeleine in the Dordogne, southwest France, where it was first identified. It has been divided into six phases, and was characterised by finds of bone implements testifying to a fishing and deer-hunting lifestyle during the final phase of the last Ice Age. It was the culture that produced most of the best known cave paintings.

Mesolithic. That part of the Stone Age between the Paleolithic (*qv*) and the Neolithic (*qv*); literally the 'middle'.

money cowrie. *See* cowrie.

mortise and tenon. Woodworking joint in which slots (mortises) are cut in one piece, into which tongues (tenons) are inserted in order to fasten another. The tenon can be integral with one of the pieces, or can be separate, mortises being then cut in both parts to be joined together. The technique was widely employed in shipbuilding in Antiquity, shell-first (*qv*) hulls being laboriously constructed by fixing flush strakes of timber together using this joint. Such a hull was light and strong, but required a high level of skill and was labour-intensive; it also made the pre-planning of hull shape difficult.

mtepe. A type of East African sailing coaster from the Lamu Archipelago which survived until early in this century, it existed in a number of variant forms but was characterised by a dowelled and sewn shell-first construction.

murus Gallicus. The form of timber-laced iron-fastened rampart that typically surrounded the late Celtic settlements known as *oppida* (*qv*) of La Tène Culture (*qv*); from a phrase in Caesar's *Gallic Wars* describing the defences of Avaricum in Gaul. The latticed timber structure stabilised and strengthened a stone-faced earth core.

Neolithic. The later (or new) Stone Age, and anything pertaining to it. It is characterised by the use of ground and polished stone tools (as opposed to chipped in earlier periods), and the employment of pottery and farming. These aspects arise in different societies at different times, so it is not in itself a precise chronological division.

Nydam boat. A heavy oak clinker-built rowing boat discovered in a peat bog at Nydam in what is now Schleswig-Holstein in 1859; it is dated to about AD 310-320 and is now displayed at Schloss Gottorp near Hedeby. The boat is about 80ft (24m) long and was rowed by thirty oarsmen and steered by a single oar lashed to the quarter. It is regarded as the type of vessel likely to have been used in the Dark Age migrations, such as the Anglo-Saxon invasions of Britain.

Oberländer. A flat-bottomed river craft of the Rhineland whose design is thought to descend from the dugout-derived vessels of the Romano-Celtic period.

oculus (plural oculi). A device in the form of an eye, sometimes highly stylised, painted on the bows of ships since antiquity for reasons of religion or superstition.

oppidum (plural oppida). Latin term for an administrative centre, but extended to refer to the large hilltop fortified settlements characteristic of late Celtic, La Tène, societies (from the second century BC). They were often princely seats of government and formed important nodal points in the trading networks of the time.

Oseberg ship. A Viking vessel found in a burial mound at Oseberg in southern Norway in 1904. With construction dated to about AD 820, the craft was of lower freeboard than the Gokstad ship (*qv*), and like that vessel can now be seen in reassembled form in the Viking Ship Museum, Oslo.

outlier. An outlying portion or example of anything.

outrigger. Subsidiary hull or hulls carried outside the main hull to provide additional stability, first noticed by Europeans in some of the native canoes of the Indian Ocean and Pacific.

Paleolithic. Pertaining to the old Stone Age. *Homo sapiens* appeared only towards the end of this period (approximately 75,000-10,000 BC), although man's tool-making ancestors can be traced back around 2.5 million years.

Plimsoll Mark. A loading gauge painted on the outside of merchant ships' hulls; made compulsory for British ships by the Merchant Shipping Act of 1876, the work of Samuel Plimsoll, MP, a tireless champion of seamen's rights.

pram bow. A bow in which the lines are 'cut off', ending in a flat transom, usually but not always above the waterline.

Punic. Relating to Carthage.

quarter rudder. Steering device, usually in the form of an oar, situated not on the centreline as in modern boats but on the side of the hull aft (*ie* on the quarters). Steering oars might be positioned on one or both quarters and could be single or multiple according to the size and design of the craft. Cumbersome and inefficient for large vessels, it had some advantages for smaller craft, where it might act as a leeboard to make the boat more weatherly.

rabbet. Shipbuilders' rendition of 'rebate', a cut or bevel (*qv*) designed to take the end or side of another piece of timber.

radiocarbon dating. A method of dating archaeological finds by measuring the state of the radioactive isotope carbon 14, which is involved in a natural cycle of replacement in all organic matter. The replacement of carbon 14 stops on the death of a plant or animal, and since it decays at a known rate, measurement of its ratio against the constant carbon 12 establishes a date of death. Results can be very precise, but are usually expressed as a date ± (plus or minus) x years – ie within the range of x years before to x years after the given date, accuracy declining further back in time the tecnique is applied. Apart from cost, the major drawback of the method is the necessary destruction of the sample of the material being dated.

ratlines. Light lines secured at easy intervals across the shrouds to provide a foothold for seamen going aloft.

red-figure pottery. Ancient Mediterranean style characterised by figures left in the natural red of the pottery against a painted background of black.

reef. The portion of a sail which could be shortened. A sail had one or more rows of reef-points along a reef band which when hauled up and secured to the yard produced a fold in the reefed area of the sail, reducing the depth of canvas exposed to the wind.

reef points. Short lengths of cordage used to secure the sail when reefed.

Rössen Culture. A Neolithic development of the Linear Pottery Culture (*qv*), dating from around the later fifth millenium BC, covering an area of the Rhineland and the Jura.

sagging. The opposite of hogging (*qv*).

scantling. In shipbuilding, the dimensions of an individual piece of the structure; the principal measurements were the sided dimension (the width of timber, usually the same throughout its length) and the moulded (thickness, shaped from a mould, which might well vary).

scarf (or scarph). A timber joint formed by two mirror-imaged bevels at the extremities of the pieces to ne connected. Ship-and boatbuilding devised many elaborate variations on the scarf, some incorporating steps or tenons (*qv*) to lock the pieces in place.

Serçe Liman wreck. An eleventh-century merchantman which probably sank in 1024/1025 discovered near Marmaris in Turkey in 1973; the wreck was excavated in 1977-79.

sheer. In the profile of a ship the upward curve towards the ends of the hull.

sheerstrake. In a plank-built boat the uppermost strake of the hull proper.

shell-first. A term used by modern historians for ship- and boatbuilding in which the hull strakes are fastened together to form the hull shape without the benefit of a pre-erected framework (although strengthening frames may be added later). Overlapping clinker (*qv*) and the ancient Mediterranean method of securing strakes with internal mortise and tenon joints are examples.

shroud. Heavy rope supporting a mast from behind and transversely.

skeuomorph. In archaeology, the survival of the appearance of a feature after its structural raison d'etre has disappeared. For example, early stone buildings might display purely decorative pilasters that reproduce the appearance of timber uprights in earlier wooden-framed structures.

Skuldelev wrecks. A fleet of five vessels discovered in Roskilde fjord on the Danish island of Sjaelland and excavated in an operation that began in 1962. The craft had been deliberately scuttled to block the navigable channel some time in the eleventh century, and were of different types: Wreck 1 was a large merchant ship, identified as a *knaar* (*qv*); Wreck 2 was a very large longship; Wreck 3 was a small coastal carrier; Wreck 5 was a smaller longship; and Wreck 6 was a small open boat. They were all old when sunk and represent a cross-section of designs from the late Viking era. The remains are now displayed in a purpose-built museum at Roskilde.

spritsail. A fore-and-aft sail extended by a spar called a sprit running from the foot of the mast to the top outer corner of the sail.

square sails. Canvas set from yards that at rest were carried at right angles to the centreline of the ship; as opposed to fore-and-aft canvas set from stays or yards on the centreline, or nearly so.

stability. The strength of a ship's tendency to return to the upright, *ie* to right herself. The righting moment in tonne-metres = displacement in tonnes x metacentric height in metres x sine of the angle of heel.

Stroke Ornamented Ware. The characteristic product of a Neolithic culture of central Europe (covering present-day Poland, Czechoslovakia and central Germany). The pottery decoration takes the form of short incisions rather than continuous lines, and developed out of the earlier Linear Pottery during the late fifth and early fourth millenium BC. Known in German as *stichbandkeramic*.

tenon. Rectangular block of hard wood, each half-length being fitted into opposing mortises (*qv*) to join two timbers side by side. Tenons may be locked into place by being drilled through and pegged.

thole, thole pin. A more-or-less vertical surface, particularly a pin, that takes the strain of the oar's pull. In ancient times the pin was sometimes used with an oarloop.

thrust oar. An oar employed by a standing man facing forward, the thrust being obtained by a stroke midway between a paddle and a conventional oar; still used by Venetian gondolas.

ton. *See* tun.

transom. Structural cross piece in the stern of wooden sailing ships; derived from this practice, a flat stern became known as a transom stern.

treenails, trenails, trennels, etc. Wooden dowels used as fastenings in shipbuilding; preferable in some situations to nails or bolts since they do not corrode.

tree-ring analysis. *See* dendrochronology.

trim. The fore and aft attitude of the ship; if the ship draws more water aft than forward, for example, she is said to 'trim by the stern'.

tun. A medieval cask, primarily used for the transportation of wine. These were sufficiently standard for the number of 'tuns' a ship could carry to become the usual measure of her capacity, from which the ton unit eventually derived.

tundra. Arctic wilderness, often virtually flat and treeless, but supporting limited flora and fauna.

umiak. Version of the kayak (*qv*) but used for load-carrying and travelling rather than hunting; in Inuit society usually the province of the women.

velum. Latin for a sail.

vicus. Latin term for a commercial settlement or market town.

VOC. Initials of the Vereenigde Oostindische Compagnie, the Dutch East India Company, founded in 1604, which survived until 1795.

volute. A scroll-shaped ornament.

votive ship. Usually a model dedicated to a church or saint as a thank offering or a mark of piety by seafarers.

wale. Thickened strakes of external hull planking acting as longitudinal strength members.

washstrake. In a boat the uppermost board of timber, designed to keep out spray; it was fitted above the gunwale and was sometimes removeable.

withy. Strictly speaking, the flexible branch of a willow, mainly used for lashings or binding, but by extension applied to other species of branch or twig with similar properties.

Yassi Ada wreck. A seventh-century AD coastal trader of about 60 tons discovered in Turkish waters in 1958 and excavated in 1960-64. It is important as an example of the transition from classical mortise-and-tenon shell-first construction to the less labour-intensive skeleton-first techniques of later centuries.

yard. A spar crossing a mast from which a sail is set. Horizontally set yards, which are primarily oriented athwartship are for square sails; those at an angle and set in the fore-and-aft line are called lateens if they cross the mast, or gaffs if they are set aft of it.

yatra dhoni. Traditional Sri Lankan sailing coaster averaging about 50 tons, a type that disappeared in the 1930s; they were of sewn planked construction.

Index